"Be Home by Dark"

How I Earned My Dime Store MBA

- + -

A 1940's -1950's memoir

Post WW II Era freedom to roam our communities provided unique Learning Opportunities

Dale Kent Phenicie

Dedication

This book is dedicated to my family and the childhood friends and peers with whom I grew up, as well as in memory of those who are no longer with us, especially my late wife of 51 years, Barbara Jean Kolb Phenicie. Their love and support over the years is much appreciated. The bonus for living a long life is the memories these special people have provided. The pain is having to lose them.

Acknowledgements

A number of people have encouraged and helped me prepare this book. I am indebted to Cynthia Petre and the Constantine Township Library staff for support and valuable reference materials. Review and draft manuscript edits by Teresa Ellis, Jim Peterson, Jon Phenicie, Pam Weir, and unending support from my wife of five years Katy Spade are much appreciated. Fellow authors, David Allman, Bill Plitt and his wife Kathy have provided valuable insight into the mechanics of getting the final volume published. Thanks to all.

"Be Home by Dark"

How I Earned My Dime Store MBA

Table of Contents

Chapter		Page
Preface		viii
	Part 1 – The Community	1
1	83 Customers - How Many Papers Are Left?	2
2	Our Move to Constantine	19
3	Walking the Business District	24
	Part 2 – The Store	92
4	Vice President of the Broom	93
5	You Can't Do Business from an Empty Wagon	126
	Part 3 – The Community Network	145
6	Finding Work and Odd Jobs	146
7	Some Adventures	164
8	School Days	187
9	Scooter Boys	219
	Part 4 – Advanced Lessons	243
10	Learning to Drive	244
11	Coming of Age	278
12	The School of Hard Knocks	305
References		337
Photo Credits		345

Growing up, we kids were often sent out to play on our own and given Just one instruction, ...

"Be Home by Dark"

Preface

This book is a memoir about growing up in a small southwest Michigan town during the two-decade period just following WW II (1940s and 1950s). It's a collection of stories about how we lived, what we did, and what those experiences taught us. It is easy to dismiss the contrast between the way we did things then versus now by saying, "Things were much different in those days." For sure, they were. But just maybe, reminders of some of those lifestyle elements may be of value for navigating today's world.

That era provided unique opportunities for those of us growing up in those times. As costly, difficult, and stressful as the war years had been, when it was over our parents drew on knowledge, skills, and capabilities developed during that time to put American society on track for unprecedented growth and exploitation. The National "get it done" attitude spawned and nurtured through global military operations and monstrous at-home support efforts, honed and sharpened our industrial might. The follow-up produced a U.S. economy and consumer-focused society of unprecedented strength. The end of rationing and shortages spurred consumers into a time when they could buy anything, and they did.

Formal school systems provided us kids with basic knowledge. That asset was augmented with life-skill lessons gained from freedom to roam our communities in an era of perceived security. Crossing age group boundaries, we observed skills, practices, and gained knowledge through networking opportunities. In addition, a myriad of available odd jobs for young people provided us, for better or sometimes worse, with additional lessons that shaped our character.

My small hometown of Constantine, Michigan, is located in the southwest corner of the state, just a few miles from Indiana in an area known locally as "Michiana." It is strategically located about "half-way" between mega cities Detroit and Chicago. The vast prairie lands in between are dotted with small communities and numerous farms developed during settlement days by pioneers who filtered in from the country's eastern birthing grounds.

This book is about our community, our experiences, and how we lived in those times. The story is told through a collection of tales and descriptions of the things we did. They come mostly from my memory, buttressed by selected documentation and references. Admittedly (and with apologies to the real people named), others will remember things differently. That's OK. They are my stories and I'm sticking to them. I am sure alternate versions are just as compelling, and perhaps of more value.

My venue for experiencing all that went on was somewhat unique. My parents ran the local five-and-dime store (dime store). This planted me in the middle of our village's business community, provided on-the-job training opportunities, and (I was told repeatedly) obligated me to practice good behavior as I traveled around town. In no uncertain words, I was informed that it was my responsibility to avoid bringing disgrace to the family name. Sternly, I was told if I misbehaved my actions could chase customers away from the store resulting in starvation of my entire family. I had my orders, "Behave yourself." Sometimes I complied, sometimes I didn't.

In my adult years, I have often said, "I wish my children had been able to have some of these same experiences." They were not unique. Residents elsewhere throughout the country would have had similar opportunities during that era. Whether they lived in town or on farms out in the country, the activities of my peers and me were typical of the times. I have always believed that our participation in running small businesses and farms, along with the interactions we had with members of our community at large, provided knowledge and a practical education similar to that acquired by business school graduates. The freedom to try, fail, and have success, along with expectations of accountability entrusted to and thrust upon us by parents and the community, served us well.

Traveling through small towns and burgs today, we often see boarded-up buildings that once housed businesses such as those described in this book. If you missed seeing them during their productive days, I hope the tales that follow will give you an idea of what once went on in those structures.

It is easy to suggest that by returning to these practices in today's society, we would be better off. But, of course, it's not that simple. I hope revisiting these times through this retrospective will be at least entertaining, if not of value. The book is not intended to be a chronological volume. It is a collection of recalled events grouped into selected categories. That, and the thought that readers may choose portions of the book and not read the entire thing, is my excuse (or explanation) for repetitions that occur.

I hope you enjoy the stories.

PART 1 – The Community

Chapter 1
83 Subscribers - How many papers are left?

Southside Constantine

I peddled my newspaper laden bicycle southward down Canaris Street. It was a bright, mid-60 degree, September 1952, afternoon. I had been delivering papers on this same route for more than a year and used some of the money earned to purchase the Schwinn Black Phantom bicycle I was riding. The sky formed a deep blue canopy overhead and my right side cooled as I entered the shadow cast by our long low school building. I had left my 7th grade classroom located in that building about an hour earlier. Leaving school, I walked to our home just three blocks away, threw my books on the kitchen table, grabbed my Three Rivers Commercial newspaper bag, jumped on my bike and rode directly downtown to pick up my papers at Armstrong's Rexall Drug Store, the starting point of my route.

Situated about 100 feet back from of the west side of the street, our two-story school building was long and sleek. I had attended school in this building since kindergarten. Anticipating the junior high school career that I had just started, I looked with some reverence at the structure I was passing. I had emerged from the elementary school section housed in the southern end of the building's first floor and would now fill my remaining time in the building in the northern first floor and second floor areas. As I peddled by, I ticked off each of the classroom windows that I could identify from the outside. I mused over recent changes to those rooms. The building now housed just grades 5 through 12. Lower elementary grade classes had just recently been relocated to a new building constructed a few blocks away on White Pigeon Road, near and across from my home. The old building had changed some, but it, and its adjoining playgrounds, ball fields, and undeveloped areas, still served as a primary activity center for our town's young people.

This being a Thursday, thoughts of the coming weekend with two days off from school, were also circling in my head. I looked for cars and bikes parked near the building that would indicate who might still be hanging out at the school. The playgrounds and ball diamonds were empty. The high school football team was practicing down in the stadium out of my sight, but I could hear the coach's whistle blowing as he put the team through its paces. Only a few cars belonging to coaches, teachers, and older students remained. I peddled onward towards the southern boundary of our flat prairieland community.

Our town was divided nearly down the middle by the "main drag," Washington Street, also designated as U.S. Highway 131. It put lots of traffic through our town. Parallel streets, about three on each side of Washington, were intersected by six or eight "cross streets" making up the grid that formed our community. Homes lining the streets dated back as far as the mid 1800s. Many were large stately Victorian style houses built of brick or wood. A few were built of "rock faced" or "rusticated" cement blocks that had at one time been manufactured right there in our town. I liked the rugged look these blocks gave the buildings made from them. A mix of "newer" modest one-or two-story frame structures were built in the early 1900s on most of the community's other house lots. Village streets were lined with huge, beautiful, hard maple trees, making our town known as the "city of big trees." Residents and visitors alike always remarked about them. They shaded us in summer and were spectacular in the fall. When everyone raked and burned leaves that fell in the fall, smoke permeated the entire community. The community gave visitors a feeling of having just stepped into a Norman Rockwell painting.

The Shootout

Approaching the southern end of Canaris, and its V-shaped intersection with Washington Street, I intently kept an eye out for anticipated assailants. Ken Spade and Rob Polleys, grade school and scout troop buddies I had grown up with, lived in this southern end of town. Their houses both faced Washington Street but were on opposite sides of the street. Ken's house and yard backed up to Canaris, just a couple of houses from the intersection we referred to as "The Point." The town's "City Limits" stretched northward from here for about two miles to the opposite end of Washington Street. We thought of our community of 1500 people as a "city" even though opposing borders on each of the four sides of town were only about two miles apart.

As I peddled past Ken's back yard, I noted that he and Rob were not at his house playing catch. This told me that, for sure, they would be doing so over at Rob's house. During late afternoons, they could usually be found tossing hi-fly baseballs to each other in one yard or the other. Later, in early evening right after supper, they organized pick-up games that included other neighborhood kids, including me. These usually occurred in Ken's yard where there was more space to lay out base lines. But we had to be careful when running or sliding on the baselines. His dog, Pudge, tended to "dress" the field just before each of our games.

Rounding "The Point," I changed both streets and directions. I was now headed north, up the eastern side of the community. I had delivered papers to about one-third of my customers. It was important that I keep moving and stay on schedule if I was to be finished with my route and home by suppertime. Rob's house was my next stop. I knew he and Ken would be there. I was also certain they would be hiding out on Rob's big front porch, just waiting for me. But I was prepared.

Downtown, after picking up my newspapers at Armstrong's, I had stopped at Read's Market, a grocery store and meat market, to purchase a large five-cent bag of dried peas. Days earlier I had purchased one of the novelty items my peers were all excited about at Armstrong's, a 12-inch-long, heavy walled, plastic pea or bean shooter. Similar to what we would today call a "plastic straw," word had gotten around that these weapons had become available. A couple of them had been brandished about on the school playground. Speculation was rampant on which style of ammo was best, beans or peas, navy or pinto, etc. I listened to the talk but was cautious about deciding whether to get involved in these combative activities. Being one of the less athletic and least streetwise of the crowd, I usually came out on the short end of such aggressive behavior. But on this day, I had decided it was time to defend myself. I was ready. My bean shooter and an ample supply of ammo was tucked away in my newspaper delivery bag.

Rob's house was the first one inside the southern village limits on the east side of Washington street. Outside the limits, the landscape was mostly farmland, dotted with farmhouses, barns, silos, and other structures typical of the 1940s – 50s era. Now inside the village, Rob's stately brick house was part of what was once an active farm. His yard included a barn surrounded by a bit of land. We loved playing in the barn and associated fields where we pursued all kinds of activities, but the lack of turf and several large maple trees didn't make for a good ball diamond. Rob's grandmother had lived in the house for a long time. It once served as a hospital. Rob, his sister, and their mother lived there with her. The large stately brick structure had lots of rooms. When we gathered there, we were frequently invited, by his grandmother, to "play outdoors." Consequently, I had been in a few of the rooms, but not all. One room we were encouraged to use was a finished basement room housing a ping-pong table. It was once used as the hospital's operating room. We each had our own mind's eye visions of what must have gone on in there. Other rooms down there were dark and scary. We didn't venture into them.

On this day, the action was focused on the sweeping front porch that wrapped around the southside of the home. Large columns and a masonry railing provided cover and shooting holes for my assailants.

As I peddled along the sidewalk in front of the house, I kept an eye out for them. At first, seeing no one, I began to doubt my suspicions. But then, I noticed a ball glove lying on the front steps leading up to the porch. They just had to be there. I was certain that each slept with their ball glove. Neither would have gone off and left a glove on the steps. They had to be nearby.

I stopped, poured a load of dried peas into my hand and thrust them into my mouth. Then I grabbed my pea shooter and forged onward, determined to complete the task of delivering a newspaper to the front door. Continuing up the sidewalk next to the street, I turned onto the short walkway that led to the steps. I tried to get as close to the steps as I could while still seated on the bike. I wanted to minimize the time during which I would have to defend myself while in the awkward position of dismounting and parking the newspaper-laden bike. It needed to be positioned carefully to keep it from tipping over while parked.

Just as the front wheel reached the first step, out from behind the columns at the top of the steps jumped the two marksmen. A dual stream of peas or beans, whatever they had chosen as ammo, came flying down the steps. The projectiles bounced off my jacket and hat. A few hit me squarely in the face, stinging a bit. But I fired back, first towards one side of the steps then the other, scoring numerous hits. I was clearly outnumbered and had the disadvantage of having to aim high in order to compensate for the three-foot difference in elevation between top and bottom steps. But the assault was short lived. They emptied their mouth-full loads quickly. I had saved a few rounds. I gained satisfaction by being able to splat them with a pea or two as I jumped off the bike, ran up the steps, and reached the front door where I placed the newspaper behind the storm door. It was over. It had been fun. We exchanged a few laughs and sarcastic comments, but I didn't stay long. I still had papers to deliver.

Heading for the Railyard

Back on my bike I continued up the street, bearing right at the intersection of Washington Street and White Pigeon Road (the second of four pie-shaped intersections on the south end of town), passed the new elementary school building that my sister attended, rode past our family's home, and went onward for several blocks, stopping frequently along the way to leave papers for customers.

At Centerville Road I turned eastward and approached the railroad tracks at Station Street. I usually arrived at the crossing about 5:30 p.m. each afternoon. Two New York Central freight trains per day traveled this north/south track. One headed north in the morning, the other came back late in the afternoon. Passenger service no longer ran through here. Industries located in area small towns relied on the freight service provided on this track. Though fading on other lines, New York Central continued to use steam locomotives on this run. The local depot was situated alongside the tracks, on Station Street, near the intersection. Sidings connected to the main line near the depot served the co-op grain elevator, the paper mill, a tank and refrigeration piping fabricator, the creamery, a casket manufacturing company, a wooden porch shade factory, and others. Some of the industries were located close to the railyard. Others, some distance away, had siding tracks that led to their location. Still others conducted loading/unloading operations in the railyard and trucked materials to and from their plant sites.

I had six customers in the "across the tracks" neighborhood. Quite often, the locomotive with its short string of a dozen or so cars, would be arriving, or was already sitting, in the railyard when I got to the grade crossing. When so, as it was on this day, I dallied a bit to watch the locomotive make forward and backward shuttle movements dropping off or picking up cars from sidings. Occasionally it stopped in front of the depot while the engineer conferred with the stationmaster. In the meantime, the fireman walked around the locomotive using a long-spouted oil can to lubricate numerous moving parts on the locomotive while it sat there breathing, hissing, and steaming as though it was alive. I was fascinated and could see the glow from coals in the firebox through small round holes near the rear of the boiler. I waved at the crew. After the locomotive moved out of sight down a siding, I placed a penny on one of the main track rails before crossing the tracks and heading up the street to make my deliveries.

Across the Tracks Customers

My route in this neighborhood was a large loop. A few houses sat on the east side of Harvey Street. It ran parallel to the tracks and continued down a steep hill leading into and around an industrial area. There, Baldwin Street ran back uphill on the opposite side of the block, reconnecting the area with Centerville Road. Customers on this loop were quite different from most on my route.

The first house was long and narrow with a porch running down its south side. Each day I rode up the short sidewalk to the front of the house, parked my bike at the steps, then walked the length of the porch to the front door where I placed the paper behind the storm door. On the way across the porch, I passed several windows that provided looks into the house. On weekdays no one was home except for a most fierce chihuahua. When I approached, it jumped up onto the back of a couch just inside the windows, barked, growled, showed it's menacing teeth, lunging at me as I walked by. This occurred both when I walked up to the door and again when I returned. It always scared me. It was inside and I was outside, but I was convinced that it could bust through the window and grab me by the throat if it wanted to. I always dreaded this stop. On Saturday mornings when I made collections there, the woman of the house corralled the dog and came to the door holding him. Though he didn't bark, the little beast glared at me and growled quietly all the time the transaction was being made. It was a scary situation. I didn't stay long to chat, nor did I receive any sort of tip from this customer.

Traveling down the hill and circling the industrial loop, my next stop was at a small tarpaper covered shack standing beside the Mill Pond. This shallow body of water, a half-mile or so across, was created by flowage from an old mill dam. We called it the Tumble Dam. It was located on the Fawn River just out of town at the opposite end of the pond and was a favored fishing site for many of us. The in-town side of the pond was a popular ice-skating place in winter and stone skipping spot in summer. Viewed as an "off-limits" area by our mothers, it was one we young explorers were often drawn to. Tony Witek, one of my older outdoors savvy friends, had set out a trapline among the reeds and cattails that encircled the pond. He caught beavers, muskrats, occasional raccoons, and made good money selling the hides he cut, stretched, and dried in his garage.

My customer's shack sat on a small strip of land between the road and the pond. A single, older man known to us only as Jack lived there with three or four dogs and a cat or two. He had no visible means of transportation. There was no car, truck, or bicycle in sight. He always seemed to be at home, was a man of few words, and was always dressed in the same plaid flannel shirt and bib overalls. When I came to collect each week, he pulled a small change pouch out of a zippered pocket in the bib portion of his overalls. Occasionally he stopped taking the paper for a week or two then flagged me down on the way by when he wanted to start it up again. He didn't appear scary, but we were instructed by our parents not to interact with him when we visited the pond.

My most memorable experience with Jack occurred while riding past his shack one day during a time when he was not taking the paper. Just as I came to the front of the shack, a small puppy ran out from under it. I was moving right along, preparing to climb the approaching hill out of the area. I couldn't stop my bicycle in time and my front wheel hit the puppy. The rear wheel skidded loudly, locked up from my sudden braking. The puppy squealed and Jack came running out of the shack. I had stopped, was collecting myself, and relieved that I had not tipped over. Jack picked up and comforted the puppy. I began apologizing for hitting it, but Jack cut me off saying, "That'll teach him not to run out from under the house again." He put the pup down, turned around and went back inside. The puppy crawled back under the shack and appeared to be doing ok. I continued on, crossed a rail siding that led to the town's paper mill, then climbed the Baldwin Street hill, headed back into the residential portion of the area.

The next house, located about half-way up the hill, was also perplexing. It was a large, square, two-story, wood-sided building, situated some distance back from the street. Surrounded by several plots that formed a large vegetable garden, there was no lawn. The remainder of the lot grew wild, covered with thistles and tall grasses. Rickety steps led up to a small front porch and the front door. There was no screen or storm door. When delivering, I simply climbed the steps and placed the rolled-up paper on end leaning against the door. Large windows on either side of the front door provided a peek at the inside of the house. The only name I had for this house in my collections book was "House on Hill." I never knew the family name.

Since I usually reached this house at dusk and there were no curtains at the windows, I could see in as I climbed the steps. The household consisted of five or six old men and one woman all about the same age. The men always wore bib overalls. The woman wore a house dress similar to ones my grandmother made out of chicken feedbag cloth. Her graying hair, rolled up around the back of her head, and her "in-charge" demeanor, further reminded me of my grandmother. Since it was suppertime, the men were usually seated around a large table. The woman was usually waiting on them, serving some kind of food or drink. The scene reminded me of caricatures I had seen of the dwarfs in *Snow White and the Seven Dwarfs* (Walt Disney Productions), except these people were full sized, and all dressed alike.

Occasionally, I saw the men out working in the gardens. They glanced in my direction as I passed by, sometimes nodded, but never spoke to me. Their long white beards stretched down nearly to their waistline. Shoulder length hair spilled out from under their straw hats. They were a scary lot.

The windowless front door was almost always closed. I never saw anyone come or go through that door. However, on Saturday mornings when I made collections, I stood on the porch and knocked on it. The men in the garden ignored me but the woman opened the door quickly and greeted me warmly. She always seemed to be baking something. Her large apron was coated with flour, and she wiped her hands with it as she opened the door. She always seemed to know it was me knocking at her door and had her long, slender, clasp-on-top, change purse and punch card handy. She chatted about the weather, opened the purse, withdrew 35 cents, and handed the money and card to me. Thirty cents covered the cost of the paper. The extra nickel was a tip for me. She was one customer that I could always count on for a tip. On occasion she also offered me a cookie. However, I always declined. Given the strange nature of this place, I was unsure what might be in those cookies. Besides the silent stares received from the men, the other thing that always accompanied my visits to that opened front door was a potent unpleasant odor coming from inside the house. My objective was always the same, spend no more time than necessary standing there in front of the door. I always took a deep breath just before it opened and held it while standing there. On one warm summer Saturday the door was already open when I approached the house. As I climbed the front steps, I saw that the woman was vigorously sweeping the floor inside. I peered in while knocking to get her attention. That's when I realized that she was sweeping a dirt floor. it was indeed a strange and unusual place.

School Principal H. Richard Johns

Continuing up to the top of the hill, I was again at Centerville Road. The small attractive one-story house on the southeast corner of the intersection was the residence of Mr. H. Richard Johns, the stern principal of our school. It made me a little nervous to park my bicycle in front of his house, walk the short distance up his front steps, and place the paper behind the storm door. What if he should be in his front yard? What if he opened the door just as I reached it? What would I say? Fortunately, that never happened. When I made my collection rounds it was always his wife who came to the door, paid me, and offered pleasant greetings. I didn't have much interaction with Mr. Johns at school, but as did all students, I knew that he knew who I was. He walked the school building halls often, always stood in the halls as we were coming and going from classrooms, and silently watched us as we walked by him. Once in a while he entered our classrooms, stood in the back of the room and observed the teacher delivering her lessons. She always smiled when he entered, kept on presenting her lesson without interruption, but appeared to give a sigh of relief when he quietly left the room a few minutes later. I was sure he was watching me anytime I saw him at school and as I came and went while delivering his newspaper, I thought I could feel his eyes gazing at me from somewhere inside the house.

I didn't see it happen, or observe any evidence of it, but a story circulating around school was, one day, just after school had started in the fall, a student in the high school senior class called the local coal company, pretended to be Mr. Johns, and ordered a truckload of coal to be dumped on the lawn right in front of his house. The story included speculation regarding his reaction, who had made the call, what happened to the coal, etc. After making my delivery each day, I smiled as I thought about these rumors, hopped back on my bike, and rode on up the side street beside his house.

I had two subscribers on this short dead-end street, directly across from each other. I always stopped at the one on the righthand side first then crossed to the other. I didn't have to get off the bike to deliver the second paper. It was a trailer-home with no front steps and located very close to the edge of the street. I rode up to the front door and simply placed the paper in the mailbox beside the door.

At this point, every day, I looked into my paper bag and counted how many papers were left. I had just five more deliveries to make. The last paper was the one I took home. If there were exactly six papers in the bag, I was ecstatic! "I'm coming out right tonight," I would exclaim to myself. I hummed a little ditty tune

I had made up. *"I'm coming out right tonight, coming out right tonight, coming out right, coming out right, I'm coming out right tonight."*

If I counted seven or eight papers that meant I had missed someone somewhere along the way. Then, the agony began. I traced back in my mind, where had I gone? What had happened along my route? Which house did I forget? Was it way back at the beginning of the route across the river? Was it a house on one of the side streets off of Canaris? Who could it have been? What had I seen or done that had distracted me?

If I was lucky, I would remember some unusual event that caused a diversion from my normal path. If so, I could loop back and fill that gap, hoping that no one noticed. If not, I was in for a rough evening when I got home.

Returning home each day a few minutes before 6:00 p.m., my mother was putting supper on the table. My father arrived promptly at 6:15 p.m., and we all sat down to eat together at the kitchen table. The first question my mother asked as I walked in the door was, "How many papers did you have left?" The magic answer was one, the "perk" I received as a newspaper carrier, a free daily paper day for the family.

If I had more than one, she sat me down before I took off my coat, grabbed my route book listing customers, and called out the names one by one. Generally, something would trigger my mind and I could remember which stop I had not made. If I couldn't come up with the answer, we would have to wait to see who telephoned to inquire about their missing paper. Occasionally, especially if I had forgotten someone on the early portion of the route, that phone call would have been received before I returned home. Then the first question Mother asked when I arrived was different. More like, "Why did you forget to leave a paper for Mrs. Carlson?" If the missed customer was not far away, I was expected to get back on my bike and take that paper where it belonged. Everyone else sat down at the table. My supper was delayed until I returned. If the missed customer was far away, we waited until my father got home and he drove me to the customer's house. Of course, along the way, I would have to explain what had gone wrong that day. In either case, disrupting the family routine at suppertime was an unpleasant experience for everyone. Fortunately, it didn't happen often.

A Good Outcome on This Day

On this day, I had the magic number. I sang the ditty and noted that efficient travel around the route, in spite of time needed to defend myself during the great bean shooter ambush, had given me enough time to stop at the railroad tracks on the way back and search for the penny I placed on the track on my trip over. During my time "across the tracks," the locomotive finished working the sidings and steamed on southward out of town. While counting the remaining papers in my bag, I heard the engineer give two long blasts on the steam whistle as he chugged out of the railyard. With any luck, the penny would have stayed on the rail and been flattened by the locomotive.

Finding the penny, squashed or not, between track ties and among ballast rocks, could be a challenge. But, again, this was a good day. I had marked the spot where I placed the penny using a distinctively shaped rock alongside the tracks. I started my search there. About three ties down the track, there it was. A thin, oblong-shaped, bright piece of copper lying between the rails. This was really cool. It gave me something to take to school the next day and show to my back of the classroom buddies. Occasionally, I placed previously squashed pennies on the track to see how thin they would become when run over multiple times. My buddies had performed their own versions of the experiment and we always tried to come up with a "one-better" specimen to brag about. There were some days when I couldn't find the penny. This would invariably be the time that someone else had a unique result to display. Today, I placed the newly flattened coin in my pocket, satisfied I had a fresh curio to show off.

My Next to Last Customer

Jumping back on my bike I continued up Station Street towards the creamery to make last deliveries before turning around to head south on White Pigeon Road back to my home.

My next to last customer was most perplexing. It was the home of Coach Turka, an assistant high school coach. He taught government and social studies, junior high physical Education, and coached junior high baseball, football, and basketball teams. He lived in a brick two-story house one block south of the creamery, at the corner of Prospect and Depot Streets. Living with him were his wife, two children, and a large, yellow, short-haired dog.

When I arrived in his neighborhood, I often found the dog out freely wandering the yard on his own. No chain, leash, or fence restrained him. He was very friendly. He always saw me coming when I was still a block away. He came running and bounded towards me with tongue and tail both wagging. When he met me, he quickly turned and raced alongside my bike back to the house. He was never aggressive. He didn't bark or try to jump on me. He just wanted to race. After I delivered the coach's paper and headed down the street, he again jogged alongside. The only way I could get rid of him was to circle back to the house, go knock on the door, and get someone to come out and corral him. This took extra time and was always annoying. If I said anything to the coach about keeping him tied up, he simply said, "That's all right, this way he gets some exercise." I didn't have any leverage in the situation so there wasn't much I could do about it.

But the most shocking experience regarding Coach Turka deliveries occurred one Saturday morning while I was making collections. As I approached the house, I was relieved that the dog was not outside. I parked my bike on the sidewalk, walked to the door, and knocked. Coach came to the door. As he opened it, I could hardly believe my eyes. He was wearing a dress! What was this all about? I didn't know what to do or say. There he stood before me, all smiles and friendly, in a brown and white checkered housedress! He was also wearing white sox and men's shoes, but with a dress! I had heard talk among my peers about crossdressers, but these tales were associated with people in far off towns, considered weird, and not expected in our small town.

I tried to act normal. I took the coach's money, punched his card, and left as quickly as possible. I wouldn't see the coach again until Monday at school. For two days I kept going over that experience in my mind. What was I going to do? Should I tell anyone? I decided the best course of action was to say nothing about it to anyone. Surely, this had been some freaky thing. Maybe I didn't really see what I thought I saw. I decided to just forget it. Two years later, the coach taught my ninth-grade civics class. One day in class, he mentioned that he sometimes liked to wear a dress around the house. He said he found it to be "comfortable." He got surprised looks from my classmates and snickers from male counterparts seated with me in the back row. I just sat and smiled. I still didn't know what to make of it, but at least now I wasn't the only one in town who knew about Coach's quirk.

Chapter 2

Our Move to Constantine

Dad's Home – "For the Rest of My Life"
My father bought the Constantine "dime store" in 1944. For those not familiar with what a dime store is, or was, think Dollar General. It was a general merchandise store where a multitude of small items used daily could be purchased. Candy, sold from a large glass binned case just inside the front door, tempted customers. They could look through the glass, see mounds of chocolates, jellybeans, and other confections, sold by the pound, and ask the clerk to weigh up their selection. Packs of chewing gum, candy bars, greeting cards, magazines, small gifts, souvenirs, knick-knacks, hair goods, sewing notions, small hardware items, paint and wallpaper, lamp shades, tablecloths made of fabric or "oil cloth," light bulbs, fuses, a large selection of toys, some clothing items, and other necessities could all be purchased there. In reverse of what is found in general merchandise stores today, 90 percent of items sold were "Made in the USA."

My dad, Walter Stephen Phenicie, was born in 1913 into a family of modest folks who worked farms and toiled at factory jobs during times that included both the Great Depression and World War II. They understood the need to take care of themselves and their families. This made Dad an ambitious self-starter. He grew up in the southeastern Michigan/northcentral Ohio area moving from place to place, on and near the shores of Lake Erie. His father worked at various jobs and always rented rather than bought property. Consequently, they moved a lot, making Dad "the new kid in school" several times. There, he was forced to prove or establish himself within the pecking order, both in and outside of the classroom. Not one to pick a fight out of necessity he learned how to take care of himself among one-room schoolhouse peers where age groups could be quite broad. He had one younger brother. They were a compact and supportive family where each member knew what was expected of them.

My mother, Gertrude Elizabeth Phenicie, was born the same year and came from a similar background. However, her family was more farm operations oriented. Her father bought and sold farmsteads, moving several times within the same Michigan/Ohio region. Each time, he increased the size of his holdings. Over the years, they became large dairy farms. Though he grew crops, and performed corn or grain growing and harvesting operations, he focused on breeding, raising, keeping, and milking cows. Mother, her five brothers and one sister all supported these endeavors, including milk bottling and distribution activities. Often, while on their way to school, they delivered milk from the farm truck. In her teen years, a bit of wanderlust prompted her and an adventurous girlfriend to leave home, forsaking high school graduation, to work as waitresses at an Ann Arbor, Michigan, hotel.

Mother returned to the Michigan-Ohio border area when she and my father married in 1936. He, having graduated from high school, was going door-to-door selling insurance policies for Michigan Farmer. These were low-cost accident coverage policies that he often described as, "One where, if you lost your leg, the company would help you find it."

Shortly thereafter Dad took a job in a "dime store" starting, as he said many times, "On the bottom rung of the ladder." From there he "worked his way up." His initial position was "stock boy," meaning he put merchandise on the shelves, swept the floor, and performed other tasks that supported the business.

While climbing the ladder, Dad worked for two different regional chain-store companies that had stores in the Michigan, Ohio, and Indiana, "Tri-state" area. He ascended to clerk, assistant manager, then manager, and was transferred many times from store to store. Each time he, Mother, and I (once I came into the world in late 1940) moved to a different town, sometimes a different state. I was born in Celina, Ohio. My memories only go back as far as residency in Buchanan, Michigan, at age three, but I was told that in my first three years I lived in several Tri-state communities. Most of the time for only a few months in each.

Dad grew tired of all the moving and working for different bosses. He wanted his own store. Messages passed around the network of dime store peers, including traveling salesmen suppling merchandise to the stores, told him that Fuller's store in the town of Constantine, Michigan, was for sale. 1944 being a late World War II year meant that merchandise was hard to get. That store had been a Ben Franklin franchise, but the owner was having difficulty stocking it. Dad was positioned solidly enough within his chain store hierarchy to work out arrangements to acquire goods for the Constantine store through them. He arranged financing with the store owner, packed us up, and moved, for his final time, to Constantine in late spring of that year. A few months after our move, my sister, Barbara Annette (Phenicie) Gray was born.

Dad was 4-F
Like all young men in the WW II era, Dad was called to take a military service physical exam. A bit older than most draftees, examiners said he had "flat feet" and wouldn't make a good infantry man. Classified 4-F, he was sent home. No sooner did he get there than he received a message telling him to report to Cark Equipment Company to work night shifts building U.S. Army halftrack vehicles. That was how he was to do his part in support of the war effort. He ran the Buchannan chain dime store during the day and reported to Clark each night.

She and I both spent our entire public-school careers in the Constantine system, graduating from high school four years apart. Dad with daily help from our mother, and during our school years the two of us, ran the store and became very involved in community affairs. He served on the village Council, helped organize and was very active in the local Rotary Club, and actively served on church committees. He always said, "You get out of a community just what you put into it."

The store was located on the west side of south Washington Street in Eureka Hall, a prominent building in one of the village's three downtown business blocks. Dad only bought the business, he didn't purchase the building. It was owned by a woman named Mrs. King who lived in another community. Her family had operated both a funeral parlor and variety store in the same building. Typical of Dad's business acumen, he never signed a formal lease. He worked out a "handshake-deal" where he had use of the building at a low monthly rate in exchange for taking care of most maintenance and upkeep needs.

One thing the store never had was a telephone. Dad said, "If I had a phone, people would call the store to ask if I had what they were looking for. I want them to come to the store to look for it. If I didn't have it, they would see other things they liked, and buy them." When customers did come for something he didn't have, he always offered to get it quickly. He either ran next door to the Walgreens drug store to use their phone or drove home to order it. He also didn't want to have to answer the phone when he was busy serving customers. While talking with someone in-person, he considered it the ultimate insult to have that conversation interrupted by the other party answering a ringing phone. "When I'm standing right in front of them, what makes the person calling more important than me?" he asked.

Dad often said, "When I moved to Constantine, I knew right from the start it was the place I would live for the rest of my life." He was right. He ran that store for 30 years, until he died suddenly and unexpectedly in 1974. Mom with the help of some fine hired clerks, continued to run the store for another five years.

Map of Constantine, Michigan Business District - Circa 1950s

Chapter 3

Walking the Business District

A Life-Skills University

The Constantine business district was developed along the southern banks of the St. Joseph River. Area waterways were important to early settlers arriving in 1828. The St. Joe, as we called it, is a major tributary to Lake Michigan and served as a transportation corridor. The new community was the last stop for flat-bottomed steamers that traveled up-river from the port of St. Joseph, Michigan. Settlers quickly built dams and raceways (canals) in the intersecting Fawn River watershed. These provided hydromechanical power that turned wheels and pulleys in newly built mills. In our mid-20th century era, the rivers produced hydroelectric power, were seen primarily as geographic markers, and provided recreational opportunities.

Most residential streets fanned out southward from the area. Only a few residential streets were located on the north side of the river. Downtown businesses served both in-town citizens and those living on family farms that stretched out across adjacent flat, fertile-soil plains. The business district was both a supply point and social gathering spot where people walked the streets, browsed the stores, visited restaurants and bars, and attended the movie theater. For my peers and me, it was also an important learning academy. As we ran the streets and visited with whomever we encountered, we picked up pointers on how to conduct business and perform a wide variety of tasks.

Stores were positioned along four streets. One block of Washington Street (U.S. Highway 131), three one-block sections of east and west Water streets, and the north side of West 2nd Street made up the area. It didn't take long to walk the entire area and visit each business. Let's take a virtual tour.

South Washington Street – East Side

Morrison's Standard Oil

Henry (Hank) Morrison's Standard Oil filling station sat at the intersection of Washington and East Second Streets. A small, brick, cottage style building, it was painted white and had a gabled roof that extended from the front of the building to shelter one side of the gasoline pump island. A car parked under the roof had access to the two pumps. A second vehicle could be serviced on the uncovered side. One of the pumps delivered "Regular" grade gas, the other, "Ethyl," a premium grade. The higher octane and tetraethyl lead levels in "Ethyl" decreased "knocking" in higher compression car engines. All engines of the day were thought to provide more power from the more expensive fuel. A motorist feeling frisky, or one who had extra cash in his pocket, was sometimes tempted to try a tankful of "Ethyl" just to see how it performed.

The station had a hydraulic lift for servicing cars. It was located outdoors on the south side of the building. A lawn area surrounding the station was neatly landscaped. A white painted curb outlined the driveway and ramp areas. When not pumping gas, Hank was usually found under a car hoisted up on the lift. He replaced rusted mufflers, changed engine oil, and injected grease into the many Zork fittings found on cars in those days. Except during downpours, cars were serviced rain or shine.

Inside, a sales counter was used for collecting money, scheduling appointments, and selling cigarettes. A floor-to-ceiling cigarette rack contained colorful packages that took up most of the space behind the counter. In total, the office was just large enough for three or four people to stand in at one time.

Hank operated the station single-handedly most of the time. He kept the building and grounds meticulously clean. He greeted drivers pulling up to the pumps with a huge smile and booming voice asking, "What can I get for you today?" He pumped gas into the car's tank, washed the windshield, and raised the hood to check engine oil. He looked at water levels in the radiator and battery and examined the fan belt. If the oil level on the engine dipstick was "low" (frequently the case in those days), he brought it to the driver's window, showed it to the driver, and asked what weight oil to add to the engine. After adding a quart (or two), and topping off water in the radiator and/or battery, he closed the hood and made sure it was securely latched.

Most sales were cash. Only a few were paid using the new wrinkle of the day, a credit card. If a card was offered, it was usually by a nonresident passing through. Once that customer left the station, Hank muttered that credit card sales were, "A real pain in the ass." They took much longer to process, and slips used to record and approve the charge had to be filled out by hand. More paperwork was required when the slips were turned into the bank.

Everyone knew and liked Hank. When not busy he sat behind the sales counter on a tall, padded stool. Passers-by stopped in to talk and catch up on village gossip or regional and worldly news that constantly blared from a radio sitting amongst cigarette cartons. Hank and visitors watched traffic rolling past the station, noted who was headed where, and conjectured about what each person was doing. Lots of wisdom, philosophy, and worldly information was exchanged in these conversations. No age limit was placed on the gatherings. We pre-teen-aged boys often joined in, sometimes learning a few new words.

The Library
The building across Second Street, fronted on Washington Street, housed the public library. Built in the mid-1800s, like most downtown buildings, it was a long narrow two-story brick building with plate glass windows on each side of the entry door.

The interior was ringed floor to ceiling with tall bookshelves. Ladders hanging from tracks bolted to the ceiling were moved along in front of bookcases to provide access to high shelves. Floor space in the middle of the room provided a reading area that included low-lying bookshelves situated amongst tables and chairs where patrons sat to read, take notes, or look through newspapers. The librarian sat at a large desk ready to check out or receive books and try to keep order. She provided constant reminders that this was to be a "quiet place." My chums and I visited frequently to obtain books and do research for Boy Scout or school projects. The musty book smell, worn titles on many volumes, and collection of newspapers and magazines available from far-off places like Chicago, Detroit, or even New York City, were always of interest and gave us the "feel" of being at the library. Of special interest was a huge dictionary that stood open on a stand right behind the front window. We gathered there to get sneak peaks at "dirty words," snickering as we read and pointing out definitions. We didn't stay long when the librarian started to glare at us.

The Beauty Shop
The next building contained the beauty shop. My mother, and most ladies in the community, went there weekly for hair washing and styling. The huge bulbous driers they sat under with

hair done-up on huge rollers were located right near the big front window. Peering in, seeing them, and smelling permanent odors that leaked out the front door always made us laugh and wrinkle our noses as we walked by. The only reason to enter the salon was to sell tickets or coupons related to school or scouting events. If we dared, we were almost always rewarded with a sale or two. The ladies were likely to know us. We took deep breaths of fresh air before opening the door and exited as soon as our business had been completed.

Park Theater
The Park Theater, a narrow, deep cavern, with a front to back downward sloping floor leading to the red velvet-looking stage curtain and screen provided entertainment before and during the era when television was coming into our homes. Though big extravaganza films shown at large theaters in nearby communities rarely came to the Park in our days, it is said that *Gone with the Wind* (Margaret Mitchell, David O.) was once shown there with tickets priced at 50 cents each. Our films consisted mostly of westerns starring Roy Rogers, Dale Evans, Hop along Cassidy, and Lash LaRue. Jungle themed movies brought us Tarzan, The Black Panther, etc.

When very young, my sister and I were sent to the movies most Saturday evenings while Mom and Dad worked in the dime store across the street. Like other downtown businesses, the store stayed open from 6:00 pm to 9:00 pm on Saturdays. It was almost closing time when we returned from our evening at the Park.

Cocky Howard owned the theater and often walked downtown streets dressed in a flashy plaid sports coat. He had a broad smile that showed off his bright front gold tooth that he often picked at with a toothpick. He or his wife sat in the ticket booth each evening selling tickets.

Bates Barber Shop

My father sent me to Bates barber shop next door to the theater every other Saturday morning for a haircut. Often a few of my grade school chums were sent at the same time so it turned out to be a place to gather and talk over latest adventures in our young lives. The deep and narrow shop had a long row of wooden straight-backed chairs lined up along the side wall. The once caned seats had been replaced with thick, embossed, hard leather seat coverings fastened to the chair frames with upholstery tacks nailed all around the seat perimeter. We sat on these awaiting our turn in the barber chair.

Five large, white, enameled, barber chairs with padded leather seats and backs, lined the opposite wall. Emery and two other barbers attended the front three chairs. Bare light bulbs hung from the ceiling over each chair. Only those hanging over chairs in use were turned on leaving the back portion of the shop dark and eerie.

Behind each chair a large mirror mounted over a white marble-topped counter provided a resting place for the barber's tools. The most intriguing item at each station was a tall glass cylinder with a chromed metal cover containing a blue-green disinfectant solution. A dozen or so combs were emersed in the liquid. When a new customer climbed into the chair, the barber turned to his cylinder to withdraw a fresh comb for use on that person. He tapped it a time or two on the cylinder top rim to knock disinfectant solution from the comb tines.

The shop was always busy. Men came in for haircuts, shampoos, and often a shave or beard trim. As we sat and watched the men in line ahead of us get haircuts, we dreaded times afterwards when the big barber chair was tipped back, its large footrest pointed towards the ceiling, and the barber began giving the customer a shave. This meant we would have to sit for a much longer time before being summoned into the chair for our simple haircuts.

The shaving procedure took longer than a haircut. Sometimes we waited most of the morning for our quick 25-cent haircuts. We had to keep a sharp eye out for who came in and took a seat on the waiting chairs. If we weren't careful, adult customers would jump ahead of us, again prolonging the time we had to sit waiting. While we waited, we perused magazines lying around the shop. *National Geographic, True Magazine, Popular Mechanics, Field and Stream*, etc., and at the bottom of the stack, a girly magazine or two. We snickered when we found these and tried to make sure no one saw us peaking at them. We eavesdropped on the banter between barbers and customers. Occasionally we learned new words.

Jonker's Accordion Studio
The building next to Emery's housed both an accordion studio and, in a small space carved out of a front corner of the building, the office of the local Justice of the Peace. From the street, the function of the accordion studio was obvious. That of Justice of the Peace, not so much.

> **The Men Looked Funny**
> The shaving ritual included steaming the beard. Hot towels were wrapped around the man's face with only his nose sticking out. Then came the sound of a shave cream brush being forcefully stirred around the inside of a shaving cream mug to generate whipped lather. It was brushed on the face after removing the towel. Next, we heard the slapping sound from the barber stropping (sharpening) a straight razor on a long leather strap that hung on the side of each chair. Then the shaving began.

The Jonker family sold instruments and taught students how to play those big, heavy, flashy, pearl finished accordions. They held accordion band rehearsals in the back room. On warm days, with the studio front door open, strains of tunes and odd sounds squeezed from the instruments wafted out onto the street. The Jonkers were accomplished players and could play accordion masterpieces such as *Lady of Spain* (Tol shard Evans). But mostly, the sounds we heard were from students learning to coordinate hands and arms to produce moving note passages and scales.

Students performed at public events. In parades, they sat on hay bales arranged on a flatbed wagon, towed by horse, tractor, or pick-up truck. Their performances were popular, and the studio attracted students from miles around. Accordions were less expensive than pianos and package-deal payment plans that included instruments and instruction were carefully designed to be affordable. Other local merchants, including my parents, marveled at the success of the operation and appreciated the "traffic" generated when parents brought students to lessons then walked downtown streets checking out merchandise and services offered. Saturdays, and after school weekdays, were busy times at the studio.

J. P. Sylas
The function of Justice Sylas was not apparent. Day after day he sat behind the window in his small office, dressed in the same suit and tie, his feet propped up on the desk, gazing out onto the street. When we asked our parents what this fellow did, they simply replied, "Don't ever find out." Pressed for more information they would simply say, "He's there to keep the peace."

Occasionally, the Justice grew tired of sitting behind his desk and walked the downtown sidewalks. He tipped his hat to approaching persons, stopped to chat, or ducked quickly into a business to see who might be available to swap tales or exchange greetings with. While he never seemed busy or harried, he carried with him an air of authority, mystery, and (to us kids) uncomfortableness. It was later in my early driving career that I came to understand his function more clearly. Though he also held a real estate license and could help people buy and sell houses, there wasn't much of that going on in town in those days.

R.F. Donley Jewelry
Next door, the bottom half of the jewelry store plate glass window was painted black on the inside so no one could see through it. Behind the transparent upper portion, a narrow platform covered with white satin fabric was a display space for small clocks, watches, fancy cigarette lighters, silver plated items and assorted diamond studded jewelry items like rings, necklaces, earrings, etc. A sign with a black background and gold lettering hung above the window. It read, "*R. F. Donley Jeweler."* Inside, a small customer browsing space consisted of an "L" shaped glass-topped counter where merchandise was displayed. Behind the counter a tall cabinet providing a small workbench topped off by several small drawers stood against the wall. Robert F. or "Moose," as he was known, sat at the workbench on a tall stool performing watch, clock, and jewelry repairs. He stopped as needed to attend to customers. A large man with thick black hair, bushy eyebrows, and a big black mustache, his friendly nature forestalled scary first impressions.

Beside the display case, a black velvet drape hung from floor to ceiling. When an item he wanted to show a customer was not located in the display case, Moose used a slit in the drape to disappear into the back of the store and quickly return with the desired material. Customer space on the front side of the display case could only accommodate three or four people at one time. Given the "L" shape of the display case, there was no access to the back side of the counter, making me wonder how Moose got around to tend to the front of the store. Clearly, I thought, he had to enter and exit his private portion of the building through a backdoor. Access to the back side of the front window display area was also limited to his side of the counter. At store closing time, almost all merchandise was removed from the window. I imagined them being placed into some large secure vault located somewhere behind the mysterious black curtain. After all, these precious items were made of gold and contained expensive diamonds.

The store always had a musty odor about it heightening the intrigue associated with my visits there. Though he had no air conditioning, it was always cool in the summer, perhaps as a result of the dark closed-in conditions. As for Moose, he was a gregarious man, who wore wire rimmed glasses that included a small magnifying lens he could flip down to examine the internals of a watch, or peer at a ring setting. He was one of the core downtown merchants that my father hung out with, both on the main street and as a hunting or fishing buddy in off hours. It must have been his physical features that earned him the name Moose. We kids really liked his nickname and used it among ourselves but were instructed by our parents to call him Mr. Donley. Any time I saw him, either in his store or out on the street, I wondered how, given his large hands and big fingers, he could handle the delicate parts of the watches he sat repairing. My father explained that he had learned his trade and developed his skills while serving in the U.S. Army during WW II. He was a proud member of the local American Legion Post, and I always had a feeling of great respect for him when he marched, in uniform, in the annual Memorial Day parade.

Wagner Furniture Company
The Wagner Furniture Company, directly across the street from my family's dime store, was owned and operated by Ora Wagner. He and his family lived upstairs. The downstairs area was split into two halves, the showroom in the front portion, the shop in the back. His shop or "factory" was where he made furniture or, more commonly, reupholstered items for customers. Orrie, as he was known, was a solidly built stocky man of medium height with bushy salt and pepper colored hair. Generally dressed in a white T-shirt and bib overalls, his slight accent suggested a north European background. The dominant feature of his shop was a large, low, flat table located in the center of his work area. Couches or chairs that he upholstered were placed on this

workbench putting them at eye level for the job at hand. Off in the corner, a large, heavy duty, industrial sewing machine was used to stitch together material cut into odd shapes to form heavy fabric, leather, or sometimes a stretchy new material called vinyl furniture coverings.

The shop was littered with all sorts of hand tools. Clamps, hammers, scissors, etc. of various sizes and shapes were seen lying around or hanging from the sides of the workbench. Though it looked to be in disarray, Orrie knew exactly where everything was. Each tool seemed to be available to him, at arm's length reach, at the exact time he needed it.

I was occasionally sent to the store to run errands for my father or to take a hand-written message from my mother to Mrs. Wagner. (That was "texting" in those days.) She was quiet, friendly, always neatly dressed, and sat at a bookkeeping desk at the front of the store. After conducting my business with her, I always took time to sneak back into the shop to watch Orrie work. I stood there quietly with him not knowing I was present. Working on furniture frames, he tied large coil springs together with heavy twine then tacked and stretched strips of upholstery webbing over them. Cotton batting was placed on top of the webbing before the covering was stretched over the item. Especially amusing was the way he took handfuls of tacks, thrust them into his mouth, then spit them out one at a time onto the head of his magnetic tack hammer. He tacked the covering to the frame using high speed motions, sinking tacks with single hammer blows at a rate of about two tacks per second.

A hard-working fellow, Orrie produced a fine product. However, customers mused that it took him a long time to get to and complete furniture pieces left for his attention. Now and then he also produced hardwood chair or couch frames that he upholstered, thereby building the entire piece of furniture. Customers "stood in line" to purchase these custom-built items. Unfortunately, Orrie also had a drinking problem. Occasionally, main street would be a-buzz with the word that Orrie was "off on a bender." All shop work stopped until sobriety returned.

The Telephone Company
Next to Wagner's and across an alleyway, a single step located on the main street sidewalk led up into the telephone office. Pedestrians walking the sidewalk had to negotiate around the step. Inside, the front half of the office included a tall reception desk for paying phone bills or conducting other business. Behind it, sitting at a 90-degree angle, a complicated looking switchboard stood against the building sidewall. An array of round-holed telephone jacks was mounted in a vertical main panel. In front of it, several corded phone plugs stood at attention ready to be plugged into jacks that connected customer telephone lines.

Working in shifts, 24 hours per day, telephone company "Operators" sat at the switchboard answering calls with the simple one-word statement, "Operator." When the caller identified who they wanted to be connected with, the operator (usually a woman) shoved the appropriate plug into the jack that connected them to the requested party.

Stacks of telephones were piled in the rear portion of the office. Many were wall hung crank phones, others newer desktop units. Large spools of wire were also stored in the area. Company lineman, Louie Richwine, worked out of there. We often saw him out about town tending pole-to-house wiring and installing or repairing individual telephones. We marveled at his pole climbing abilities. Using climbing spurs attached to his boots, he "shinnied" up poles to reach connections at the top in no time at all.

The operators were mostly unseen but always a part of our lives. We couldn't make a phone call without speaking to them and relying on their connections. During slow periods they filled us in on latest news or hot topics in town. I liked going into the telephone office with one of my parents to pay their bill. I looked over the equipment and watched operators plug and unplug calls. If busy, their skillful motions looked like something that could be set to music.

One operator was the quiet and kindly mother of my friend Ken Spade. Another was a bit of a sensation in the eyes of some of my older peers. Younger than the others, she dressed in provocative clothing. These fellows referred to her as "Two-bits Betsy." I wasn't sure what this meant, but they sure enjoyed talking about her. One summer day as we rode bicycles through the downtown area, these fellows knew that Betsy was working the switchboard. They dared me to go up to the open office front door and yell, "Hey, two-bits Betsy." I didn't want to do it, but they kept pushing me in that direction, calling me "Chicken." So, I did it. I pushed my bike up near the screen door and yelled the phrase. Instantly, the door flew open, and she came after me. I peddled like crazy up the main street sidewalk and turned the corner onto to the east Water Street walkway where I finally got away from her. No, I didn't know what those words meant, but I sure learned not use them again.

We lived in town for a while before getting a phone. When we did, it was a modern desk style unit. Mother didn't want one that hung on the wall. A 10-inch square black metal box containing the bell ringer did hang on the wall but was located discretely down near the floor. The handset sat in a cradle placed on a small table that disguised the box on the wall. Fabric-covered wire connected the two.

We didn't need to turn a crank to reach the operator. We simply lifted the handset and waited for her to answer. When she did, we told her who we wanted to call. For a local call, we gave her the party's name or, if we knew it, their telephone number. If making a long-distance call, we needed to know the number and location of the party we were calling. The operator used out-of-town trunklines to connect. Frequently, they were busy. She would have to wait until they cleared before putting our call through. We were asked to hang up and wait for her to call back when she had an open line. Often that was sometime later, perhaps an hour or more. (Just like when calling the cable company or airline customer service agents today.)

When receiving calls, we had to pay attention to the "ring." Ours was "two-shorts-and-one-long." The bell rang quickly twice, followed by one long ring. The duration or tempo of longs and shorts varied between operators. It was the ring pattern that was important. When we heard our ring, we picked up the phone to be connected with the caller. Our number, 2-1-R, described our ring. Two short rings followed by one long one. I thought the R stood for "ring," but other customer numbers used the same digits, but a different letter. Individual phone companies had their own numbering schemes in those days.

When the system was converted to dial phones, long distance calls still required operator assistance, but we direct dialed in-town calls. Phone numbers were changed to four-digit numbers. Ours was 4386. Our new telephone had a black cradle that held the handset and had a numbered dial in its base. The bells were still in a box on the wall. When we picked up the handset we were no longer connected to "Central." Instead, we listened for a "dial tone." If we heard party line persons speaking, we had to wait our turn. As a part of the change, the local phone company merged with General Telephone, a regional company. The local office closed. Operators were located nine miles away in Three Rivers.

Crater Guarded Razon Company
The disheveled looking building abutting the telephone office was home to Crater Guarded Razor Company. The appearance of the once white wooden facade with peeling paint never changed. Two front glass windows as well as those in the centered entry door were covered on the inside with brown wrapping paper. No one was ever seen coming from or going

into the abandoned looking building. However, my father knew what went on in there.

Starting in 1917, the company manufactured and repaired straight razors. Modified by Mr. Crater, these patented shaving instruments were unique. The "razor sharp" shaving blade folded into a bone-colored plastic handle when not in use and had a spring steel guard that the beard passed through before it was cut. This prevented direct contact of the sharp blade with the face, yielding a close but "safer" shave. My generation didn't have much experience with these. Once mature enough to grow our whiskers, we learned to shave with "T handle" Gillette safety razors and electric shavers. Straight razor use was on the wane. However, they are now regarded as rare collectables.

I remember my father "lathering-up" and shaving with his Crater when he wanted a close shave not provided by early electric razors. Skill was required to strop the blade on a long leather razor strap, hold the guarded blade in one hand at just the right angle – with pinky finger sticking out just so, then gently shaving the face under a thick layer of shaving cream. The lather was whipped up in a shaving mug using a round half-dollar-sized soft bristled shaving brush to both produce the foam and apply it to the face. The company played a starring role in this personal care act practiced by men around the world.

The Post Office
When old enough to cross main street on my own, I was sent to the Post Office to mail letters or buy stamps. I especially enjoyed those trips when Postmaster Fred Davenport was available. He was also my Boy Scout leader and Sunday School teacher. A tall man with a soothing voice, he had a way of talking with young fellows. He was inviting, educational, and authoritative all at the same time. We really liked and respected Fred.

The Post Office lobby was a long narrow shaped space with row upon row of small postal box doors mounted in the back wall.

The knobs and small glass windows on the front of each box made it look as though eyes and mouths of a thousand faces were staring at you as you entered the lobby. Three service windows along the right-hand side of the room served customers. Usually only one, the largest near the back of the lobby, was open. Fred's desk sat behind the first, a smaller bar-covered window. It was only open when he was available to chat with customers. The middle window was only open during busy periods such as Christmas card or income tax mailing time.

Greetings from Fred were always a treat. He knew I was working on a Boy Scout stamp collecting merit badge and often alerted me to availability of new commemorative stamps. He sold me a plate block or two to add to my collection. We also exchanged small talk. It was a sad day when he lost his job due to a change of U.S. Presidents. Postmasters were politically appointed positions in those days. When a new president was elected, persons who held Postmaster jobs could quickly change. I thought that was unfair, but it gave me a quick Civics lesson. Fred was resilient. He quickly took a job selling cars at the local Ford dealership. I still saw him often since the Ford garage was located near the back door of the dime store.

Later, the Post Office was moved to a new building one and a half blocks south of the business district, next to the Congregational Church. The lot and the new building were owned by the local funeral director. Among grumblings about moving the Post Office out of the business block, it was suggested that this too was the result of political connections. Another Civics lesson.

Gambles Store
The Gambles store at the corner of Washington and East Water Street had large display windows and featured appliances and furniture. A modest facade between the corner building and the Post Office served as the main entrance. The Gambles chain of stores sold hardware, appliances, and furniture. Headquartered in Minnesota, local stores were franchised, but individual owners

stocked them as they saw fit. The Constantine store had a large auto parts department, modest hardware and toy offerings, and focused on large ticket items such as mattresses, furniture, appliances, and electronic items of the day. Radios, record players, and the latest sensation, television sets, were available. Owner John Susko was a personable, always smiling, sort of fellow. His merchandise brand names tended to be unfamiliar, reflective of Gambles discounted lines.

My first bicycle was a 24-inch Gambles Hiawatha bike. Several of my friends had more popular brands like, Schwinn, Columbia or Roadmaster. Mine was a basic model, red in color, with no light, horn, luggage rack or other accessories that my buddies had.

I went to work on it, adding an "Ahh-oh-gah" horn, headlight, and rear reflector. Doing so, I made repeated trips to the Gambles bicycle parts counter. I used allowance and saved-up odd-job money for each item.

Besides the smaller diameter wheels (which I quickly outgrew), a major issue with this bike was frequent rear wheel flat tires. About once a week, when I went to hop on my bike for daily rides, I found I had a flat rear tire. The leak was almost always at the innertube valve stem. The fix required a trip to Gambles for a new tube. To install it, I removed the rear wheel, pried the tire from the rim, and swapped the tubes. I had to be careful not to poke holes in the new tube when using screwdrivers to stretch the tire back over the wheel rim.

I used a hand-pump to put air back into the tire. If I had inflicted a wound-causing a leak to the new tube, I had to remove it, walk to the gas station a block from our house and have it "hot-patched." That process intrigued me. The station attendant stretched the tube over a curve-shaped anvil, roughed up the rubber with a wire brush, smeared nice-smelling rubber cement on the tube, placed an oval-shaped metal cup and rubber patch over the hole, clamped it down, then used a match to ignite flammable material contained in the cup. The sizzle, smoke, and gunpowder-like odor produced were impressive. This vulcanized patch cost me 10 cents. I required so many of them that once in a while the station attendant felt sorry for me and didn't charge.

My father concluded that when I jammed on the coaster brake, as I often did to make skid marks, the rim stopped but the tire kept turning. That tore a hole in the tube at the valve stem causing a flat.

The bike's coaster brake intrigued me. Located in the rear hub, it had a short metal arm attached to one side of the wheel that was bolted to the bike frame. Each time I fixed a flat, I removed a bolt to free the arm, calling my attention to the brake. I wondered what was inside the hub that made it work. One day, I decided to find out.

As I removed the large flat nuts that kept the brake and its numerous parts inside the hub, a whole bunch of thin metal rings started falling out. I was bewildered. How would I get them back where they belonged? I gathered them up off the garage floor and put them in an empty cigar box that my father had left lying around. When he came home that evening, I presented him with the box and asked him to put the brake back together. His response surprised me.

He was a very handy fellow that I was certain could build or fix anything. But, after questioning me about why I had taken the perfectly good working brake apart, he said, "Since I didn't take it apart, I don't know how to put it back together." He said "we" would have to take the parts to the Three Rivers bicycle shop, and "I" would have to use my allowance to have it put back together. Dad continued to fuss, making the trip an uncomfortable journey. But it turned out to be a watershed event. On arrival, I found my next ride. There it was, a Schwinn Black Phantom, the top of the line among new bikes. I had been saving my money for quite a while. After the shop owner offered a modest trade-in allowance for my Hiawatha, box of brake parts and all, I had just enough to buy the bike. The deal was struck, we returned home, loaded up the rest of the Hiawatha, and headed back to Three Rivers to load up the new Schwinn. That made my visits to the Gambles bike parts counter much less frequent.

East Water Street – South Side

South Washington St.	Gambles Store	Beer Store		Engles Market	Stephenson Dry Cleaner	Alleyway	White Pigeon St.	Fire Station
	Post Office							
	Crater Razor							
	Telephone Office							

Alleyway

The Beer Store

Among the half-dozen small store fronts behind Gambles on the south side of East Water Street, the first one housed what we called "The Beer Store." Besides beer, it also sold liquor. Occasionally, Dad stopped there to purchase a bottle of Four Roses bourbon. Using it primarily when guests were entertained, he didn't drink much of it. One bottle could sit in the kitchen cupboard, high-up over the refrigerator, for a long time. I had been in the beer store a time or two with Dad but had no reason to venture there on my own.

Engles Market

Engles Market stood next to the alleyway behind Gambles. This small grocery store had a nice meat counter. Mr. Engles, a quiet man dressed in all white and a full-length blood-stained apron was usually found working at the back of the store. His large chopping block stood behind the refrigerated meat counter. The collection of sharp knives and meat cleavers lying on it were intimidating. I was glad the glassed display case separated customers from the chopping block. I didn't want to go near it.

Mom liked shopping there. When she made selections from his well-stocked cooler, he used a large Toledo self-calculating scale and its multicolored pricing chart to weigh and compute the cost of each purchase. With great fanfare he tore a big sheet of white butcher wrap from a large paper roll at the end the counter, wrapped the meat in it, and sealed the package with white paper tape that was moistened with water when pulled from its dispenser. Using a red grease pencil, always tucked behind his right ear, he wrote the price on the package. The showmanship involved with these actions made the store interesting to me.

Engle's also offered blocks of cheese cut from giant cheese wheels. My father loved to go there for the latest in strong smelly cheese. Limburger was a favorite. He also brought home Blue cheese and others, most of which Mother found offensive. The odors and tastes sparked much conversation around our kitchen table. I liked some, didn't care for others, but always expressed approval to support Dad's side of the debate.

Stephenson Dry Cleaners
Mark Stephenson ran the laundry/dry cleaning store located across an alley from Engles. It was our place to get suits, pants, and other "good" clothing items cleaned and pressed. Large items like draperies, comforters, or tablecloths were also taken there to be washed or dry cleaned. Besides Mr. Stephenson, several ladies worked in the hot smelly area behind the front counter. Large steaming and rumbling machinery used for cleaning and washing continuously whirled and hissed back there. Adjacent pressing equipment included large ironing boards and heavy irons, heated by placing them on steam-fed hot plates. Steam-heated mangles were used to press wrinkles out of cleaned items. It was hot work for the ladies, but fun for me

when I stood at the front counter watching steam inflate trousers threaded onto a mandrel that removed wrinkles as they were withdrawn from the dry-cleaning drum.

Despite the steamy atmosphere, owner Mark always looked dapper standing behind the front counter. A large apron covered his white dress shirt and neatly pressed pants, accented by a crisp bow tie. He did the heavy work loading and unloading the machines. Though frequently wiping sweat from his brow, he never looked stressed and was always jovial. Out on the street, a fedora, smart-looking jacket, and a big cigar completed his outfit. He served as town mayor and enjoyed walking through the business district greeting constituents and hanging out at the Walgreen's Drugstore coffee counter.

The Fire Station
A two-story brick building at the intersection of East Water Street and White Pigeon Streets was the closest thing we had to a town hall. Formerly an auto dealership, two large bays with roll-up doors housed two fire trucks. One belonged to the village, the other to outlying Florence Township. In town, volunteer firemen responded to fire calls using both trucks, but only the township truck responded to rural area calls, unless extra help was needed. Two-way radios frequently crackled, buzzed, and beeped in an unmanned office adjacent to the trucks. Our scout troop met on the second floor each week. We frequently heard voices coming from the radios during scout meetings. Our imaginations conjured up thoughts of what those conversations were about.

The meeting room was stark. Long plank tables with screw-on pipe legs and straight-backed chairs were randomly arranged. Single bare light bulbs in porcelain sockets dangled from the high ceiling. They cast shadowed lighting in the room. In winter, the room was always cold. The firemen occasionally held public suppers there. They used a sparsely appointed kitchen at the back of the room to prepare or reheat simple meals. A large walk-in closet was used for disorderly storage of scout camping gear. Tents, cooking sets, back packs, duffle bags, shovels, hatchets, etc. were piled on the floor, one pile for each scout patrol. Handmade signs taped to nearby walls identified each. Much of it was army surplus gear. Some tents were a two-piece affair. They had to be buttoned together at the peak. They had no floor. We used separate canvas tarps for that. Larger walled tents were also made-up using sections buttoned together. If put together right, they were somewhat watertight, but we could count on getting wet. It rained on most of our outings. Only younger scouts used the Army surplus tents. Once we advanced, we were privileged to use new one-piece pup tents with sewn in floors. That led to a more pleasant camping experience.

Occasionally volunteer firemen were training or maintaining equipment when we arrived for meetings. They gave us close-up looks at the trucks and even let us sit in them. Switches that ran the siren and red lights were always of special interest. We helped them stretch out or roll up canvas hoses used to fight fires. Better yet, when a truck was running with hoses hooked to it, we took turns trying to hold onto the nozzle and spray water out onto the street. Fighting pressure produced by the truck's powerful pump was hard.

When the village bought a brand-new pumper, we saw it before other residents. The shiny red 1950 Chevrolet was equipped with the latest equipment. We shared the pride of the firemen as it was shown around town. We could quote statistics regarding pumping rates and describe attributes of the truck as it rolled by in parades or screamed by responding to a call.

East Water Street – North Side

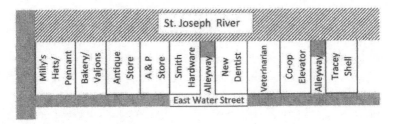

Lee Tracy's Shell Station

Lee Tracy's Shell Oil station was right across the street from the Fire Station. Larger than Hank's Standard station, a pair of gasoline pumps sat out in the open on the station ramp. The building included a small office area and two indoor service bays. One was equipped with a hydraulic lift. Lee was a kind and likeable man who stuck to business when waiting on customers and servicing cars. We walked beside his station to get down to the riverbank behind the co-op feed mill. On the way, we bought soda pop from Lee and exchanged a few greetings. He asked about our fishing successes, but conversations didn't last long.

Lee had two sons, Walter and Ron. Walter was older than I, Ron younger. In my early teen years, Walter had a car. It was a late 40s-early 50s model Chevrolet coupe. He kept it in spotless condition. Quiet, thoughtful, and always friendly, he played clarinet in the high school band. When not in school, he worked at the station. Initially unbeknownst to me, he had a 1948 Cushman motor scooter stored at home in the garage. One day when I stopped by the station to check in with Walter, I learned he was selling it. That got my attention! Discussions with him, and negotiations with my dad and mom resulted in my getting that scooter. That story follows in Chapter 9.

The Co-op Feed Mill

The co-op feed mill was a busy downtown focal point. A member owned business, farmers brought harvested grain to the elevator to sell or have processed into feed. Feed production from stored grain, sale of seed, fertilizer, and supplies supported the business during non-harvest seasons.

Tractors pulling grain-filled wagons into town created a busy traffic pattern on East Water Street. School chums living on farms were often drivers of these loads. We town kids were envious of their opportunity to start driving at an early age. Our primary interest in the place was the riverbank behind the large, corrugated metal-sided building. Municipal sewers and co-op waste materials discharged directly into the river made it a messy and somewhat odoriferous place. However, carp, red horse, and freshwater garfish liked the washed-in grain and were plentiful. They quickly struck "doughballs" (a dampened lump of bread molded around a large fishhook) that we used as fishing bait. In addition to our day-time fishing trips, buddies Jim Smith and Barry Swartwout ventured down there to spear fish after dark. I never participated. My curfew was always, "Be home by dark."

The Veterinarian's Office
A modern looking building just west of the co-op served as the office and residence of town veterinarian, Dr. Wescott and family. Doc and Mrs. Wescott were friends of my parents and very active in the community. During my early teen years, they left town and a new "lady vet" moved in. Dr. Jacoby was an interesting person. Besides the novelty (in those days) of being a woman in that profession, she was German in origin and spoke with a strong accent. She was slight in build and a chain smoker. A cigarette always dangled from her lower lip. She carried cigarette packs rolled up in the sleeves of her T-shirts. Though very friendly, Dr. Jacoby was always in a hurry. Conversations with her, including office visits, were brief. Much speculation circulated about how she managed large farm animals while making rounds in her always mud-covered car. In summer when she wore no jacket, her bulging biceps suggested she could physically handle the beasts. Her husband, Mr. Martin Hammond, taught high school science classes. He was an animated instructor known for his intellect and tough questions

on biology, chemistry, and physics tests. We didn't socialize with either of them much, but both taught us a lot through their professional roles.

The New Dentist's Office
Dr. Robert Carter built a new brick office building on the river front. Very modern looking, the building had a low-pitched roof and small slit-like windows high up on the outside walls, just below the eves. New buildings in town were always a novelty. Besides its architecture, this one became a place of curiosity for other reasons. Stories circulated that Dr. Carter used new and unusual techniques in his practice. But most folks in my circles used dentists in neighboring communities, Sturgis or Three Rivers.

Smith Hardware
Smith Hardware had been in close friend Jim Smith's family for a long time. His grandparents started it and lived on the second floor of the building. Though they continued to be involved, the business was primarily run by Jim's father, Ted. Grandfather A J served as a clerk. Jim's grandmother and his mother took care of bookkeeping in an office located at the back of the store. The store carried a full range of hardware items and had well-stocked hunting and fishing departments. The latest rifles, shotguns, ammunition, fishing rods, reels, and tackle were always available. When working on various projects, either at home or in the dime store, I went to Smith Hardware for nuts and bolts, hinges, catches, or handles. Occasionally, I needed glass and putty to replace a broken window pain or perhaps a piece of pipe. Pipe could be cut to length and threaded as we waited using a machine in the basement. Elbows, unions, flanges, and other fittings were available in tall bins at the back of the sales floor.

My father and I always kept a keen eye out for new items in the hunting-fishing departments. I bought 22-gauge rifle bullets, shotgun shells, and fishing lines and lures for adventures with Dad and my peers. When we young fellows gathered for outings,

Jim always had an advantage over the rest of us. He came equipped with the latest in tackle, tools, or other items.

The A&P Supermarket
The local A&P store (officially named The Great Atlantic and Pacific Tea Company) was located next to Smith Hardware. It was the best known, largest, and first national grocery store chain in the USA. A wide variety of food products were all available in one store. Back then, the brand was as familiar as today's McDonalds, Amazon, Google, or Walmart stores. Our A&P had the largest sales floor and was the only out-of-town owned store in town. All others were locally owned. My mother shopped there, took me with her, and later sent me there to pick up a bag of sugar, loaf of bread, or other items she ran out of while cooking or baking.

I was impressed by the store's vastness and store-brand products offered, especially Eight O'clock coffee. I was amused by the name. Were you supposed to drink it only in the morning? My folks drank coffee all day long. It also came in a paper bag. Other coffee brands were packed in vacuum sealed tins. The bag contents were not ground coffee but whole coffee beans. When someone took a bag off the shelf, they opened it and dumped the beans into a large machine located next to the packages. They turned a large dial on the front of the machine to select the desired "grind," then pressed a button to produce freshly ground coffee. The empty bag was placed under a spout to catch the grounds. I loved the process, but I could only experience it by watching others grind their coffee. Despite my urging, Mother didn't buy that brand. She preferred Maxwell House, claiming it was "Good to the Last Drop!" just like their ads said.

A&P store manager Brown Witek was one of my father's hunting and fishing buddies. Always super friendly, he struck up conversations with all who entered the store, including kids like me. One Saturday afternoon, when the local bank was closed, my father needed change for dime store cash registers. He handed me a $20 bill and asked me to walk over to the A&P and ask Mr. Witek to exchange it for a roll of quarters ($10) and two rolls of dimes ($5 each). When I approached him and made the request, he replied sternly, "Ask your dad what he thinks this place is, the First National Bank?" Then smiling, he gave me the rolled coins. When I reported what Mr. Week said, Dad replied, "Next time tell him, 'No, it's only a branch office.'"

The Always Dark Antique Store
The next storefront was occasionally vacant. For a time, it housed an antique store that, when open, sold furniture and other items. There was rarely any activity in the building. It was always dark inside, except for a mysterious single light bulb that glowed in a floor stand located at the back of the store. It was spooky and reminded me of what I understood stage actors said about theaters: "The theater stage should never go dark." I had seen movies that highlighted this superstition, showing a single bare bulb lamp placed on stage when the theater was empty. I thought of this every time I walked by and peeked in the closed store front windows. When it was open, I walked in and looked at the unusual items on display. They included ornate doorknobs, hinges, large keys, etc. Today we call these items "restoration hardware."

The Bakery and Val Jon's
Wilbur Mann ran the bakery next door. He produced fresh breads, rolls, cakes, doughnuts, cookies, etc. He and his family lived in the building upstairs. Every morning at 4:00 AM, Wilbur was downstairs producing baked goods and aromas that wafted out onto the street, attracting morning customers. That's when you could see him and hear his jokes and stories. In afternoons he was not to be found. That's when his wife and, after school, his daughter tended the sales counters. Now and then, Wilbur baked salt-rising bread. My father loved it. When he proudly brought a loaf home, I enjoyed it too. I liked the taste and strange odor. Like with his cheese, Mother wasn't impressed.

When Wilbur died, his wife, Rita, closed the bakery. She came over and worked in the dime store for a number of years and continued to live in her upstairs apartment. I helped her with chores such as putting new license plates on her car. She kept the 1953 Hudson Hornet in the bakery building basement. It was long and sleek, had a plush interior, and sunken floor panels. Very stylish, it really impressed me. It was way ahead of its time.

Rita rented the bakery space to the Went family who started a combined flower and phonograph record store. Named Viljoen's, the flower portion was run by the mother Val Went, the record portion by her oldest, out of school, son Jon. Younger son Terry was in my class at school and also worked there. It was a happening' place. We guys bought flowers for special date occasions like proms and sweetheart dances from Val. Jon stocked record albums and 45 rpm records, including the latest pop music hits. One day a regional recording artist stopped in to play and sing along with his new rock and roll recordings that were blasted out of the store sound system. The store was packed with gawking teenagers but there was no squealing or whistling. The guy wasn't that good.

Jon Terry and I were all "into" new high-fidelity (HI-FI) record playing developments, especially the latest, stereophonic sound. We built our own equipment using purchased kits to assemble turntables, tone arms, amplifiers, and speaker systems. We experimented with different phono cartridges, always looking for the best sound. The Went brothers had an advantage over me. They had access to wholesale sources of high-end equipment. Heath kits and Electro-voice loudspeakers were made nearby in St. Joseph and Buchanan Michigan. They were top-of-the-line components, and expensive. I had to stick with lower cost mail-ordered Knight Kit equipment sold by Allied Radio in Chicago. I mailed in an order and items were delivered by United Parcel Service (UPS). (The Amazon experience of the day.) I watched the Went brothers solder their kits together in the back room of their store, then went home and assembled mine.

The Pennant
The Pennant anchored the northeast corner of East Water and Washington Streets. A combination ice cream shop, restaurant, and newsstand, it was popular and run by the Baechler family. It was also a hangout for teenagers, before I had become of age.

My parents were friends of Mr. and Mrs. Baechler. On Saturday evenings when the dime store was open, we occasionally went there for supper. I liked their hamburgers, fries, and, of course, the ice cream. My parents' objective was to get in and out as quickly as possible so they could be back at work. One evening my father was particularly anxious to get back, but I had ordered French fries, the only one to do so. It took longer to produce the fries than the rest of our order, so I was the one holding up progress on our food getting to the table. To make matters worse, it meant we would not have time to order an ice cream sundae for dessert, a real disappointment for my sister. I was unpopular with all three of them that evening.

Milly's Hats
Milly's Hats located upstairs over the Pennant sold ladies and young girl hats. Mother visited the store now and then, taking me with her on just one occasion. I found it to be a very boring place, and apparently expressed that reaction. From then on, she went there by herself, or with just my sister. They proudly modeled their purchases on return. I didn't really care to look.

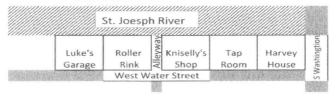

The Harvey House

The main downtown intersection of Washington and East/West Water Streets was, and still is, offset. West Water is positioned about 100 feet north of East Water. The Harvey House Hotel, the most prominent downtown landmark, anchored the northwest corner of the intersection. Built in 1903, the heavy stone foundations had supported a warehouse during the town's river port days. In my time, the Harvey House had a few rooms for rent on upper floors but was primarily known for its restaurant and popular bar named the Tap Room. It was run by the Thornton family. They lived on the upper floors. Depending on who was cooking, the restaurant waned in and out of popularity in the eyes of my mother. We also went there on Saturday evenings, especially once The Pennant closed.

Separated from the restaurant by a beaded curtain hanging in the doorway between the two rooms, The Tap Room was a curiosity. We youngsters were barred from entering the area. From laughter and conversations that filtered through the curtain, I concluded that a big crowd gathered there. That heightened the mystique and my young mind's eye visions of what must be going on back there.

Knisely's Barber Shop

Roy Knisely ran his barber shop in a second Harvey House side room. Accessible only from the street, it was just large enough for one barber chair and a small waiting area. Plate glass windows on either side of the front door provided good visibility from the street to determine how busy he was. Roy, a friendly and younger fellow than Bates shop barbers, was always up to date on high school athletic happenings, and even hotter topics like who was driving what car, who was dating who, etc. In our junior high years, my peers and I switched to Roy for haircuts. Mother thought the Bates shop produced better cuts, but the conversations and networking experiences at Roy's were much more to our liking. No one wanted to be seen coming or going from the Bates shop once we reached that mature age. I still recall the aroma of the Red Rose hair tonic that Roy liberally sprinkled on my hair at the end of each haircut. For my daily routine, I used the more lightly scented Wildroot Cream Oil.

The Roller Rink
The roller-skating rink just west of the barber shop had been there for a long time. It opened occasionally, but mostly stood silent. I skated there on a few occasions. I was impressed by the rink's smooth hardwood floor, amused by the old oblong shaped bare light bulbs that hung from the ceiling around the perimeter of the skating floor, enjoyed the view of the river through large windows in the back of the building, and intrigued by the antique sound system that provided music for skaters. Behind the rental skate desk, a huge audio amplifier sat in a wire cage with its large amber glowing vacuum tubes producing sounds from the system. An old-style microphone stood on the desk. Three springs held the sound capturing element within a circular metal ring. I had only seen this style microphone in the movies, but this one sat right there on the counter still in active use.

The rink was open occasionally on Saturdays and on some school vacation days. Scout troops, school classes and other groups used the rink for special parties. We could use our own wooden wheeled high-top shoe skates, which no one that I skated with had, or rent the worn and cracked-leather ones available at the rink. They had seen lots of miles and, on my extra wide feet, were very uncomfortable. We all used steel wheeled clamp-on skates to skate on the town's cement sidewalks but couldn't use them in the rink. Wearing a clamp-on-skate key on a string around our neck was a symbol of streetwise behavior in our middle-school age days.

By the time I was in my teen years, the rink had permanently closed. Our skating venues became rinks located in neighboring communities, 10 to 20 miles away.

Luke's Garage and Bait Shop
Luke Irwin's garage was a free-standing structure built of "rusticated" or "rock faced" cement blocks. Once an Oldsmobile dealer, he had been in business for a long time. He still performed a few oil changes, grease jobs, engine tune-ups, and exhaust system repairs, but mostly served other functions. He was a wastepaper dealer, fur trader, and sold bait and tackle out of the shop.

The building consisted of two main-floor rooms and a cavernous basement. His small office looked out onto the street and contained about three chairs where he and cronies sat to debate the issues of the day. The shop didn't have a hydraulic lift for working under cars. Instead, Luke used a long narrow hole in the floor as a pit that he drove cars over. From downstairs, he reached up to perform under-car service. Always an active place, locals brought in old newspapers, magazines, and corrugated boxes to sell for a few cents per pound. Trappers sold stretched and dried hides. Sheep farmers brought-in wool. Luke bailed these materials and resold them through wastepaper, cotton fiber, and fur trade markets. I sold him shipping cartons emptied at the dime store.

One of my early jobs was to flatten emptied boxes in the back corner of the stockroom, load them on my express wagon, and pull them up the alley behind the store and over to Luke's. Frequently, they fell off on the way, causing me to stop and reload. Once there, I took them down the steep alleyway between Luke's and the roller rink to his river's-edge basement door. I piled the boxes on an old platform scale so he could weigh them. We went up to his office to complete the transaction. I came away with about a quarter per load. On days when I made multiple trips I ended up with as much as a whole dollars' worth of change in my pocket.

I enjoyed visits to Luke's office. He collected odd but interesting things. He used the wall dividing his office from the shop to display them. Small objects such as unusual keys, odd or fancy doorknobs, auto license plates from far-off places, a strange can or bottle opener, unusual silverware, and peculiar or antique tools were hung on the wall. Centered above them was a collection of dried fish heads cut from bragging sized specimens he or others had caught. They were flanked by shells from turtles caught on the riverbank or other places. Luke was an expert at cleaning turtle meat from the shells and bragged about his recipe for turtle soup and other turtle meat specialties.

The office wall displaying the collection was made of Celotex, a light, soft, easy to work fiberboard material about three-quarters of an inch thick. The wall was only finished on the office side. Bare studs and unpainted Celotex faced the shop side. To mount his treasures Luke wired them in place by poking small holes in the Celotex, passing the wire through the holes, then twisting the ends together on the back side. In all, 100 or more treasures were on display. Most had been there for a while, but now and then a new object would be added. It was always fun to examine the collection and try to identify each object, especially if its purpose was not obvious. Spotting something new was a special treat.

West Water Street – South Side

```
| Municipal Light Plant | Advertiser Record | Alleyway | Parking Lot          | Read's          |              |
|                       |                   |          |                      | Teft's          | S. Washington St. |
|                       |                   |          |                      | State Farm      |              |
|                       |                   |          |                      | Perry's Appliances |           |
|                       |                   |          |                      | Vail's          |              |
                                             Alleyway
```

West Water Street (top) / Alleyway (bottom)

Constantine Municipal Light Plant

The Municipal Light Plant stood across the street from Luke's, at the end of West Water and its intersection with Canaris Street. This square brick industrial building had large arched windows on all four sides and looked more modern than most other downtown structures. The village established this diesel-powered electric generation plant and distribution system in the late 1930s. It provided what was described as "less expensive" and "more reliable" power than that supplied by Michigan Gas and Electric Co. that also served the community. The plant occupied about one-quarter of the block, nearly abutting the rear of the dime store building diagonally across the block. Three huge diesel engines powered the plant. Two big Nordberg engines of the type used to propel ocean going ships were original. Standing 10 or 12 feet high, they had 6 or 8-foot diameter flywheels and large exposed crankshafts. A third modern looking engine/generator set, the latest in Nordberg design, was added in the early 1950s. Smaller in physical size, with all moving parts encased, it produced more electricity than the other two combined.

We could feel vibrations and hear the constant exhaust rumble from these monsters inside the dime store. My father, a village councilman at the time, served on the committee to select the new engine/generator set when it was added. He fussed that "Vibrations from the plant caused items in the store to walk right off the shelves."

Intrigued by the plant and its operation, I often walked out the dime store back door over to the light plant to watch the engines run and strike up conversations with the operators. At least one man per shift was always on duty. They invited me in to check things out and get up-close looks, sounds, and the feel of all that powerful machinery. One operator really liked to explain and demonstrate the tasks he performed while on the job. He kept logbooks full of readings taken from the vast number of dials and gauges located on the engines and switch panels standing around the interior of the plant. He and other operators managed electricity outputs by turning numerous knobs and switches. Some tasks, such as shifting electrical load from one operating generator to another, without causing a community-wide power outage, were tricky. Once in a while, when outages did occur, I headed over to the plant at my next opportunity to ask what the problem had been, what caused the outage. Operators usually gave me a complete description. On one occasion, the massive crankshaft on the largest of the two old engines failed, breaking into two pieces. That engine was out of service for several months while a new crankshaft was manufactured and installed. I followed those developments with great interest.

Switching loads between generators usually occurred in the middle of the night when electrical demand was low. On Sunday mornings, that activity took place later, about 6:00 a.m. On one of my visits, the operator invited me to observe the task on the next Sunday morning. When the day came, I hopped on my bicycle and rode down to the plant, arriving early to make sure I didn't miss the event. When I arrived, the operator got up from his chair and took me over to the panel used for the switchover. He explained the function of each gauge, dial, knob, and lever and just how he would make the change. Then, using compressed air to turn the newer engine over he got it started. I could just barely hear him over the loud clatter of the old engine running at the time. Then came the more muted sounds of the new one coming to life. Two large white lightbulbs located on the operators panel began to blink on and off. They alternated, one on, the other off, back and forth between the two. Each one represented one of the two generators being synchronized. The objective was to keep them blinking in a constant rhythm to make sure that the load change between units occurred smoothly. A meter indicated the alternating current frequency produced. It needed to be held constant at 60 cycles per second. There were no computers to assist. "If I don't do this right I can cause a power outage, or your clocks won't run at the right speed," the operator said. I was fascinated. Those plant visits gave me a background useful when working around industrial power plants later in life.

The Advertiser Record
Just east of the light plant, a combination brick-and-metal-sided, warehouse-looking building housed *The Advertiser Record*, the town's weekly newspaper. It was owned and operated by Joseph A. Cox. A friendly fellow, Joe was short in stature and always on the lookout for news to print in the paper. Just inside the front door a reception area consisted of a high-topped main counter equipped with a telephone. If not engaged in printing or typesetting operations, Joe was usually found standing behind the counter talking on the phone. Dressed in a businessman's white shirt, protected by a large denim apron, he took handwritten notes destined to become parts of news stories. Working from their respective homes, one or two writers also contributed material. They tracked what townspeople were doing, who traveled where to visit which relatives or some notable landmark, then wrote short news items describing the events. Joe personally covered bigger stories such as town council or school board meetings. Every week, he physically set the type, printed, folded, and distributed each copy by mail. As editor and publisher, he had final say on what got printed.

Like most downtown merchants, Joe was a coffee break buddy of my father's, a member of the local Rotary Club, active in local masonic organizations, the Methodist Church, etc. His ability to keep up on the news of the village while tethered to the shop was remarkable. He also provided print shop services to the community. Anyone needing event tickets, posters, programs, letterheads, envelopes, or other printed materials, got them from Joe.

The front door to the building was on West Water Street but the back end abutted two alleyways that met behind the dime store. I visited the office often. I used an old stockroom sign press to print signs for dime store merchandise displays. I obtained poster board and other materials needed from Joe. For 10 cents each, Joe sold me large sheets of poster board that I cut up into sign blanks. Each visit gave me a chance to check out Joe's printing operation.

His linotype machines stood just behind the front counter. He had two, but only the second one was generally in use. These behemoth and complicated looking machines produced lines of lead type used to print the newspaper and other items Joe produced. He sat in front of the machine at its typewriter style keyboard entering text he wanted to print. Through a series of mechanical processes, the machine melted solid blocks of lead and recycled used type to produce lines of reverse face type that were put into printing presses. Experienced typesetters like Joe (and I) could read the backward lines of type as they were locked into printing press frames. Others might need to look at the type in a mirror to read it. My father obtained a few linotype produced blocks from Joe that I used in my sign press. I used both individual pieces of wood block type and the lead blocks to print my signs.

Joe's two platen presses and a newer flatbed press stood near the linotypes. Each had unique moving parts and intricate ink supply systems. They were fun to watch. The hissing sound made by ink rollers running across large round plates on the top of the platen press was unique. They picked up ink and transferred it to the typefaces just before the press closed down on paper automatically placed in the press at just the right moment by metal arms that were always moving. The precision associated with all this was fascinating, much different from the manual process I used on my sign press. Joe patiently answered my questions on how it all worked.

In a large unheated room at the back of the building, Joe kept a huge, long, press used just one day per week to print the newspaper. During one of my visits, he took me back there to see it. A large roll of paper was fed into one end of the machine, the newspaper was printed in the middle section. Folded newspaper copies came out of the other end. Not running at the time, Joe described in detail how the huge machine worked. He invited me to come and watch when he ran the press on Tuesdays. However, he did so at 4:00 a.m. I was an early riser, but I never got around to going in to watch the printing operation. However, my frequent visits taught me a lot about printing. That information came in handy later on in my paper industry career.

South Washington Street – West Side

Read's Market

Read Langworthy, a close fishing buddy of my father, ran his meat market on the southwest corner of West Water and Washington Streets. He was a tall, thin, very friendly fellow who was thought of by many as the source of the best meat products in town. He tended the store from behind his large, refrigerated meat cabinet, wearing a full-length blood-stained apron. A checkout clerk at the front finalized sales.

Standing at a maple chopping block, Read wielded a large cleaver, used sharp knives, and an adjacent band saw to produce steaks and chops from whole sides of beef and pork kept in a large walk-in cooler at the back of the store. Other tools included a cold-cut slicing machine and menacing looking meat grinder used for producing ground beef. Shelving units in the center of the store were stocked with common grocery items, but in smaller quantities and with less variety than the A&P.

In high school years, Read's two children and other school chums worked at the store. They tended the checkout counter, stocked shelves, and occasionally performed some meat-cutting tasks. They also handled waste materials. Chunks of fat, bones, etc. were boxed and piled behind the cooler or placed in barrels out

62

in the alley. These were later, sometimes much later, taken to the dump. They could get "pretty ripe," especially on hot summer days. It was best not to walk or bike behind Read's Market on these days.

My mother did some meat shopping there and my father kept an eye out for bargains on prime cuts or specialty items. Read stocked items such as oysters when they were in season, and occasionally, special cheeses. I was the gofer, sent to pick up deals Dad had cut with Read when they met at the Lakes drug store coffee bar. As I entered the store and headed towards the meat counter, Read flashed a broad smile, stopped what he was doing, and retrieved a butcher paper wrapped package from the cooler to hand to me. I dropped off the cash I had been given at the checkout counter. If there was change involved, I shoved it in my pocket and didn't mention it when I returned with the goods. I hoped to keep it as a tip for my services. Sometimes that worked, sometimes it didn't.

Every year, Read saved beef tenderloins for Dad to grill on Christmas Eve. For four to five weeks prior to Christmas, the dime store stayed open until 9:00 p.m. This made for long days. On Christmas Eve, Dad closed at the usual time, 6:00 p.m.. He decided that he and the family had earned a nice steak during this busy season. He headed home to start a fire in the back yard grill. It made no difference how cold it was or how heavily the snow was falling. Read supplied the best cuts he could find, and Dad grilled them to perfection. When asked how he came up with those special steaks, Dad said, "I just asked for the ones that the meat cutter saves out for himself."

Dr. Raymond Zimont
Community physician, Dr. Ray Zimont's office was upstairs over Read's Market. He was a jovial fellow, and quite a fixture in town. Everyone knew him. He and his family were active in social circles and most residents were patients of his. My family was not. At the time we moved to town, my mother was expecting my sister.

Somehow, the search for doctor/hospital arrangements to address her needs led to us becoming patients of Dr. Fortner in Three Rivers.

However, when I was nine, I did make one visit to Dr. Ray's office. It was time to prepare for the annual scout trek to summer camp. One registration requirement was a physical exam. Scoutmaster Fred Davenport asked Dr. Ray to provide troop member physicals at no charge.

Having been made aware of the appointment at one of our weekly meetings, discussions among us centered on what to expect when we reported for the exam. Of most comment was the anticipated hernia test. Some of the more informed members of the troop professed to know all about it. They regaled in introducing us uninformed lads to what was to happen. We would, they said, experience the "drop your drawers and turn your head and cough" test. They added, "Doctor Ray is going to examine your private parts!" We anguished, "Are we really going to have to do this?" "Yes, you are," they insisted.

On appointment day, with great trepidation, we all lined up on chairs along the wall in the waiting room. One by one, we were called into the exam room. There, a nurse who most of us knew, stood dressed in her starched whites wielding a clipboard. She was ready to write the information to come from the exam on our camp forms. "Oh no! This woman would be present for 'the test,'" we thought. The exam began with Dr. Ray peering into our eyes, ears, and throat. He took our temperature using an alcohol tasting thermometer that he had shaken down vigorously before sticking it into our mouth. Using his stethoscope, he listened to our pounding heart and noted our pulse rate. Then, he asked us to stand and turn to the side so our backs would be to the nurse. Sure enough, he calmly asked us to lower our pants and underwear, turn our head to one side, and cough. We barely felt him do the check. Then, we quickly pulled up our pants and returned to the waiting room. Fellow troop members stood there snickering and awaiting our reactions. Unphased, each one of us gave a self-assured nod indicating we had passed the test, become a bit wiser, and were now ready to head for camp.

Teft's Shoe Repair and Clothing Store
Mr. and Mrs. Frank Teft ran their shoe repair and clothing store by themselves. They and their family lived upstairs over the store. Just inside the front door, floor to ceiling shelves were stuffed with boxes of new shoes. Clothing racks and counters filled the center and opposite wall areas. The rear portion of the store housed the shoe repair shop. A pleasant odor of leather goods greeted customers as they entered.

Frank was a talented shoe, and other leather products, repair technician. My father always said, "If Franky can't fix a shoe for you, he can make you a new one just like it." I never knew that to happen, but I took full advantage of his repair skills. I was hard on shoes. My extra wide (EEE) feet made it very hard to find shoes that fit. There were none to be found among those stocked at Teft's. I had to wait until we traveled to neighboring and larger town shoe stores to find them. When I did, there would usually be only one pair in the entire store that fit. When we walked in and the salesman greeted us asking what style of shoes we were looking for, Dad would say, "Just bring him the box."

Once I got new ones, it wouldn't be long before the soles came unstitched in the front, the heals were worn down or pulled off, or the leather soles wore through. Then, I was sent to see Mr. Teft and ask that he fix them. Frank would see me coming, smile, and for minor repairs, invite me to sit in the chair near his work area while he went to work on my shoes.

He wore denim clothing including a long heavy apron. Tools laying on or attached to his workbench were really interesting. Steel shoe-sole shaped anvils of various sizes stood at the corners of the bench. He placed shoes upside down on these to nail on heels or trim new sole edges using sharp, curved, knives. Using a heavy-duty sewing machine, he stitched layers of leather together. Along the shop sidewall, a 6- or 8-foot-long rotating horizontal power shaft, driven by a single electric motor and wide belt/pulley arrangement, held numerous grinding and buffing wheels. Frank stood in front of the turning wheels and moved back and forth between them grinding, buffing, and polishing the shoe he was working on. While it didn't take long for him to fix minor problems, I had to leave shoes for more involved repairs such as half-soling or, once in a while, replacement of entire soles.

When he was finished, the shoes always looked as good as new, except in the case of the half-sole job. This repair, which cost considerably less than one that replaced the entire sole, left a telltale seam under the arch where the new leather joined the old sole. Though only visible when one looked at the bottom of the shoe, I hated this. While the upper portion of the shoe looked new, my peers were always tipped off to the fact I was wearing repaired shoes if that seam was seen. That was certain to draw comments and jeers and was traumatic for me. When other kids wore out their shoes, they got new ones. Because of the short supply of shoes in my size, my frequent need for repairs, and cost issues, I had to have mine repaired. In class, I sat erect with my feet placed flat on the floor, trying hard not to expose the bottom of my shoes until they became scuffed enough to make the half-sole seam less noticeable.

State Farm Insurance
A small office building just south of Teft's was home to Tom Wagner's State Farm Insurance Agency. When we first moved to town, this building housed Gracy Skrimshaw's restaurant, pool hall, and billiards parlor. As the insurance agency, the building front had been remodeled and had a more modern look than most other downtown buildings.

A large plate glass window ran across the front at an angle, providing a view of the furnishings in the office. Tom, furniture maker Orrie Wagner's son, sat sternly, at attention behind his desk, meticulously dressed in a suit and tie. When approached, he was soft spoken and always very polite. Fully visible behind that huge window, he and an office assistant sat, all day, handling papers, typing, and talking on the phone conducting their business.

Since my father had filled his insurance needs with the Noecker Insurance Agency located two blocks south of the business district, he didn't use the State Farm Agency. Consequently, I had only occasional contact with Tom. He and his wife were active members of village social circles. She, the more outgoing of the two, was a frequent dime store customer. I stopped by the office now and then selling tickets for Boy Scout events, ad space in school publications, etc. Tom was receptive and supportive. I always left with a sale and impressed by the "business like" atmosphere in his office. Exceptionally neat, tidy and business like, I thought to myself, "That's the way to run an office."

Armstrong's Rexall Drugstore
Armstrong's Rexall Drugstore was a happening place. There were two drugstores in town, and they were very different. Each had their own distinct character and cliental. Ross and Mary Armstrong, assisted by their son George, had been in business for a long time. The building exterior, as well as the layout and furnishings inside, had an old, comfortable, and traditional feel. In part, it was a newsstand. A large rack just inside the front door held newspapers, magazines, and additional printed materials pertinent to the area. The sales floor had areas devoted to gifts, jewelry, and personal care products. A prescription drug counter was located in the far back corner. It also had a unique, and attractive, soda fountain accompanied by a few booths and tables, where customers sat to enjoy drinks, ice cream sundaes, malts and shakes, and other treats.

In late summer of each year, Armstrong's also became the only supply point for textbooks used in all classes in the village's K-12 school system. In those days, families had to buy books used at school. Come August, we all headed down to Armstrong's, returned (for cash) books we had used the previous year that we wanted to dispose of, and bought either new or used books for the new school year. Though this created lots of traffic for the store, my father always wondered if all the planning, coordination, and headaches associated with providing this service was offset by the sales rewards received. For sure, it disrupted the store's layout and was an intense time for the sales staff during several weeks each summer.

For us young people, the soda fountain was the big drawing card. The long darkly stained wooden bar and about eight red leather-topped circular barstools, permanently fastened to the floor, stood at attention along the righthand side of the sales floor. A wall hugging counter behind the bar had tall, mirrored panels, flanked by marble pillars, and capped by a cornice near the ceiling. The booths, tables, and wire framed chairs provided group seating. Soda fountain drinks such as cherry or chocolate Cokes, lime phosphates (for the more macho or adventuresome), and 7 Up floats were mixed by the attendant, usually a teen-aged peer. Ice cream treats such as sundaes, malts and shakes, or simple ice cream cones of various flavors were also available.

After school, during school lunch breaks, on Saturdays, during school holiday periods, and on summer vacation days, we met friends, caught-up on news of the day, and arranged dates at Armstrong's. Mary Armstrong (Mrs. A, we called her) assumed the role of Sergeant at Arms. A diminutive lady with brilliantly white hair, she was always neatly dressed, had sharp eyes and a way of nodding, shaking her head, or pointing a single finger to let us know when we had crossed the line and were about to be spoken to. Her husband, Ross, the pharmacist, was a short, stocky, and quiet man always dressed in a white shirt and tie. He went about his business compounding and filling prescriptions in his small work area across from the soda fountain. He observed happenings across the room but mostly watched, smiled, and carried on brief conversations with anyone who approached him. Son George, on the other hand, was in the thick of things. A good-sized, good-looking and good-natured middle-aged fella, he was casually dressed and served both as host and bouncer, whichever was appropriate at the time. He was not married but had a male partner. The partner, Chuck, a blond-haired good-looking guy younger than George, occasionally stocked shelves, etc. He was quiet and didn't engage much with the crowd. Among our parents there was a bit of a buzz about the relationship between George and Chuck. We teenagers were left to figure this out on our own. No one wanted to explain it to us. We just enjoyed our rendezvous there, using it as our "social media" and launch point for many happenings.

Newspaper carriers who delivered daily papers door to door throughout the community did so out of Armstrong's backroom. They gathered there late in the afternoon, every day except Sunday, picked up newspapers printed in several adjacent communities then fanned out across town on appointed routes.

The Masonic Lodge
The Masonic Lodge met upstairs over Armstrong's. Three large rooms and a kitchen area could only be reached by climbing a long flight of stairs. There was no elevator. My father was a Mason, and Mother a member of the Order of the Eastern Star. Each met on different nights. Many downtown businesspeople and other residents were members. The Masonic groups were part of the community social structure. Participation varied between individuals. My father often said he was a "Belly Mason." He would say, "Yes, I'm a member, but I generally only attend meetings when dinner is served." My mother was more engaged. For many decades, she held the Eastern Star office of "Organist." I always wondered why she was called organist since the room had no organ. She played a piano at meetings.

The only time I was involved in these activities was during installation ceremonies when members brought guests or when the Masons were planning a dinner and tables and chairs had to be set up. My father often volunteered me to go up and help the men move heavy tables and chairs. He had hoped I would one day join the Masons. I wasn't opposed to doing so, but we never got around to it.

When my mother, and once my father, were installed as Eastern Star officers, my attendance was required. I had to get dressed up in a suit, climb the long flight of stairs, go sit in the long row of hard uncomfortable "plank seat" chairs that lined the perimeter of the room, and endure a very long ceremony. I tried to sit in the chair furthest back from the front of the meeting room where I could watch the guards who stood at the meeting room door. Once the meeting was called to order, the door was closed. One guard stood outside of the room, the other inside. There was a small speak-easy style opening in the door. During the ceremony, when someone was to enter the chamber, a loud knock would come from the guard outside. The inside guard peeked through the opening and loudly asked who wished to enter. The outside guard announced the individual's name and office. The inside guard then turned and repeated the announcement. When prompted by the Conductress (the woman in charge of the meeting), he opened the door. I never understood all the secrecy around these activities. It seemed pretty silly to me. I knew practically everyone who attended these functions. I saw them on the streets in town all the time. I found it amusing that inside this mysterious place, everyone had to get all dressed up and act and address each other in strange ways. There were even secret handshakes that had to be exchanged between members. These were people who had known one another nearly all their lives. I guess one had to be a member to understand. However, I have always felt that I did miss out on something important or worthwhile by not having made the effort to join and share that experience with my father.

Perry's Gas and Electric Company
Perry's Gas and Electric Company sold appliances. They stocked kitchen stoves, refrigerators, washing machines, even clothes dryers (if one could afford such a luxury). Radios, record players, and the latest craze, television sets, were also available.

My parents bought appliances there. A stove, refrigerator, and one of the first automatic washers in town were among their purchases. My mother had done laundry using an old ringer washer out on our back porch on Mondays. It was a labor-intensive process. She soaked the clothes in a washtub (filled with hot water using buckets) then hauled the waterlogged garments out of the tub and placed them in the washer where they sloshed around for several minutes in soapy water. She ran them through the washer's wringer, refilled the washer tub with clean water, and put the clothes back in to slosh around in a rinse cycle, then ran them back through the wringer once again. Drying was done outdoors on a clothesline. Laundry had to be done on sunny days if clothes were going to be dried.

My father saw the new automatic washer as a way to lighten her load and make the task safer. Several stories chronicled women, and children, getting hands and arms caught in wringers on those old-fashioned washing machines. Despite uncertainties and misgivings about this new "gadget," Mother agreed to let him have Perry's install one in our kitchen.

It was noisy and somewhat quirky, but it worked, mostly. When the machine entered the spin cycle it was VERY noisy. I said it sounded like a B-29 bomber. If the load had become unbalanced, as it often did, the machine thrashed and jumped around making me think it would bust through the floor or adjacent walls. The worst problem was the machine's tendency to throw a sock up over the edge of the washer tub and down into the area of the machine where the pump was located. Sometimes the machine stopped working mid-cycle and all progress towards the weekly laundry chore ended until my father came home and ran his arm down into the machine to extract the sock from the pump. Mother was quite frustrated, but Dad was still pleased. After all, by using it, she had more time to spend working in the dime store rather than spend the entire day doing the family's laundry.

Way in the back of Perry's store, a room was home to Glenn Pashby's radio-TV repair shop. He was a small man, balding, very quiet, and afflicted with a nervous system condition known in those days as the St. Vitus Dance. As he worked or talked with you, every now and then, his hands, head, eyes, or feet made quick jerky movements. At times, they were quite violent. But he was known as the best radio, TV, or other electronic device repairman for miles around. He always had tons of work to do. Non-working radios and TV sets were stacked up all around his workbench waiting to be fixed. He also worked on car radios. When not at his workbench inside the shop, he could be found outside in the alleyway, lying on a car floor, under the dashboard, changing tubes or performing other repairs on car radios. If more extensive work was needed, he removed the radio from the car and took it into his shop for diagnosis and repair. Car radios required lots of repairs in those days and were not universally installed in vehicles. One of the great debates of the time was whether or not having a radio in the car was too distracting for the driver.

Glenn's skills, knowledge, and command of his tools were impressive. Stacked up on and around his workbench, an array of specialized instruments and materials were used in his work. The voltmeters, vacuum tube testers, stacks of paper circuit diagrams, and most interesting a couple of oscilloscopes were all impressive. Glenn probed around inside the bird's nest of wires, resistors, capacitors, and other components that made those electronic things work. He checked voltages and looked at "sine curves" displayed on oscilloscope screens and compared them with information printed in schematic circuit diagrams published by manufacturers. I was amazed at how he understood all of this and used that information to determine which component, among hundreds involved, needed to be unsoldered, removed, and replaced. His ability to use a soldering iron in tight places while having involuntary jerky hand motions was remarkable. My peers and I wandered into his shop at odd moments to watch him work and ask questions about what he was doing. Though he didn't talk much, he was patient and passed on tidbits of information that we could add to our fledgling electronics knowledge. He showed us how to read circuit diagrams, understand their funny shaped squiggly lines, make good solder joints, etc. The knowledge obtained helped me assemble the Allied Radio Knight Kit amplifiers and other parts of my homemade stereophonic sound system.

Radio/TV repair was Glenn's day job. Evenings he ran the movie projector at the Park Theater. Always unseen, cloistered upstairs in the projector booth, he was responsible for presenting most of the movies that entertained local residents. Among us kids this sideline job earned him the nickname "Pushbutton Pashby." When theater owner Cocky Howard, sitting in the theater ticket booth selling tickets, decided it was time to start the movie, he pushed a button on an intercom linked to the projection booth and let Glenn know it was time for showing to begin. While attending movies, my peers and I, sitting in our seats, turned around squinting up into a little window near the ceiling in the back of the theater. We hoped to catch of glimpse of "Pushbutton" as he went about his duties.

Vail's Department Store
The P. L. Vail Dry Goods store had been in business next to Perry's for a very long time. When I initially visited the store with my mother, Mr. Vail, (P.L.) was an elderly man who sat at a large desk at the back of the store, smoking a cigar. His two clerks, daughter Maribeth Stephenson and another lady, tended to customers and stocked shelves. The store sold ready-to-wear clothing, a large assortment of fabrics, garment patterns, and sewing notions (thread, needles, buttons, zippers, hooks and eyes, etc.). In this respect, Vail's was a competitor to the dime store. We too

sold sewing notions. My mother also found a source of fabric remnants she could sell, further increasing the dual merchandise offerings. However, the competition was not stiff or acrimonious. Quite often when a customer couldn't find the thread or rickrack color, style, or another sewing item they were looking for, Mother would tell them to try Vail's. We believed the opposite suggestion was provided by Maribeth.

The store layout provided a window back into mercantile history. Merchandise was kept behind the counters on tall shelf units that stood around the perimeter of the store. An Item could be viewed when the customer asked a clerk to bring it to them. A few racks held ready-to-wear items on hangars near the front of the store, but most were in armoire style cabinets with glass doors. Near the back of the store, fabrics were displayed in long bolts stacked on end in free standing shelf units that arose nearly from floor to ceiling. A large flat wooden table positioned amongst the shelving units provided a surface to unfurl, examine, and cut a length of fabric from the bolts. Nearby, filing cabinets contained a large selection of patterns that could be used to make any kind of garment. Other racks and cabinets held the spools of thread, cards of buttons, zippers, needles, and other sewing supplies.

What attracted me was the huge cash register that sat squarely in the middle of the store. A bright, shiny brass behemoth, it was nearly three feet wide by three feet tall. It sat on a wooden cabinet containing a stack of six or eight cash drawers. Several rows and columns of keys on the register's curved front panel were used to enter the amount of the sale being "rung-up" and open one of the cash drawers where the clerk to put the money. Each clerk was assigned their own drawer. The machine did not total the cost of items purchased by the customer or calculate any change needed to complete the sale. All of that arithmetic was done off to the side with pencil and paper. The register was powered by a large crank on the side of the machine. After pushing the keys, the clerk turned the crank, the machine rang a small bell, opened a cash drawer, and printed a record of the sale on paper tape that rolled up on a reel kept for store records. I was familiar with how cash registers worked since we had three in different places on the dime store sales floor. But they were small single drawer units in painted metal cases. I wondered why such a large machine was needed for this quiet store. I came to realize that it reflected early days when the store was a general store, selling groceries, hardware and other items, and was a much busier place.

By the time I was a pre-teen, P.L. had passed away and Maribeth became the primary proprietor. She was a tall, slender lady with hair rolled up into a bun. Always very neatly dressed in a suit jacket, long skirt, frilly white blouse, and appropriate hat, she maintained an air of being "in charge" of all she did. Her personality was completely different from her husband Mark Stephenson, owner of the dry-cleaning shop. While he was an out going, slap-on-the-back, sort of fellow, she was always erect and reserved.

Active in the community, she was treasurer of the First Congregational Church where my family attended. During pre-teen years I was custodian of the church. Fridays after school or on Saturday I went to the church to perform my duties. When finished, I went to Vail's to report in with Maribeth. That was an uncomfortable experience. She grilled me extensively before paying me. But after a while, my self-confidence was bolstered, and I learned to communicate with adults, saying "yes ma'am" or "no ma'am" as appropriate.

Lake's Walgreen's Drug Store
An alleyway separated Vail's from Ken and Florence Lake's modern looking Walgreen's Drug Store. Ken, a very friendly fellow, was the pharmacist. He always wore a white lab coat as he worked away counting pills or compounding medicines behind his elevated prescription counter in the back of the store. Florence had a broad smile and was always impeccably dressed

while tending her cosmetic, costume jewelry, and personal-care product counters. The store was an epitome of neatness. No speck of dust or out of place items could be seen. Ken and Florence were younger than Ross and Mary Armstrong, about the same age as my parents.

They also had a soda fountain, but it was really more of a coffee bar. Tended by an adult uniformed server, one could order a Coke or ice cream treat, even a sandwich or pastry. But the most common item sold was a cup of coffee. The store served as a hangout for adults, especially businesspeople from other stores. At mid-morning and again in mid-afternoon, they gathered for coffee break periods. Greetings, tales, and news items of day were swapped. It was a mixed crowd of both men and women. Attendees depended on who had help to leave in charge of their businesses. Folks who managed factories in town, the funeral home, the church ministers, and even the superintendent of schools also stopped by to share what were the social media posts of the day.

The store also served as the stopping point and ticket agency for the Indiana Motor Bus Company. Four times a day, the bus stopped in front of the store to discharge or board passengers, and unload freight brought into town by this service. Buses two or three hours apart headed north in the morning and returned in the afternoon heading back to South Bend.

Young people of my generation were not barred from the store, but the adult atmosphere made it a bit uncomfortable for us. If we had business there, we conducted it quickly and went on our way. When my sister and I were young, our parents took us there on Saturday nights after both the dime store and drugstore had closed. Ken or Florence locked the door and we all sat at the soda bar enjoying an ice cream treat of some sort. Occasionally our father went behind the counter to create a special treat. The Lakes didn't have children and enjoyed talking with the two of us. I liked the ice cream and was always interested in Mr. Lake's prescription counter activities. I liked watching him mix chemicals together for prescriptions. Conversations with Mrs. Lake could be somewhat uncomfortable. She took a schoolteacher approach to conversing with us. I turned my connection with her into an advantage and consulted with her on which small cosmetic or jewelry items I could buy my mom for birthday, Christmas, or Mother's Day gifts. It was a lesson in networking.

Phenicie's 5 Cent to One Dollar Store
My father was certain that the brick wall between Lake's drug and the dime store was a common one. He always said if either of the two buildings were taken down the other would have no wall on the adjoining side. The two-story dime store building, identified on its upper cornice as Eureka Hall, housed two storefronts. The second was The Men's Store. They were separated by internal wood framed partitions. The building was owned by a woman named Mrs. King who lived in another town some distance away.

"Phenicie's 5 Cent to One Dollar and Up" store, as the sign on the front of the building read, occupied three-quarters of the building, "The Men's (clothing) Store" filled the remainder. This made the dime store layout "L" shaped. The sales floor occupied the complete length of the north side. It ran from the South Washington Street entrance nearly all the way to the alleyway behind the building. This narrow but deep layout prompted Dad to advertise the place as "A Half-block of Bargains." The Men's Store occupied about half the length of the south side of the building. The space behind The Men's Store served as the stockroom for the dime store.

Merchandise display windows flanked either side of the dime store entryway. Inside, the forward portion of the sales floor was devoted to greeting cards, gift items, a magazine/comic book display area, and shelves displaying souvenir items, etc. But the defining feature greeting customers was the large bulk candy counter centered just inside the entryway.

The three-sided glass horseshoe-shaped enclosure had separate bins for mounds of candies of various kinds. Chocolate-maple and chocolate-vanilla peanut clusters, caramels, chocolate covered peanuts, malted milk balls, wintergreen and/or peppermint lozenges, gum drops, orange slices, marshmallow circus peanuts, red-hot cinnamon drops, candies called burnt peanuts, and of course, jelly beans were sold from the bulk case.

A clerk standing behind the counter scooped customer selected candies onto a self-calculating scale that weighed and priced the purchase that was poured into a plain-white paper bag. A flat tabletop area on the fourth side of the counter served as a "check-out" area for candy and other items brought forward from elsewhere in the store.

A long row of counters extended down the center of the sales floor, flanked by front-to-back aisles on either side. Display counters, shelving and hanging spaces for merchandise in the numerous store departments stood along the outer walls. Sewing notions and personal care items were displayed just beyond the candy counter. Ready-to-wear items, followed by school supplies, light hardware and electrical items (inexpensive tools, lightbulbs, lamp sockets, extension cords, plugs, switches, etc.), housewares such as dishes, pots and pans, cooking and eating utensils, lamp shades, etc. led customers into the toy department. Toy cars and trucks, ready to assemble model cars, airplanes, and even battleships were on display. Bags of marbles, skipping jacks, jump ropes, metal clicking frogs, and more aggressive playthings like squirt guns, cap guns, bb guns, and cap and bb ammunition, "Chinese" finger locks, etc. were also available. As were passive amusements like board games, playing cards, and a rack of children's books.

Wide ledges above outer wall shelves displayed tricycles, radio express wagons, and peddle cars. The very back of the store was devoted to paints, wallpaper, and associated supplies.

The huge variety of merchandise, packed into the long narrow space, prompted Dad to boast "My store can't be described like most in square feet, it has to be thought of in cubic feet." Front to back he stacked merchandise from floor to ceiling. Maintaining inventory was a priority for him. He treasured a framed pen and ink drawing hanging on the wall near his desk in the store's office. It depicted a merchant standing next to a mule driven sales wagon. The caption under the picture read, "You can't do business from an empty wagon." (Chapter

Dad and Mom were joint proprietors with each taking care of separate departments. They ordered merchandise, stocked shelves, and helped customers make selections or find items. Dad focused on the hardgoods, Mother the soft goods (ready-to-wear, sewing notions, greeting cards, etc.). They employed one or two clerks, depending on seasonal traffic. For my sister and me, it was our home away from home. We spent many of our non-school daytime hours at the store, either in the small "apartment" area Dad established in a portion of the store's stockroom, or when older, working at assigned tasks and tending the check-out cash register. I even earned a title from my efforts. That story follows in Chapter 4.

The Men's Shop
The Men's Shop was operated single handedly by Vernie Loomis. It was a small store selling men's clothing, mostly of the good, business, or formal varieties. Though some casual items were available, he didn't stock work clothes or hunting/fishing attire. These were sold up the street at Teft's. A short fellow, Vernie was older than my father. They were hunting and fishing buddies and Vernie was also quite the philosopher. Traffic in and out of Vernie's store was always pretty light. Quiet and observing, he often stood out on the sidewalk at the entrance to his store watching people and traffic pass by. Walkers stopped to chat and hear thoughts running through Vernie's mind. He reported who or what had passed by and speculated on what that activity was likely to mean. One day, he noted a number of people coming and going from Lake's Drug Store, two doors up the street. After watching this activity for a while he said, "I would have more

business If every time someone went to the doctor they left with a prescription telling them to go buy a pair of pants." Other observations included who had just driven by in a new car, where the fish were biting, statistics from the latest high school ballgames, or which attractive ladies had recently walked by. We learned a lot chatting with Vernie.

Inside, his store had a mixed odor of new woolen clothing and mothballs placed in the backs of cabinets to protect the merchandise. It was spotlessly clean with merchandise neatly folded, stacked on counters in the center of the store, or hung in armoire cabinets lining the walls. Suits, topcoats, and pants were in the armoires. Shirts, neckties, sox, and underwear were displayed on center tables.

His desk was located at the back of the sales floor. When not standing out on the sidewalk, Vernie sat there, reading newspapers or a book while keeping an eye out for occasional customers. An old treadle sewing machine sat in a small room behind the sales floor. When someone purchased a pair of pants, or suit, Vernie used it to sew cuffs and make other minor alterations.

We had access to Vernie's side of the building through a shared stairwell leading to the basement. Doors on both sides were usually locked but provided a "cut-through" when desired. We entered the stairway area from our side, knocked on Vernie's door and if not busy, he responded by opening it. If I needed a pair of paints or dress shirt, my mother sent me over to pick out what I wanted. After some discussion between Vernie and Mother, a deal was struck, and I had what I needed.

The wall between respective stockroom areas was quite thin. Conversations in each could be overheard on the other side. My father always kept a radio turned on, blatting away, on his side. This, he said, would "make it harder for Vernie to hear conversations on our side." Once my sister and I had outgrown the need for the "apartment" that abutted Vernie's stockroom, Dad moved his office there. He wanted to keep business discussions with staff or merchandise suppliers confidential.

The Nip and Sip
The Nip and Sip, on the other side of The Men's Shop, was declared completely off limits to my sister and me by our mother. While the Harvey House Tap Room was a happening place, The Nip and Sip was the primary "watering hole" in downtown Constantine. Just walking past on the sidewalk, one could breathe-in the combined aromas of beer and fried food.

Though they were not "teetotalers" by any means, to my knowledge, my parents never set foot in the place. I knew little about the establishment but found the "hubbub" regarding it a curiosity. I peered in through the front door anytime I walked by but continued to walk. I didn't want to be caught standing on the sidewalk looking in. For sure, I would hear about that from Mother. She used the place, and her perceived frequency with which clientele visited it, as a lesson on how NOT to live. "Those people get their paychecks, then head directly to the Nip and Sip to spend it on booze rather than take care of their families," she exclaimed.

From my quick looks, I saw people sitting at a long bar drinking beer and eating burgers. When television came to the area, a TV set was placed on a high shelf, over the bar, near the front entrance. I could get glances of it in the days before my family had a TV. One of the first sets in town, it was quite the item of interest. Later, it was replaced by the first COLOR TV in town. Some of my chums claimed to have entered the bar to get a close-up look at that. They had more nerve than I did.

A Competing Dime Store!

The building just south of the Nip and Sip housed a number of businesses over the years. For a short time, a children's clothing store was operated there by Bess Robertson. Our mothers were excited to see it open. However, Bess' husband Robert who worked at the local funeral home, bought his own parlor in Schoolcraft, Michigan. They moved away.

Another venture caused quite a stir. A lady from out of town, and worse yet someone from Elkhart, Indiana, started a second dime store. A sign announcing arrival of the business appeared on the door. For several weeks we watched as boxes of merchandise were stacked in the building. Customers coming into our store boldly asked what we thought about the coming competition. They speculated on what the new store might sell and at what price. They did so in hushed conversations among themselves, not engaging us, but making sure we could hear it. My father, a veteran of many years in the business, remained philosophical. He said he welcomed the challenge.

The store turned out to be quite small, offered limited merchandise, and lasted only a few months. However, it livened up conversations on main street and ultimately focused more attention on Phenicie's 5 cent to $1.00 Store. A good byproduct of the experience.

El-Rose Cafe

The El-Rose Café was operated by a couple named Elwood and Rose Mills. He had been a cook in the military. It was said that she had been a nurse. Some say that they had owned and operated the Nip and Sip but sold it and started the restaurant seeking a more laid-back career later in their lives.

Rose was a large lady who always wore a spotless white dress. She single-handedly ran the dining room, jotting orders on a small green-paper order pad. El, dressed in a white T-shirt and jeans, did all the cooking in the partitioned-off kitchen. He was a small man, always smiling. All we ever saw of him was from the waste up, looking out through his serving window. If he was not busy cooking, he sat at the window, on the kitchen side, peering out into the dining area.

The dining room had a counter with bar stools lining the south wall. A few tables and chairs, neatly arranged, filled the center of the room. Three uncomfortable straight-backed homemade booths hugged the north wall. The place was always spotless, rarely busy, and had a simple diner-style menu.

It wasn't fancy food. A typical daily special was the roast beef dinner. It consisted of a single slice of roast beef cut from a cooked roast using a slicing machine, a dollop of mashed potatoes with a brown-gravy lake pressed into the top, and a scoop of mixed vegetables (corn, diced carrots, and peas) all presented on the same plate. Items like burgers, soups, or fried egg sandwiches were also available. Desserts such as pies, cake slices, or a dip of ice cream (three flavors available - vanilla, chocolate, or strawberry) completed the offerings.

We ate there fairly often, sometimes on Saturday evenings, but more often for lunch in summer or on school vacation days. Rose kept up on street news from customers that came and went. She shared it with my parents as they sat taking a break from the store. I wondered how the restaurant stayed open given its quiet level of activity. The blandness of the decor, menu, and quiet lives of El and Rose seemed boring to me. When I asked my father how they could stand to do what they did day after day, he replied, "El takes a break from cooking now and then. He also washes dishes."

First Commercial Savings Bank
The stately First Commercial Savings Bank building anchored the southwest corner of Washington and Second Streets.

Constantine was founded as a center of commerce when William Meek built his mill and harnessed area waterpower resources in 1828. As the community developed, banks were prominent institutions. First Commercial Savings Bank was formed by consolidation of two pre-existing banks in 1925. The organizers were proud that their bank was one of the few that didn't go broke during the Great Depression.

The original building was an ornate gothic style structure with cement pilers and highly arched window moldings making up its outer façade. A large two sided, lighted, clock hung from the corner of the building. It loudly chimed the hour to keep downtown patrons informed of the time of day. Inside, tellers stood on marble floors, working from marble counter tops, behind brass grille enclosures, interacting with customers through pass-through grille openings.

In the 1950s the building was remodeled and the clock retired. It became a modern looking structure with a smooth brick outer façade, accented by a high strip of thin windows stretching across an angled front building wall. Inside, modern open-topped counters made it easy for tellers to converse with customers during transactions.

Foster Daugherty, a gregarious, slap on the back, firm handshake fellow, served as bank President. He greeted customers entering the lobby and people out on the street with broad smiles and glad handshakes. His omnipresence was aided by the fact that he and his large family lived just a half block away on East Second Street. His son David, a bit younger, was one of my buddies.

My father knew the importance of establishing a good relationship with the bank when he bought the dime store. He told of introducing himself to bank officials on the day he bought it. He immediately took out a several hundred-dollar short term loan, then sat on the money before paying it off several days early. From then on, when it was time to buy seasonal merchandise, he was assured of getting sufficient backup capital to keep his shelves stocked, especially when buying Christmas season items.

Dad instilled the importance of saving and practicing benevolence through banking in my sister and me. He gave us a weekly allowance of 50 cents. We could do as we wished with half of that, but the other 25 cents had to be deposited every week into a bank Christmas Club account. Each Saturday morning, she and I walked to the bank with our coupon books and quarters to make our payments. In early December, we collected our annual Christmas shopping check, all $12.50 of it. We were to use it to buy gifts for others.

We were also expected to maintain savings accounts and deposit money accumulated from odd jobs or gifts from grandparents. We could make occasional withdrawals for carefully considered purchases but were to see that our account balances grew over time. In that era, banks facilitated these lessons by offering youth accounts. By the time my own children reach that age banks no longer offered them.

West Second Street – North Side

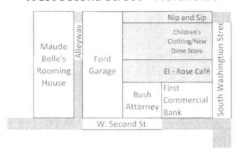

Franklin Bush Attorney at Law
The law office of Franklin Bush occupied a small, flat roofed, brick building that stood behind the Bank. The Bush family lived on Klinger Lake, several miles southeast of town. Franklin hired my friend Rob Polleys to tend the law office furnace on weekends. Rob lived on the south side of town near my family's home. He went to the law office twice a day on Saturdays and Sundays. Now and then he asked me to go with him on Sunday evenings.

Just as I had been entrusted with a key to the dime store, Rob had a key to the law office. He didn't want to attract attention on the street when he entered the building after dark, so he did not turn on lights once we stepped inside. We felt our way through the front reception area, walked through a bookshelf lined conference room in the center portion of the building, and entered Franklin's private office space at the back. There, Rob turned on the lights. A large, stately, wooden desk centered in the room was accompanied by a high-backed leather desk chair and a couple of large leather client chairs. The walls were lined with bookshelves containing rows of law books. The furnace was located in a small room adjacent to the desk area.

It didn't take long for Rob to shake down the furnace grates, shovel hot ashes into a bucket, recharge the furnace with fresh coal, then take the ashes out the back door and dump them on a pile accumulating behind the building. Once these tasks were completed, we sat for a few moments in the private office, Rob behind the desk, me in one of the client chairs. We conjectured about what crimes or other situations made people need to consult a lawyer. Rob had more knowledge and familiarity about that than I. His father was a judge. We took-in the odors from the chairs and leather-bound law books and imagined the clouds of cigar smoke encircling those engaged in high-level strategic discussions that we assumed took place there.

We speculated about how much danger there might be in this profession, thinking that not all clients were upstanding citizens. We thought some might even be dangerous criminals. We never touched anything on the desk, but before leaving, Rob slowly pulled open the top righthand drawer revealing a revolver strategically placed there by Lawyer Bush. We simply gazed at it and surmised that he needed it for his own protection.

Our fantasies completed, we turned out the lights and worked our way back through the dark building to the front door. After making sure no one was lurking in the shadows outside, we made a quick exit onto the street and began our walk back to our homes. These were good evenings out, a way to exercise a bit of independence with a legitimate purpose while, though we didn't know it at the time, increasing our sense of responsibility.

The Ford Garage
The Ford Garage abutted the mid-block alleyway. A huge structure, it had once been the town's Opera House. In garage mode the building provided a showroom large enough to display two or three cars, a couple of offices, a steel fenced-in two level cage serving as the parts department, a body shop that included an enclosed paint booth, and four mechanic's repair bays. I tried to imagine what the building looked like in its Opera House days and wondered how this small community could have supported such a large performance space. In my time, it was a busy center of mechanical activity that I visited often.

The back door to the building opened out onto our outdoor space directly behind the dime store. We had room to park two cars back there. In one corner of this space, an earthen ramp led up to the Ford Garage back door. Large enough to drive a vehicle through, the door was rarely used for that purpose, but was often left open for ventilation and foot traffic to and from the building, especially in warm weather. I used the open door to stroll up into the garage and observe what was going on.

My father had paved the way for me. When changing-out candy case varieties he used the back door to take what he wanted to get rid of to the mechanics. They loved to see him coming with an armload of white candy bags that he left with them. In return, I assumed that they didn't object to my wandering in now and then to quiz them on what they were doing.

Mechanic Sammy Rentfrow worked in the bay closest to the back door. He had a reputation of being the best mechanic in town and was the go-to-guy for engine overhauls. Those Ford flathead V-8 engines were popular and fairly reliable but required rebuild often. At about 25,000 miles they needed "valve jobs." New piston rings were a requirement at 50,000 miles. Sammy always had one or two cars torn down performing these tasks. I liked checking to see whose car he was working on and watched him remove, grind, and replace valves, hone cylinder walls, install new rings on pistons, etc.

I also checked in with the body man, Harry Ware. Harry, also known to be extremely good at his job, repaired damage from collisions, or more commonly, rust. He matched paint so well the finished product showed no signs of restoration. Rocker panel rust repair was a daily activity. I often found him sitting beside the vehicle on the floor using a small grinding wheel to cut out rusted panels. He replaced them by brazing in new ones, then filled cracks and seams with lead. He heated both the car body and small blocks of lead with his acetylene torch. When molten, he applied the lead to the joint, then skillfully smoothed it out with a small trowel he repeatedly heated with the torch. It took lots of coordination for him to handle the lead, trowel, and torch through motions that reminded me of a ballet. I concluded that I would need at least three hands to do all he did with two. I also watched him mix paint to match colors and stood outside the paint booth, peering in, when he sprayed primer or finish-color onto his workpieces. He handled the spray gun gracefully as well. His spray-painting technique reminded me of waltz melodies. Watching these masters at work, I collected hints on how to proceed with Cushman scooter projects and, much later, cars. But I never stayed long. I spent just enough time to briefly watch, exchange a few words, then head back to the stockroom before anyone missed me.

Maude Belle's Rooming House
Across the alley from the Ford garage loomed a large structure known as Maude Belle's rooming house. It was a long narrow building extending down the alley almost all the way to the back of the lot. Occupants of the building's small apartments or one room flats turned over quickly. My mother kept a keen eye out for who was coming and going. She always told my sister and me to steer clear of those folks. Since no one in town seemed to know them, or was able to vouch for them, she was wary.

Johan Johanson's Refrigeration Repairs
Behind Maude Belle's house, nearly directly across the alley from our dime store parking spaces, a pair of garages associated with her property were located. One of these roll-roofing sided structures had been rented to Johan Johanson. It housed his refrigeration system repair business.

Johan had operated a dairy down on the south end of town and developed refrigeration repair skills while working on systems needed to keep his milk bottling business going. When he closed the dairy, he opened the repair shop. He often sat in that old, dark, dirt-floor garage with outward swinging doors propped wide open, working on compressors or other components he was hired to service. Wearing heavily stained bib overalls, he was always up to his elbows in grease and oil. He loved to talk with anyone who strolled by. Given his strong Swedish accent he was a little hard to understand but was always welcoming and liked to talk about what he was doing.

My father was impressed with his self-taught mechanical skills and the fact that he had started this business during a time of fast-growing need for commercial refrigeration system servicing. "He has gotten himself in on the ground floor," Dad said. Between the two of them they hatched a scheme whereby I was to go over and talk with him about working in his business as an apprentice. They concluded that I could become skilled in this relatively new trade, fill a need, and in their minds anyway, "make good money."

Well, I wasn't impressed. The visuals were not enticing to me. Though I liked mechanical things and activities, that job appeared to be the most messy and dirty of any I could think of. Though I was frequently directed to go over and have a talk with Mr. Johansen, I never did. I had no idea what I was going to do with my life. However, I didn't think what I saw going on in that garage was it. I passed up that learning opportunity.

Part 2 – The Store

Chapter 4

Vice President of the Broom

A Full Time, Family Affair

My parents, sister, and I lived nearly as much at the store as we did in our home, one-half mile away. It was open from 9:00 AM to 6:00 PM Monday through Friday, until 9:00 PM on Saturdays, but closed on Sundays. Dad relished his "one day a week off," but always found reasons to have to go down to the store on that day too, if only to stoke the fire in the furnace. Mom and Dad's discussions around our dinner table often included things like which items were selling well, which not, what shelves needed restocking, when to go to the wholesale house for resupplies, selection of seasonal merchandise, etc. It was a 24-7 occupation – for all four of us.

We were up early on Sunday mornings to dress for Sunday school and worship services at the First Congregational Church. Mother played the organ, so weekly attendance was somewhat mandatory. Often, my father skipped out to attend his favorite services, at the lake fishing. In the fall it was pheasant hunting. In winter, ice fishing was a treasured activity. He said he could commune with God while being out-of-doors just as well as he could sitting in a church pew. But he had to be home by noon. Mother insisted that Sunday afternoons be devoted to family outings. When he did join us in the church pew, I liked sitting next to Dad. He taught me to read the bass line in the hymnal when singing along with the congregation.

Though she always tried to "be a good sport" and participate in Dad's out-of-doors activities, Mother preferred more urban recreational pursuits. On Sunday afternoons we often headed off to nearby larger communities, usually Elkhart or South Bend,

Indiana, to a restaurant for dinner, then an afternoon movie. Occasionally, especially on holidays, we traveled to southeast Michigan to visit relatives. Both parent's families lived there. It was a two-hour drive over and two hours back.

No matter where Sunday adventures took us, we came home after dark. Since our travels almost always took us southward, we reentered our neighborhood first when back in town. But we never went straight home. Since we had been out of town for a significant portion of the day, we drove downtown, traveled slowly past the front of the store, and peered into the windows and front door to make sure all looked to be in order. I don't recall ever seeing anything amiss but knowing all appeared to be in order meant Mom and Dad could sleep well and would be ready to be back at work on Monday morning.

Open for Business

Although the store didn't open until 9:00 a.m., Dad was always out the door and on the job before 8 o'clock. On arrival, he let himself in the front door, locked the door from the inside, tended the furnace, put change in the cash registers, took his morning bathroom break, then sat at his office desk for a few minutes before turning on the lights, unlocking the door, ready to receive the first customer of the day. I wondered why he hurried down there so early every morning. I was certain most of those tasks could be completed in less time than he gave himself to do them. But after reading the Steinbeck novel *The Winter of Our Discontent*, I understood. In that story, the main character, Ethan, managed a grocery store. He too, went in early every morning before opening. He did so because in his troubled and busy life, those moments before opening gave him time to be alone with just the bottles and cans on his shelves. They didn't give him any grief or problems to solve. This, I concluded, was how, why, and when my father found his quiet time. Those moments before he unlocked the door and opened for business each day were special.

Once open, the first thing dad did was sweep the sidewalk in front of the store. That served two purposes. Yes, it cleaned the sidewalk for pedestrians walking past, and customers entering the store, but more important, Dad said, "It signaled that the store was open." Anyone walking the length of the business district could clearly see him out there, know he was open, and be drawn onward to the store. In winter, the ritual became snow shoveling, but the mission remained the same. Keep the sidewalk clean, present a welcoming image, and let the world know the store was open.

A Home Away from Home

Our store stockroom "apartment" was to be "home" on Saturdays and non-school days for my sister and me. We remained there until nearly closing time each evening. Furnishings consisted of an old studio couch, a table and chairs, a sink, and a hot plate Mother used to heat soup or other canned specialties for lunch. Chef Boyardee Spaghetti was one of her favorites, but not ours. I had a strong dislike for that spaghetti. Mother was a good cook, but it wasn't until I went off to college that I learned there were other ways to make spaghetti, and those versions were really good. If we were lucky and Mom and Dad could both break for lunch at the same time, we were spared "apartment fare," and went for lunch at a nearby restaurant.

At ages three and seven, my sister and I were to stay in the apartment area most of the day, read books, do coloring, or otherwise entertain ourselves. There was no TV in those days. I quickly became bored and milled around in the remainder of the stockroom finding tools, merchandise (broken toys) that couldn't be sold, or empty boxes that I found interesting. Along one wall, a pair of large wooden boxes, the size of a desk, were stacked on their sides, one on top of the other. Their open tops faced out into the stock room. The bottom one was used to store merchandise, but the top one was difficult to reach and left empty. I stretched an old blanket across the front of the upper box and "camped-out" up there in my own special "cabin." It was a great place to read comic books and get away from my sister who couldn't, or didn't want to, climb up there.

A better hiding place was located at the front of the store near the front entrance just beyond the greeting card cabinets. A set of tall display shelves devoted to magazines and comic books, hid a flight of stairs that led to the second floor. We used the upstairs for off-season merchandise, unused store decorations and furnishings, and family personal items. Dad had a workshop up there that included a collection of bench mounted power tools, some of which he had built himself. The stairway, accessed from the sales floor through a small passage at the end of the greeting card cabinets, was not often used. I could sneak back there, sit on the stair treads and read comic books borrowed from the shelves. I put them back for sale once I had looked through them.

We sold most of the popular comics of the day. The adventures of Spiderman, Batman, The Three Musketeers, and Captain Midnight were of special interest, but we didn't call them superheroes back then. Mysteries involving characters such as Dick Tracey, Red Ryder, The Lone Ranger, or Wyatt Earp, were fun. But Donald Duck, Scrooge McDuck, Mickey Mouse, Bugs Bunny, Casper the Friendly Ghost, and Popeye tales were my favorites, as were stories about Archie, Lucy, and Jughead's activities. When new comics arrived, I spent a few hours up there digesting latest issues.

Magazines and comic books were delivered via U.S. Mail. Bundles of plain brown paper wrapped packages contained a dozen or more copies of each title. The bundles were secured by a length of string that salesclerk Rita Mann saved and wound on a ball kept under the candy case. She and I mused over how large the ball grew over time. New issues arrived once a month. Title arrival was staggered. There were always new issues of one or more of the magazines to attract buyer attention.

When new ones came, unsold issues were removed from the rack. The store only paid for books sold. We got credit for those unsold. However, the books were not returned to the supplier. Instead, one of my first store jobs was to use a straight edge ruler to tear the cover page title from each book. These 2 ½- or 3-inch-high strips were mailed to the supplier. Credit received was based on the number of title strips mailed. I could keep the de-titled books if I wished, but I was not to give them to my friends. Dad wanted them to come in and buy their copies. A selection was left in the "apartment" for my amusement. But mostly, I preferred to read the new ones as they came in. For the most part, old issues were thrown away in the back corner of the stockroom along with empty boxes and other wastepaper.

More Work to Do

Another of my first store jobs was to clean out wastepaper stashed under Dad's desk. A raised platform tucked in the back corner of the sales floor behind merchandise display shelves provided Dad's office space. It was cozy, just wide enough to accommodate his rolltop desk and a file cabinet. A swivel chair and one straight backed guest chair were the only additional furnishings. When up there, Dad could not be seen, but he could stand up to look out over the sales floor, gazing all the way up to the front of that long narrow space. He didn't spend a lot of time up there, but used it to open mail, make sales entries in his daily ledger book, count money from the cash register, prepare bank deposits, and perform other clerical tasks. Among things he didn't have was a wastebasket.

As he sat opening his mail, he examined each item and decided if he wanted to keep it or throw it away. If it was to be kept, he placed it on top of a stack of papers growing on the desktop. About twice a year, or whenever the pile tipped over, he took time to file them. If a paper was to be thrown out, he tossed it under the desk in the knee space. While sitting at the desk counting money, coins occasionally rolled off the desktop down amongst the discarded papers. He never attempted to pick them up. When the pile of papers got out of hand, he asked me to crawl under there, box up the papers, and take them to the stockroom where he used them as kindling to start fires in the Round Oak stove that heated the area. Office shredders were not in vogue back then, so that was how Dad disposed of confidential business papers. When I came across coins mixed with the papers, I got to keep them. I usually came up with about 75 cents worth of the dimes, nickels, and pennies, a nice supplement to my 50 cent per week allowance.

As I got older, the complexity of my tasks increased. By the time I was 9 or 10, running errands took me to other main street businesses. I was sent to the Post Office to mail items and buy stamps. That required crossing the busy main street. Dispatched to the bank, I was asked to exchange a $20 dollar bill (about $200 in today's money) for coins or smaller bills needed for cash register change.

Working in the Stockroom

Merchandise arrived in various sized corrugated boxes. When unpacked, these were thrown in a collection bin in the back corner of the stockroom. When it became full, I broke down the boxes, and took them to Luke's Garage to sell them. Sometimes I made a full dollar, or perhaps more, performing that task.

At age 11 or 12, I learned to unpack merchandise and check off items received against the supplier's invoice. The objective was to confirm we had received everything we were billed for. I also applied price tags to items. Prices, set by my father, amounted to about 40 percent more than his cost. This "margin" was what it took to cover costs of doing business. Building rent, the electric and heating bills, wages paid to the help, local and federal taxes, etc. all had to be paid. Anything left over amounted to some level of "profit" for him. Dad was a good business expense manager. Though he always found ways to end up making a profit from the business as a whole, he sometimes lost money on certain "loss leader" items used to bring customers into the store.

Juggling figures to make profits happen was all done in his head. Sometimes he did the arithmetic needed on the back of an envelope or other scrap of paper. He didn't have a computer, just a prized mechanical pencil he kept tucked into his shirt pocket. He rarely let me use that out of concern that I might lose or break it. To help him keep track of merchandise cost, price tags included a set of letters printed or neatly written on each one. These came from a code that could be translated into his cost. One of his wholesalers was the Grand Rapids, Michigan based J.W. Dykstra company. Dad used the letters "jwdykstra" to represent numbers 1 through 9. Zero was represented by the letter "o." If the invoice showed that an item cost him $7 per dozen (about 58 cents each), I was to put both the price he gave me (79 cents) and the letters KR (58 cents – his cost for each item) on the tag. Just as we have to keep track of passwords today, Dad wrote the "key" to the code on the stockroom worktable top.

Merchandise Cost Code Key									
o	J	W	D	Y	K	S	T	R	A
0	1	2	3	4	5	6	7	8	9

I used a hand crank Monarch Marking Machine to print price tags. Tiny lead type was "set" by inserting individual type pieces into the machine's tiny printing frame. Setting mirror image type using correct

numbers and letters was a key part of the job. Both peel and stick and pin-on tags could be produced by the machine.

I also printed signs used for counter displays. An old sign press had sat behind the Round Oak potbellied stove forever. When not in use, it was covered by a full-length denim apron. Both the press and apron were dobbed with ink. I felt important each time I put on that apron, preparing to print signs.

The top of the cabinet served as the printing area. Under the top, metal drawers contained pieces of wooden type, one letter on each piece. The top drawer also contained inking blocks. Ink was squeezed from toothpaste style tubes onto one of the blocks. A small hand roller was pushed back and forth across the block to pick-up an even ink film on the roller before running it across typefaces arranged in the press bed.

Arranging typefaces was tricky. They had to be set backwards in a mirror image of the sign text. When I ran the ink roller across the type, I had to be careful not to misalign individual type pieces. The signs I printed were about 6 by 10 inches up to 12 by 14 inches in size, printed on white posterboard acquired from Joe Cox at the *Advertiser Record* newspaper office. Wording was simple. Messages like, **Ladies Hosiery 69¢, Back to School Special, Boxed Candy 59¢,** or **Lay Away for Christmas**, called attention to sale items, seasonal promotions, new merchandise, etc.

To print them, the correctly sized sign board was fastened to a hinged platin and lowered down onto the type. Then in one swift motion, I pulled heavy chrome steel rollers attached to the press frame back and forth across the platin. Ball bearings in the roller mechanism made them run smoothy over the printing area. When returned to their resting place, the rollers continued to whirl emitting a decelerating whine as they spooled down. That sound made me feel powerful and gave me a sense of satisfaction after having completed the tedious "make ready" steps.

Raising the platin off the type, I hoped to see a perfectly printed sign. But often individual type pieces had moved or become stuck to the paper. This required a do-over. My rejection rate was about 40 percent. The real prize from my efforts was seeing the signs placed in standards and set out in merchandise displays.

It took a lot of effort to keep sales floor shelves stocked. I used dollies and push carts to move items from the stockroom out to where they were displayed by Mom, Dad and the salesclerks. Occasionally I was asked to set up a special promotional display, but mostly, I was the "gofer" who carted the merchandise from the stockroom.

Merchandise not trucked from the supplier to the store in Dad's station wagon arrived via semi-trailer trucks. Two over-the-road freight companies served our community, Allied Trucking and OIM (Ohio, Indiana, and Michigan) freight lines. When making deliveries, trucks came up the alleyway behind the store and stopped right behind the stockroom door. When I heard airbrakes hissing while working in the stockroom, I knew a truck had arrived. Shortly thereafter, a driver came in the back door to announce that he was about to unload.

In those days trucks didn't have hydraulic tailgates to lower boxes to the ground. Instead, the driver climbed up into the trailer, brought cartons to the back then jumped down and used a hand truck to bring them through stockroom doors. My job was to help with the lugging. OIM drivers were often different people each time and not particularly friendly. However, the Allied driver was almost always the same super friendly fellow named Chuck. He came in, announced himself in a loud voice, and immediately started looking for me. "Hey Muscles," he yelled. "Come on out here, we've got freight to unload."

As we brought cartons into the stockroom, we lined them up and counted them, checking to see that the number of cartons received matched the number printed on the driver's bill of lading. When we agreed the numbers matched, which took some jeering and joking with Chuck, I signed the driver's copy, and he was on his way. I enjoyed encounters with Chuck.

Window Displays

Dad had artistic talents and loved producing spectacular window displays. He developed window dressing skills while working in the chain stores. His displays highlighted each holiday season, special community events, and new lines of merchandise. My role was to take down displays being removed from the window, put the merchandise back on counters or shelves, clean up the display space, then bring him materials needed to create the new display. They always attracted attention from passers-by and sparked conversations around town. Dad had won awards for his chain store displays and once received special recognition in a nationally circulated variety store magazine. Once in a while, I was given the opportunity to produce my own display. Highlighting things like "back to school" supplies or "summer fun" items, Dad coached me, and I did OK, but I couldn't match results produced by the expert.

Keeping the Shelves Stocked

Every few weeks, my folks went to go to the wholesale house to buy merchandise. Located in Elkhart, Indiana and Grand Rapids, Michigan, they (in some ways) resembled the Costco or Sam's Club stores of today. Upon arrival, Mom and Dad met with a salesperson who checked them in, then pushed a large cart down the aisles to help them find items on my father's shopping list. Hair care goods, other personal care products, simple housewares, and hardware items were selected, in case lots, and loaded on the cart. After checkout, Dad loaded most of it into his station wagon for transport back to the store. Large cartons were set aside and shipped via freight haulers.

Dad was an expert packer. He hauled an amazing amount or merchandise in that station wagon. He packed things around the spare tire, under folded down seats, and if no one was with him, stacked cartons on the front seat and in the floor well next to him. When he got back to the store, it was my job to unload it. I always groaned when I first looked into those loads. It seemed it would take forever to unload it. Once I had it all inside, I checked off items received against the wholesale house invoice, marked their prices, and got them ready for the sales floor.

Most of the time, I didn't enjoy going to the wholesale house. Going down aisles devoted to mundane items like hair curlers packed in plain shipping containers was boring. Dad and the sales agent debated which style was likely to be the best seller or could be sold at the best price. That didn't interest me. However, my sister and I did want to be a part of the mid-July trip when Christmas toys were purchased.

Wholesalers set up large displays showing the latest and hottest toys of the year. We got to try them out, determine which passed the "kids test," and improve the odds that what Dad and Mom purchased would be good sellers. Items shipped to the store usually arrived in August on one of the hottest days of the year. As I labored and sweated to unpack and cart these items upstairs for storage (we had no air conditioning), I was told, "Just think of the cold winter days when we will be selling these toys. That should cool you off." Hmm, not so much.

The riding toys came to us unassembled. In September, after the annual back-to-school promotional period, I started putting these together and getting them out on the high display shelves. I put axels, wheels, and pulling tongues on wagons, wheels and handlebars on trikes, bikes, and scooters, and assembled peddle crank assemblies on riding cars, fire trucks, and tractors. Dad's policy was that these items were to be sold completely assembled. I spent many after school and Saturday hours putting them together.

In those days, Christmas sales didn't start in earnest until the day after Thanksgiving. However, regular customers often shopped early, buying items using our lay-away plan. Sometimes items were chosen right out of the packing cartons in the stockroom. Customers made a small down payment, and I put them in lay-away storage up on the second floor. They made periodic payments and picked up their purchases when paid off. Again, I was the gofer that trudged up the long staircase to retrieve them when they went out the door.

A Title to Fit the Job

In my early teen years custodial duties earned me a title. One day as I was sweeping the floor, a customer who knew my father well came in and noted that I was frequently present, always engaged in one task or another. He asked Dad what my position was. Dad replied, "Oh, him? He's Vice President of the Broom." It was the first time I had heard that, and I liked the idea of having a title.

Vice President of the Broom was much better than what dad often called me when we were in the presence of other adults. During our many outdoor treks, when coming off the lake after fishing, or out of the field when hunting, Dad compared results with other sportsmen. In doing so. he invariably said something like, "Kid here, caught one or two nice ones." In these conversations, I was always "Kid." I once told him that I did have a name and preferred being called something other than "Kid." That didn't stick. Until I was older, he seemed unsure how he was to acknowledge me. There was never any question in my mind about how he felt about me. I certainly knew he loved and cared deeply for me. I was his "right hand" companion. He was proud of me and any of my accomplishments at the store, in school, or out in the community. Typical of the times, parents didn't continuously heap "I love you" statements on us. We took it for granted that they did love us, otherwise, how did we get here? Nonetheless, I liked the Vice President of the Broom title. It confirmed that I was an official store team member.

Floor Sweeping 101

Floor sweeping required special skills, training, and had to be done with finesse. The store had a wooden plank floor that was periodically treated with floor-oil. Dad special ordered the oil in five-gallon buckets at Hank Morrison's gas station. They arrived bearing the Standard Oil logo and labeled "Floor Oil." He applied it once every few months using a garden sprayer. The treatment enhanced the floor's appearance and kept the dust down when we swept at the end of the day. He applied it late on a Saturday night after closing or early Sunday morning. This allowed time for it to soak in before the store reopened Monday morning.

Daily sweeping was done about 5:45 p.m., just before closing. Using a 24-inch-wide, fine bristled, push broom, we started at the front entrance and swept down the left aisle. We stopped along the way to sweep cross aisles. When we reached the back of the store, we returned to the front and swept the length of the right aisle.

Proper broom strokes were essential to produce a clean floor. We placed the broom flat on the floor, pushed it forward several inches, lifted the head off the floor, then gave it a sharp tap or two back down on the floor right behind the spot from where we picked it up. Continuing down the length of the store, we used the push-tap strokes to move the accumulated dirt piles to the back of the store. There we used a conventional broom and dustpan to pick up and dispose of them in the stockroom potbellied stove. The oil in the dirt flashed brightly when dumped on the fire. The same push broom was used on the sidewalk in the morning for the "store is open" ritual. Again, the push-tap stroke was used to produce cleanly swept walks.

I still have a couple of push brooms in my garage and basement. I've demonstrated the push-tap stroke to my kids and grandkids. I'm not sure I've convinced them to use it, but I show them how it produces a cleaner floor and bestows an air of authority on the pusher.

Tending the Furnace

After sweeping, I headed to the basement to tend the furnace. It was a pretty scary place down there. Divided down the center just as upstairs, the dime store side was further divided into four sections front to back. I never ventured into the middle two, Just the front one with the furnace and a storage area at the very back.

Our door to the shared front stairway was located about one-third of the way back from the store front and disguised by a sales rack displaying belts, umbrellas, and other hanging items. I had to push the belts aside to open the door. The stairwell light switch turned on the few lights hanging on our side of the big black hole. At the base of the stairs, an opening to the left led to our side, one to the right went under The Men's Store. I never went into the dark Men's Store side but wondered why it appeared filled with stacks of boxes visible from the opening. I didn't want to look very far into that scary black hole.

Our basement floor was mostly dirt. A cement walkway led from the stair landing to the furnace and coal bin areas. The basement stretched out under the stores' street level sidewalk. About half of this area served as our coal bin. This separate room had its own door and one lone lightbulb hanging from the ceiling. Up on the street, a manhole built into the sidewalk was used by the Co-op to dump loads of nugget-sized stoker coal into the bin. For deliveries, the driver pulled up to the sidewalk, lifted the manhole cover, placed a chute down the hole and raised the truck bed to dump the load. Hopefully we had shut the coal bin door so nuggets didn't flow out into the basement. More than once I had to clean up after forgetting to do this. Shoveling spilled coal off the dirt floor back into the bin was a real pain. When ordering big loads, we placed horizontal boards across the inside of the bin door, covering a portion of the opening. This prevented coal from piling up against the door and flowing out when we opened it.

I loved the distinctive sound of the coal flowing down the delivery truck metal chute. It could be heard up and down the main street, calling attention to the delivery. In my mind anyway, it suggested importance of the store. It was one of few buildings in the business district that had a manhole cover in the sidewalk. Decades later that sound came back to me during the 1970s era oil shortages. My own family and I were living in Maine at the time. Due to the shortage and high costs, some people had returned to the use of coal to heat their homes. One evening while out shoveling snow from our walks I once again heard that sound. A neighbor three houses up the street was receiving a coal delivery. I knew immediately what the sound was and quickly stopped in my tracks. Vivid memories of days in the dime store coal bin came rushing back.

The store furnace was modern looking. Encased in a large, square, blue metal cabinet, it sat on a concrete pad connected to the walkways that led to the coal bin and staircase. It looked nothing like the round octopus monstrosity that heated our home. A huge furnace fan pushed heated air into a single duct that ran the length of the sales floor. A square cast iron door on the front provided access to the firebox.

The stoker sat directly in front of the furnace, encased in a matching blue metal cabinet. Two six-inch diameter pipes ran at floor level from the stoker into the front of the furnace. One encased a screw auger that carried coal into the furnace. The other blew air under the grate to fan the fire. Opening the firebox door while it was running, I could see the inferno created.

I used two five-gallon buckets to take coal from the bin and dump it into the stoker. It usually took about three trips to fill it. It was a twice per day task, once first thing in the morning, and once at closing time. Dad took care of it in the morning. It was my turn in the evening. On extra cold days, we needed to keep a keen eye on how much coal remained in the stoker. If the stoker became empty, the fire went out. It took lots of effort to get it started again. That was Dad's job. He knew how to start a fire that kept going.

Dad said stoker filling would "build muscles." But in my mind, the clinkers that formed in the fire box were more challenging. After filling the stoker, I opened the firebox door and used a long-handled steel poker to break up clinkers that formed on the grates. Using a long-handled steel claw, I reached in and removed them, one piece at a time. The four to five chunks that came out were red-hot. As I brought them out, I dipped them in a bucket of water kept nearby. This cooled them down before I dumped them on a pile that accumulated on the dirt floor. The dousing produced a cloud of steam and interesting odors. I fantasized about being a steelmaker tending Gary, Indiana blast furnaces as I poked around in the furnace.

The real muscle building exercise occurred about twice a year when I had to haul clinkers out of the basement. I shoveled them into the five-gallon coal buckets, lugged them up the stairs, carried them the length of the sales floor, and out the stockroom back door, to dump them onto another pile in our parking area. When that pile became substantial in size, Dad brought his trailer to the store, and I shoveled them (again) into it to take them to the town dump. There, more shoveling was required to unload them.

The Back Basement

Though I never explored middle sections, the back basement was intriguing. Access was gained through a trapdoor in the stockroom floor. A section of floorboards next to the Round Oak stove, could be raised up to reveal the cavern below. Grabbing a heavy metal ring and lifting the 4 x 8-foot panel exposed the stairway. Several small boxes sitting on shelves adjacent to the stairway contained items left over from many years past when the building was used as a funeral parlor. The undertaker also built caskets. The boxes held silver plated casket handles, hinges, and decorative metal pieces. Those, undisturbed in their boxes and still wrapped in tissue, were bright and shiny. Any that had been unwrapped had become coated with dark-grey silver tarnish. I marveled at how those items had sat on the shelves for 50 or 60 years and fantasized about old men with long beards at work building caskets down in this hole.

We stored unused display racks and shelving down there. My father also kept a collection of items used in his numerous fix-it or build-it projects there. Obtained at auction sales, junk yards, or picked out of the local dump, they included pieces of sheet metal, lengths of pipe, steel boiler flues, and manufactured items such as automobile transmissions, hand push lawnmowers, large and small pulleys, electric motors salvaged from old washing machines, even a gasoline powered single cylinder Maytag washing machine engine. Dad loved to tinker and if he wanted something like a garden tractor, or a put-put car for me to ride in, he built it, relying on this storehouse to provide many of the parts.

We didn't go down there often but when we did it was always an adventure. I never wanted to miss an occasion when the floor-door was raised. Dad did the lifting. I went down the stairway to hand up or grasp items coming out of or going into storage. Though lighted with only a single lightbulb hanging at the base of the stairs, the large trap door opening to this chasm provided additional light and air making it seem less scary than the front basement with all of its dark shadowy corners. I always took a few extra minutes to explore the odd collection stashed there. I took boy scout cronies down there to find parts to build a soap box derby style car. They grabbed a couple casket handles and fastened them to our vehicle, "just in case we crash and need a coffin," they said.

Window Washing 101

Keeping the store's front display windows clean was a big deal. We washed the inside each time the display was changed. Except in cold weather, we washed the outside about every other week. This too was one of my jobs.

To produce results acceptable to my father, special techniques were needed. The process started in the stockroom where a bucket of tepid water was drawn from the tap. The only soap used was a shot of household ammonia added to the water.

When I asked Dad how much ammonia to use, he said, "Oh, a couple of glugs will do it."

Lugging the bucket, a long-handled soft bristled brush, and wide rubber squeegee out onto the sidewalk, I got to work. I dunked the brush into the bucket, soaked up some water, then scrubbed the window using circular motions. The brush handle, about four feet long, reached all the way to the top of the windows. To keep the water from running down the handle and, as my father said, "Dripping off my elbows," he had equipped it, about half-way down its length, with a clever shield. Made from a small diameter, sink drain sized, plumber's plunger, he had cut the center out of the handle socket and slid it down to the middle of the handle. People walking by looked quizzically at this arrangement. They thought it amusing, clever, and it worked.

With the window thoroughly wetted, I removed the brush from the handle and replaced it with the squeegee. Drying the window was the most critical part of the task. Skill was required to avoid streaks or smudges. Placing the squeegee at the top of the window, I forced the rubber squarely against the glass, then I slowly pulled it down to the bottom of the window – not stopping on the way. I repeated this over and over, lapping side-by-side strips, until the entire window had been dried. With a bit of good luck, I produced "squeaky clean," streak free windows. But the true test was approval of my mother. She usually stood inside, arms folded, watching me work and pointing to any area I missed or streak I had left. I had to do those areas over before moving on to the next window. This ritual continued way past my time at the store. Even my sister's children were trained to perform the task. When mother closed the store in the late 1970s, she took the brush and squeegee home and made us use them to wash her picture windows. Any member of the family could be drafted to do so during a visit. The procedure was the same, and best of all, Mother continued her oversight, standing inside, arms folded, critiquing and approving the results throughout the remainder of her 100-year life.

Becoming a Popcorn Vendor

One summer, my father bought a popcorn machine and announced that I was to become a sidewalk vendor out in front of the store. I was to operate the venture as a separate business, learn business principles, and make money in the process. The machine wasn't one of those fancy stand-alone units like movie theaters and large variety stores had. It was a small tabletop model. The central heating/popping unit at top of the machine was not motorized. I had to turn a crank on the back of the machine to stir corn kernels as they popped. I dumped cooking oil and popcorn into the unit, turned the crank clockwise while kernels popped, then cranked counterclockwise to dump the popped corn into a lightbulb heated chamber. I sprinkled salt on the popped corn, scooped it into bags, and stored them neatly in the warming chamber, ready for sale. To make the machine a stand-alone unit, Dad built a plywood, caster equipped, bottom cabinet. Sized to just fit the machine, it included a cash drawer and storage space for supplies. We rolled the combined unit out onto the sidewalk each time I set up shop.

I wasn't all that thrilled with the idea of sitting out there tending the machine. I knew my teenaged peers would be passing by and expected some jeering from them. The arrangement put me in a conspicuous spot at a pretty self-conscious age. But, in Dad's eyes, it was an opportunity for me to learn more about how to run a business.

He made it clear that I was in charge of the entire operation. He drove me to an Indiana Amish farm where I bought a 25-pound bag of popcorn, a case of popping oil in gallon cans, a few one-pound containers of fine-grained popcorn salt, and paper bags used to package the product. For several weeks over two summers I went into production, handled sales, counted and banked daily proceeds, and kept the books on the business. I didn't become rich, but I did learn something about doing business and gained some respect from adults that became frequent customers. On Saturday nights they walked the streets, visiting with friends and neighbors, and checked out downtown stores – all the while munching on my popcorn.

As a result, I could add "Professional Popcorn Vendor" to my resume. I still have the stenographer's notebook used to keep daily income and expense records. Looking at it now, I see that I didn't learn all that much about bookkeeping.

Popcorn Vending – Take Two

Following my second summer on the street Dad retired my machine and replaced it with an automated machine that dispensed "warm" popcorn from a bubble shaped compartment at the top. He kept it filled with pre-popped corn purchased in large 5-foot-tall heavy-walled paper bags. A lightbulb in the center of the holding chamber provided the "warmth." Customers placed a dime in the machine, pulled an empty bag from a slot and placed it under a spout to fill.

The machine required no operator and remained "on-station" outside the dime store 24-7. It also didn't require the daily wash-up that my manual machine needed. That was always a sticking point between my mother and me. I quickly wiped down my machine at the end of the day and declared it "clean." She inspected and pointed out places I missed. Ultimately, she took over the task. I was fine with that arrangement, but she wasn't.

However, the life of the popcorn vending machine didn't turn out to be all that long either. A year or so later Mom and Dad went out of town for a weekend. I was left "in charge," and the vending machine was "on duty." As I was getting around on Sunday morning, there was a knock at the door of our home. A Michigan State Police patrolman said someone had called the Police Post to report that the popcorn machine was found lying in the ditch on Featherstone Road, about two miles out of town. He said we needed to take care of it. I jumped into Mom's '57 DeSoto and drove out there. The machine was lying in the ditch, just as the Trooper described. The top still contained popcorn, and at first look, the remainder of the machine appeared not to have been damaged. Closer examination revealed that the coin box had been forced open and, of course, all the dimes were missing.

I tugged, pulled, and loaded the machine into the DeSoto trunk, took it to the store, and carted it into the stockroom. Dad made some effort to repair the damage but didn't really pursue it all that much. I guess he decided there wasn't going to be the money made from popcorn sales that he had envisioned. I have always wondered how many dimes the thieves obtained in the heist, and whether or not it was worth all their effort.

Checkout Clerk

Serving as checkout clerk was a multi-task assignment. As candy case attendant, I scooped, weighed and bagged candy sales, totaled up prices on items brought to the checkout, handled the cash involved, and was expected to be personable with customers.

We used pencil and paper to total up sales. To cover a 3 percent state sales tax, we used a four-tiered sliding scale arrangement to collect the pennies. No tax was charged on sales less than 10 cents. One cent (¢) was added to sales totaling 10 to 29 cents. Between 30 and 69 cents, we added two pennies, three cents were collected between 70 cents and one dollar. Above one dollar, we added three cents for each additional dollar, plus what was needed to cover the less than a dollar amount. We computed all this in our heads. We could use Dad's manual adding machine for really big orders and breathed a sigh of relief when he finally bought an electric cash register that took care of all this arithmetic. It was a major investment. I still have the receipt showing he paid $400 for the machine ($4000 in today's dollars).

Sales Tax Scale	
Amount of Sale	Tax
0 - 9¢	0
10¢ - 29¢	1¢
30¢ - 69¢	2¢
70¢ - $1.00	3¢

Nearly all sales were made using cash. Credit cards were just coming into use. Dad resisted, but finally gave in, accepting one Michigan brand card supported by the local bank. No automation was associated with these sales. All were done filling out credit sales slips by hand. It took time and good penmanship to correctly record the sale. Fortunately, that didn't occur often. when it did, it was usually someone from a larger community, perhaps as far away as Chicago. It always produced a stir among the staff once the customer left the store.

Cash sales required checkout clerks to "make change." To complete a sale, cash offered by the customer was not put directly into the cash register drawer but placed on a shelf on the front of the register. It remained there until change had been counted back to the customer. This guarded against disagreements over what denomination of coins or bills was presented, and how much change was due.

If a customer handed the clerk a $5 bill for a $1.89 sale, change was counted out from the drawer. A penny brought the amount up to $1.90. Grabbing a dime brought it up to $2. Finally, pulling three one-dollar bills from the drawer, made the exchange total $5. Rather than just hand the customer the change, the clerk counted it back to them. Handing them the penny first, the clerk said, "one dollar ninety," the dime, "two dollars," finally giving them the three one-dollar bills, one at a time, said, "three makes five. Thank you."

The "thank you" was required regardless of whether or not change was needed. "We always thank customers for shopping with us," Dad repeatedly told the clerks. Today, I'm always frustrated when a store clerk hardly speaks to me, or worse yet, ignores me completely and keeps talking on their cell phone while checking me out.

Embarrassing Sales

I was comfortable checking-out customers buying most items, but some sales were awkward. Ladies' undergarments presented issues for me. There was always a mystique associated with displaying these or tending the counters where they were kept. Bras were carefully folded and placed in glass bins on the display counter. Similar bins contained panties. The counter was stocked and tended by our most senior lady clerk, Rita Mann. Every evening before closing, she covered these items with a white bed sheet to keep dust from accumulating on them. She removed it each morning when opening. When she worked at the counter, she referred to these items as "hum-hums." At closing time, she announced, "Time to cover the 'hum-hums'."

When a customer brought them to the checkout and I was on duty, I had to examine the price tags, ring up the sale, and touch them to place them in a bag. I'm sure my face turned red in the process.

As uncomfortable as "hum-hums" made me, another item was much worse! We sold feminine hygiene products, primarily Kotex napkins. Packaged in boxes of a dozen or so, they arrived at the store with about three dozen boxes packed in one large shipping container. Before each box was put out for sale it was wrapped in plain brown paper. Fortunately, I didn't have to do the wrapping. The lady salesclerks did that, during slow periods, up at the checkout counter. My job was to lug the large 3-foot square shipping container up to them. Once I dropped off the carton, emblazoned with the word "Kotex" in about 4-inch-high letters on all sides, I opened the top then disappeared while the clerk unpacked, wrapped and stacked individual boxes on an out of the way bottom merchandise shelf located very near the checkout counter.

The bigger issue came up when I was tending the checkout and a woman, or much worse a high school girl I knew, brought one of those boxes to the register. I was totally flustered. My legs turned to rubber. I didn't know what to say. I quietly muttered the price marked in pencil on the brown wrapper, stammering "92 cents including tax," I took the money, rang up the sale, and quickly thrust the item into a plain brown paper bag. This was not the time for chatter or pleasantries. I needed to complete the transaction as quickly as possible. I'm sure the experience was also awkward for the customer. I hoped the next sale was for a half-pound of jellybeans or couple of light bulbs. Then, I could relax and enjoy interaction with the customer.

Cashing-up

Dad usually cashed-up at closing, but occasionally I handled it. A small drawer in the top of Dad's rolltop desk served as the cash drawer. In it, a small muffin tin was used to separate the coins into their respective denominations. Currency bills, sorted and stacked together in order of their denomination, were placed next to the tin. Dad insisted on proper bill handling, both within the drawer and in the cash register. This, he said, "improves accuracy when counting mixed denominations and also shows proper respect for U.S. currency." Each bill was placed face up with the bill bottom positioned at the bottom of the stack, or if vertical, to the right.

To cash-up we took the drawer to the register, recorded and zeroed the total displayed on the register sales counter, then removed the cash. However, we never left it completely empty. Twenty pennies were counted back into the register drawer, and it was not closed tightly. Left ajar, the register could easily be pulled open to reveal the pennies. Dad said this was a safety measure. In the event of a break-in, it might prevent a robber from smashing up the register or keep him from doing additional damage, he said

Back in the office, money was counted, the daily sales total recorded in a stenographer's notebook, and most cash put into a canvas, bank bag. A small amount went back into the drawer. Those coins and bills served as change for the next day. Ten nickels, ten dimes, eight quarters, two 50-cent pieces, ten one-dollar bills, and two five-dollar bills were held, ready to be placed in the cash register the next morning, to start the day.

Dad didn't have a safe. Instead, he used hiding places for overnight storage of the cash drawer, and if it was not taken to the bank night deposit box, the bank bag. The choice between bank night deposit or hiding place depended on how much money was in the bag. On early weekdays that tended to be slower sales days, it was more likely that the bag ended up in the hiding place. On Fridays and Saturdays, during the Christmas season, or on special sale days, it was taken to the night depository.

A special key was needed to open the night depository. A nook located at the front of the bank building housed the night deposit box. It was lighted, but sidewalks leading to it could be dark. It was scary carrying the bag down the sidewalk at night. Once we used our key to open the deposit box door and dropped the bag into a safe sitting inside the bank we could relax. Perceived threats regarding potential robbers had been extinguished.

When I accompanied Dad on these walks, he referred to me as his "bodyguard." But he also addressed this concern in another way. A small, nickel-plated revolver was kept in one of his desk drawers. I don't know where it came from, and he didn't make much of it since my mother never liked the fact that he had it. To my knowledge he had never fired it. He kept one small box of ammo tucked away on a nearby shelf, but I never knew the gun to be loaded. When the bank bag was heavily loaded, he slipped the unloaded revolver into his pocket before heading for the bank. When I asked what good an unloaded gun was, he replied, "Pulling it out of my pocket will scare away any robber. He wouldn't know it wasn't loaded."

In-store cash hiding places were unique. Initially, when Dad's office was located on a platform at the back of the sales floor, a wall panel beside steps leading up to the desk could be easily removed. Before leaving the store, when everyone but family had left, Dad removed the panel, and placed the cash drawer, and sometimes the bank bag, in the cavity then replaced the panel. My sister and I were admonished to never tell anyone about this secret place. After moving his office to the stockroom apartment space, a new hiding place was needed.

The sewing notions counter at the front of the store included a display cabinet for spools of thread. Four cascading shelves held numerous spools of various colors. Arranged as stairsteps, the shelves could be moved forward revealing an empty space at the back of the cabinet. That became the hiding place. Who would have thought to look under a stack of thread spools to find a cash drawer? However, moving the shelves forward, then back after hiding the cash, had to be done carefully. Otherwise, the spools spilled from the shelves and ran all over the floor. I learned this the hard way more than once.

Manager "Pro Tem"

During my late high school years I was "left in charge" when Mom and Dad ventured out of town. Dorthey Snyder, a long-serving adult salesclerk could also perform opening and closing tasks, but on school holidays I did both. Otherwise, she opened and I closed. This was a little awkward for me. I didn't want to act like "the boss" around a woman nearly as old as my parents. However, she handled the situation better than I. If questions came up regarding how to price or display something, she always consulted me before acting. We were a team and got along fine. On these occasions, I had Mother's repeated admonishment ringing in my ears, "You'll be in charge, but don't let that go to your head!"

The arrangement was really put to the test in November of my senior year. Mom and Dad went deer hunting in Michigan's

Upper Peninsula. Mother had relatives there that ran a commercial hunting lodge. They went up to take advantage of the accommodations. They had been gone a few days, Dorothy and I were running the store, and things were going smoothly. On the evening I expected Mom and Dad to return, I was home talking on the phone with my favorite high school gal Barbara Kolb, when there was a knock on the door. Again, it was the Michigan State Police. This time they had more troubling news. Mom and Dad had been in a car accident. Both were injured and in a Grand Rapids hospital. My sister and I contacted Dad's mother and brother in Adrian. They came over that evening. The next day we all got in the DeSoto and headed for Grand Rapids. It was several days before Mom and Dad were discharged. They came home bandaged and in casts. I had made a couple of trips back and forth to the hospital to take mail and store supplier messages to Dad. He sorted through things and gave me instructions. Dorothy and I kept the store open, things went well, and we were busy. It was time to get ready for the Christmas season. Yes, we were a team.

My Key to the Store

I was quite young, probably in 6th grade, when Dad gave me a key to the store. He instructed me to "Never tell anyone you have it." I put the key on a small keyring and carried it in my pocket. The primary reason he gave it to me was so I could begin rolling down the awning over the front display windows early on summer mornings.

The store faced the east. Soon after the sun came up, about 6:00 a.m., the awning needed to be rolled down to prevent merchandise displayed in the windows from fading. I was always an early riser. Since I got up every morning before anyone else in the house, Dad thought I could get dressed, hop on my bike, and ride downtown to roll down the awning.

That suited me just fine. I went out for morning bike rides then came back and put the coffee pot on the stove so Mother could have a cup when she got up. During the school year, the sun didn't rise as early so the awning didn't need to be rolled down until Dad arrived about 8:00 a.m. Then, I used my early morning time to finish schoolwork not completed the evening before. I have always used the philosophy, "Don't do today what you can put off until tomorrow." Even today.

My key was also useful at store closing time. The large double outside back doors into the stockroom were ancient. Their appearance suggested they had been there as long as the 1845 Eureka Hall building itself. A crude latch mechanism secured the two and kept them from blowing open but did not serve as a substantial lock. To increase security Dad fashioned a barricade that we placed across the inside of the opening each evening. He bolted heavy metal brackets to walls on either side of the doors. To "lock up" he dropped a wooden 2 X 4 stretching across both doors into the brackets. In the center, where the two doors met, he wedged a wooden hammer handle between the doors and the 2 X 4 to secure both. This "locking" exercise had to be done from the inside, forcing us to leave through the front door then walk down the alleyway next to the neighboring drug store to the car parked out back. Since I had a key, Dad could go out the back door, drive the car around to the front, and pick me up after I locked both doors. My only problem with this was walking through the dark empty store by myself to get to the front. That was spooky. I hurried up the aisles hoping not to encounter anyone hiding out in there waiting for us to leave.

An Era Fades

Despite Mother's fear that misdeeds committed while I roamed the community would impact income and cause the family to starve, the store provided my family with a good living for 35 years. I was pretty much out of the operational picture after I headed off to college. My sister was there for another four years, finishing high school and working in the store, then she too left for college.

With the exception of things like installing a telephone and offering widespread credit card sales, Dad strived to "stay current" with business trends. He remodeled the store interior a couple of times and even had a new vinyl floor installed. But one pressure that proved formidable was discount department stores, the precursors of today's "Big Box" stores. Discount retailers in Kalamazoo, Elkhart, and South Bend, drew customers to them with perceived "low prices" and huge stores. Dad held on by concentrating on customer service and the ability to get things for customers when they couldn't find them elsewhere. But he felt the store's viability slipping away.

His 30th Christmas season was a defining point. I was with him when he turned out the lights to close on Christmas Eve of 1973. As he flipped the switch turning off perimeter lights over giftware display shelves, he said, "There, that ends my 30th Christmas season. I wonder if I'll have another one." It turned out to be a prophetic statement. Shortly after the new year, while riding his snowmobile on local trails, he died of a massive heart attack. Mother, and loyal salesclerk assistants ran the store for another five years. She held a big "Going Out of Business Sale" and closed the store in 1979. I was with her when she turned the key in the front door lock for the last time.

The store was gone, but that didn't stop Mother from serving her community. She quickly started a new career, serving lunchtime meals to "senior citizens." She managed the local "Meals on Wheels" program for 25 years. Most of her clients were younger than she. Always referring to them as, "My seniors," she finally retired at age 96.

Chapter 5

"You Can't Do Business from an Empty Wagon"

Dad was a natural-born salesman. He loved to talk with people and had a warm outgoing personality. Though at first meeting he could quickly size-up anyone, he always saw the best in them. Mom was a bit more cautious. She too was quick to strike up conversations and was always most cordial. But she sought reassurance that those she had contact with were authentic and not about to take advantage of her. These traits came from their backgrounds.

Because Dad's family moved around a lot when he was growing up, time and time again he had to prove himself to both peers and superiors. He said, "I learned not to go around with a chip on my shoulder, for surely someone would want to knock it off." As for teachers and mentors, he wanted them to know that he was willing to learn, had useful skills, and could get the job done regardless of the task.

All but one of Mother's five brothers and one sister were older than she. She quickly developed the intuition to know when she was being taken advantage of. In addition, each member of her family was expected to pitch in and share the workload associated with her father's growing dairy farm enterprise. She got up early, helped with morning chores (both in the home and out in the barn), delivered milk on the way to school, put in a good day at school, and went back to work when she got home. These experiences and her work as an Ann Arbor, Michigan waitress taught her business skills.

The eras in which they grew up and established themselves included both the Great Depression and World War II, with its rationing and requirement to simultaneously live both corporate and personal lifestyles. Dad's insurance salesman background taught him persistence and the need to tailor his sales pitch to customer interests. His work as a "stock boy" in variety store chains taught him rudiments of shopkeeping. Working his way up from this "ground floor" position to store manager provided his graduate level business education.

Keeping an Attractive Shop

The rituals of keeping sidewalks clean, display windows washed, floors neatly swept, and merchandise neatly displayed were all part of keeping an attractive shop. "It's all about drawing customers into the store," I was told when sent off to perform my Vice President of the Broom tasks. If I didn't sweep cleanly enough or missed a smudge when washing the windows, I was sent back to "finish the job."

We couldn't just stack merchandize on the counter. We had to build a display from the bottom up. Our counters had sunken tops, making the countertop surface about two inches below the edge of an attractive molding. Before placing merchandise on the counter, we placed black rectangular wooden boxes on the counter surface. Called "shams," they allowed us to place long narrow pieces of "counter glass" on edge between shams and form bins. Merchandise was neatly placed in the bins. Often, the bottom of the bin was lined with white or colored paper to produce a contrasting background. Shelving received similar treatments to highlight items and attract customer's attention as they walked by.

Every interior store detail was important. Lighting, temperature, some sort of background music or sound (sometimes just the drone of a powerful fan on a hot summer's day) were designed to establish a comfortable atmosphere inside the store. Dad didn't want adjacent customers to be able to overhear conversations of others regarding the items they purchased or the amount of their transaction. Each visit was to be a personal experience that enticed customers to return.

Likewise, he was careful about the store being a billboard or display spot for information about local events or causes. Always supportive of community activities, he agreed to place some school or civic function posters or announcements in windows or near the checkout station. But only if they were non-political or not related to a controversial topic. Posters seeking votes by public office candidates were always rejected, regardless of who Dad or Mom may have favored. They didn't want to be seen as supporting any particular candidate, thereby driving away business from opposing candidate supporters.

Selecting Merchandise

Because the store was a "five and dime store," customers expected it to carry certain low priced "sundry" items. In addition, there was considerable flexibility in the range of items that could be offered. Stocking the right selection and quantity of merchandise was critical. Dad often recited the mantra borrowed from the old-time traveling merchant pen and ink drawing that hung beside his desk. Below his merchandise stuffed horse-drawn wagon the caption read, *"You can't do business from an empty wagon.* Though they handpicked many items based on customer requests, Mom and Dad also relied on suppliers to stock some departments. Sewing notions (spools of thread, packages of needles, buttons, bias tape and rickrack, etc.) were inventoried by the salesman who came in monthly. He restocked displays and understocks and left behind new items that were selling well elsewhere. He managed this department,

You Can't Do Business From An Empty Wagon!

Mom and Dad just signed-off on the order book when he left the store.

Another salesman came to the store quarterly and checked the lampshade display. He wrote-up orders to restock the inventory of fast selling shades and added new designs consistent with current decorating trends. This fellow was impressive. He always wore a neat suit and tie and arrived in a late model Cadillac. I asked dad how he could afford to drive such an expensive car by just selling a few lampshades. Dad said, "Since the car is used for business, he gets to claim it as an expense. It doesn't cost him any more to drive a Caddy than a Chevy." I countered, "Yes, but doesn't it cost more to buy the gas it uses?" Dad replied, "No, a Caddy gets good milage, they know how to build them."

Twice per year, a salesman selling souvenir items came to the store. His knickknack inventory was stuffed into a large van. He parked out behind the store and spent two or three hours showing Mom and Dad what they could sell on souvenir shelves. These imported items, mostly from Japan, were packed in flimsy cartons with lots of excelsior. I was intrigued by the fact that any metal used to make the items was likely to have come from a recycled can or other item. The backside of the item often carried painted logos or wording from its previous life.

The salesman was a fiery fellow who rushed through the inventory jammed into his truck using a fast banter. Mother called him the "Plunder Man." She liked the merchandise but dreaded his visits. He always came unannounced, forcing her drop whatever she was doing and go to the van to pick out "plunder." Invariably he showed up on the hottest or coldest days of the year and the van was not air conditioned or heated.

These eye-catching, impulse buying, items could be sold at high markup. They included ceramic, wooden, or metal ash trays, statuettes, salt and pepper shakers, napkin holders, etc. Many were comical characterizations of animals or people. Some artistic, some erotic. Mom quickly rejected items she thought inappropriate or too racy for her shelves. On some, we applied decals (the stickers of the day), labeling them a "Souvenir of Constantine Michigan." Located next to the check4out area, no one could miss seeing them on their way out of the store.

Adding New Lines
The Plant Man
One day, a small, thin, quiet-speaking man came into the store asking to see the owner. Mother stepped forward. He said he ran a nursery over in St. Joseph, Michigan and would like to provide a selection of house plants that she could sell in the store. They talked details, and she agreed to give him some counter space if he would come by often enough to keep up the inventory. He set up a nice display and was on his way. Subsequently, he came by every two weeks, inspected the plants and restocked the shelves. Always dressed (winter or summer)

in a plaid long sleeved flannel shirt, baggy pants held up with suspenders, and wearing a fedora, he was quite critical about how the store cared for his plants. He complained that they hadn't been watered enough, received enough sunlight, or maybe got too much sun. He grumbled his way through each visit. When he finished restocking the shelves, he presented a scrap of paper on which he had scribbled how many plants had been sold and were to be paid for. Dad or Mom went to the cash register, retrieved the cash, and handed it to him as he went out the door. His name was Grover, but we called him "The Plant Man." He drove an old station wagon that he parked behind the store. One day as he drove in, I noticed smoke wafting out from under his hood. He got out, opened the hood, pulled out and examined the engine oil dip stick, then went to the back of the car, pushed aside several plants, and grabbed a two gallon can of recycled engine oil. After pouring half of the oil into the engine, he slammed the hood shut. After he left, I recounted the incident to my father. He said, "Yeah, he gets about 16 miles to the gallon of gas, and 10 miles to the quart of oil."

Paint and Wallpaper
Both the Smith Hardware Store and Gambles sold paint. But Dad wanted to add some home care items to his inventory that were more upscale than what the other stores offered. He began selling Pittsburgh Paints and a selection of wallpaper.

Pittsburgh Paints had a unique color system. They had just two base paints to choose from, but a huge selection of colorant tubes provided a wide array of colors. Color selection was limited at the other stores. Similarly, no other store in town offered wallpaper.

Dad remodeled the rear of the store to display the new lines and built needed stockroom storage spaces. My job was to keep wallpaper rolls and paint color tubes sorted and properly stored so they could be easily retrieved when customers made selections. When a sale was made, I climbed stockroom bins to retrieve the needed rolls. I felt like a monkey when tending this department.

Dad handled paint and wallpaper sales. Mother and the other clerks wanted nothing to do with it. It was up to him to determine how many rolls of wallpaper were needed to cover a room and add exactly the right amount of color to base paint to get the desired color. He did a good job with this and had many satisfied customers.

Fabric Remnants
Although Vail's Department Store, two doors up the street, stocked a large selection of fabrics, Mother discovered a source of fabric remnants. These pieces of bolt-width fabrics varied in length and came in a wide variety of styles and colors. She obtained them in bulk lots and sold the pieces individually at attractive prices. One countertop was devoted to this merchandise. Mother sorted them in accordance with length, color and style, priced each one, then neatly arranged them in the display area. The response was astounding. Women loved to paw through the stacks and choose their favorites. The downside was keeping the display area neat. The counter was a jumbled mass at the end of most days.

For me, there was another huge downside. Mother liked to sew and often did, for my sister, when she could find the time. As she sorted the remnants, she pulled out patterns she liked for her own use. "Some would make nice shirts," she said. Not having time to make shirts for me or my father, she hired a customer who did lots of sewing to make them. I had two problems with this. One, Mom did not consult me on choice of color or pattern, and two, I didn't want to wear "homemade shirts" to school.

Whenever someone showed up in a new shirt or pair of pants, peers compared labels and boasted about which "men's store" the items came from. Though I tried boasting that I was having shirts "custom made" or "hand tailored," that didn't impress this crowd. To them, the shirts were made out of "dime store

material." Worse, a couple of times, mother had matching shirts made for my father and me. On Sunday family outings, she insisted we wear them. I didn't want to be seen in this mode. A family picture of one such outing still haunts me.

Seasonal Merchandise

Procuring seasonal merchandise required precise timing to secure best prices and timely arrival. As spring arrived, we kids were thinking about getting out of school and having summer fun, but my folks were talking about "back to school" merchandise. Having bought their textbooks from Armstrong's drug store, families also had to purchase pencils, pens (straight pens – not ball points), erasers, paper tablets, notebook paper, binders, crayons, rulers, protractors, etc. Armstrong's stocked some of these items, but the dime store had the best selection. Dad's Car Ferry paper products, (lined paper, bound notebooks, and paper tablets), produced on the other side of Lake Michigan in Manitowoc, Wisconsin, were high quality. The paper was thicker, had a nice pen and pencil feel, and could be erased without tearing. Dad's careful pricing and well-stocked inventory made our store "the source" for these things.

One year, a Car Ferry papermill strike delayed shipment of our order. That caused great angst as school opening approached, but materials arrived in the nick of time. At school, keeping my observations to myself, I always noticed when fellow students pulled out Car Ferry notebooks in class.

Obtaining Christmas merchandise required the most careful planning. The "black Friday" concept was a definite reality. The extent to which the store had a profitable year really did depend on a successful Christmas season. We had to have the right merchandise in stock at just the right time.

Annual toy shows occurred in July. While most folks were focusing on firecrackers, grilled hot dogs, and jumping into nearby lakes, my family was thinking Christmas and visiting wholesale houses. All four of us made the trip. My sister and I enjoyed trying out the latest toys. Shipments were scheduled for late summer and early fall. That's when I was kept busy assembling wagons, scooters, and tricycles. I lugged cases of decorations and gift items upstairs to be stored until display time. Dad worked with the bank to secure short term loans to pay invoices that arrived shortly afterwards. From then on, the pressure was on. When Christmas sales began on the day after Thanksgiving, Dad's blood pressure was high. Sales receipts had to pay-off those loans. Fortunately, he was successful most years.

Maintaining Core Inventory

While most merchandise came from the Grand Rapids wholesaler, Dad occasionally dashed to a small supply house located in Elkhart to secure items he had suddenly run out of. Selection was limited, and prices were higher. He called it his "pinch source." Once I had my driver's license, he occasionally handed me a list of needed items and sent me there to pick them up. The staff helped me pick items off their shelves. When done, I made out a check Dad had signed to pay the bill, loaded up, and left feeling like a "real businessman."

Quality Matters

Pittsburgh Paints and Car Ferry school supplies were just two examples of Mom and Dad's "stick with high quality" philosophy. They sold only Brach's candies. These chocolate peanut clusters, nougats, jelly beans, gum drops, chocolate stars, burnt peanuts, candy corn, marshmallow circus peanuts, and orange slice jellies were a premium brand made in Chicago, Illinois. They came to us in 20-pound bulk cases. We sold them one or two scoops at a time. Other stores stocked various brands of prepackaged candies, but not Brach's. Regardless of what customers came into the store to buy, they rarely left without a white bag of freshly scooped treats. My sister often tended the candy counter. As customers pointed to their selections, she scooped them up, weighed them on the price-calculating candy scale, and poured them into a white paper bag. Between her good looks and the tempting treats, who could resist buying at least a small bag?

Greeting cards were another of Mother's merchandise passions. Display racks at the store entrance held a robust supply of cards for all occasions. American Greetings Publishers and Ambassador Greeting Cards were her suppliers. She liked the quality and the fact that she could sell them at lower prices than Hallmark cards offered at the two drug stores. Card supply arrangements were by subscription. Cartons of cards arrived automatically, and Mom did the hard work of filling display racks. Though she drafted store clerks to help, she was never completely satisfied with how they kept the racks. "If you want something done right you need to do it yourself," she muttered as she tweaked the many rows of cards. Mom's dime store racks were widely known as the place to go for finding exactly the right card.

Ready-to-wear items included children's, ladies, and men's stockings. Durand Hosiery Mills supplied high-quality socks in a wide variety of colors and sizes (no one-size-fits-all in those days). They could be sold at attractive prices. The Durand salesman came to the store monthly, checked stocks and ordered replacements. Though he and his family lived in Fort Wayne, Indiana, they were from Chattanooga, Tennessee, Durand's home base. He loved to talk and fish, so he and Dad became instant friends. During summer, when he was done working on the sock counter, he and Dad sneaked off to go fishing. Sometimes they did more fishing than store tending. Those events were culminated by a big fish fry in our back yard. On one occasion, the salesman's wife came along. She, a very proper southern lady, really liked to cook fish. She insisted that they be accompanied by "hush puppies." In her deep southern drawl, the emphasis on the word was placed on the first syllable making the statement sound like a command. We had never heard of "HUSH puppies" and didn't understand what she meant. But she said, "Make no never mind, I brought along everything we need." She mixed a batter and poured "dabs" of batter into the fry pan to cook along with the fish. Mother concluded, "Oh, I could do that. I just have to mix up a corn meal batter." But the southern lady replied, "It's not that easy, you have to use the right corn meal, it's only made in Tennessee at water ground mills. You can't buy it up here. My momma sends it to me."

We asked, "Why are they called hush puppies." She replied, "When we go fishing, catch a mess of fish, and come home to cook them, the dogs all stand around wanting to be fed. We can't give them fish, so we fry up the corn meal and throw it to them saying, "HUSH puppy.'"

Business Trips Became Vacations

Despite they're 24/7 occupation, Mom and Dad valued time off for family vacations. Dad's idea of the perfect vacation was a trip to the north woods (including Canada) for fishing. Mom complained that we never went any direction besides "up north." Sometimes they found ways to find something they both liked and turned business trips into family vacations.

Durand Hosiery and the Great Smoky Mountains

The Durand Hosiery salesman invited them to visit the hosiery mill in Chattanooga. Mother was elated. We could head south instead of north and see some new sights. Our spring school vacation came along at just the right time. I looked forward to seeing new states. My sister wanted to see "some mountains." Our travels took us first to Chattanooga, then eastward over to the Smoky Mountains before turning north up through Ohio, towards home. It was 1952. I had to get someone to take over my paper route while I was away.

There were no interstate highways or expressways in those days. It took two long days to drive to Chattanooga. Along the way, sides of barns or other buildings were painted red and turned into huge billboards reading "SEE ROCK CITY." We wondered if we would get to do so.

The sock salesman met us at our Chattanooga motel and drove us to the hosiery mill. He introduced us to Mr. Durand, owner of the company, telling him that Dad was one of his "best customers." Mr. Durand gave us a tour of the plant. Stockings were woven on special looms that he himself had adapted to produce the Durand product. These complicated machines spun yarns around a circular frame. Within seconds they produced freshly woven socks that had no seams. Dozens of machines were located in one big room, each attended by an operator, all women, who sat all day long retrieving socks of various colors and sizes from the looms. Noise in the knitting room was near deafening. We wondered how these women could sit there eight or more hours per day and not lose their hearing.

Finishing the tour, the salesman took us on a ride around the city, past a huge dam and water reservoir recently built by the Tennessee Valley Authority, then up the side of Lookout Mountain to Rock City. We toured natural rock formations and multiple mountaintop shops that Mother termed "tourist traps." We paused at Pinnacle Overlook to "See Seven States." The salesman pointed in various directions and identified each for us. I had been keeping a log of states seen on the trip. I knew I would have to give a report to my 6th grade class when I got home. This gave me a bonanza of states to put on the list.

We also visited important Civil War sites on top of the mountain, providing additional information for my classroom report. He dropped us off at the Lookout Mountain Inclined Railway, bought us tickets, and said "I'll pick you up down below." Down the mountain we rode. It was a thrill ride. My mother and sister kept their eyes closed all the way down.

Leaving Chattanooga, we headed to The Great Smoky Mountains National Park to fulfill my sister's objective of seeing "some mountains." We had already seen and been to the top of Lookout Mountain, but she said, "That doesn't count, there was no snow on it." She insisted that we would see "real mountains" when we got to the Smokies. Her definition of a real mountain was one with snow at the top. It was a day's drive across eastern Tennessee to the park and raining when we arrived. We hoped for clearing skies, but as we drove through the park the next day, skies remained cloudy. On and off we saw tops of the Smokies but there was no snow. I was looking forward to seeing bears. I had seen many pictures of bears knocking over the park's trash barrels. But we didn't see any. We were both disappointed. "Someday I'll see some real mountains," sister said.

Dad played violin, mandolin, and harmonica and liked country music. Mother played piano, organ, and sang. She liked classical music. She said country music performers sang "with clothespins on their noses." Every Saturday night Dad tuned the dime store radio to the Renfro Valley Barn Dance station. He loved the "high steppin" music and Mother tried to ignore it. Proceeding across Kentucky we passed through Renfro Valley. Dad was elated. We found the Barn Dance building and drove all around it. Mother was relieved that it appeared to be closed with no one around. Dad persevered. He stopped the car, got out and went to the door. It opened. He got us all out of the car, and we went inside. A lone fellow was straightening up things. Dad struck up a conversation with him and he took us on a tour of the building. He showed us the stage and pointed out where the various Barn Dance stars stood for the broadcast. For Dad, it was a highlight of the trip. For Mother, it was cornbread.

Back in the car we were soon in Ohio. Early in Dad's dime store career he worked in several northwestern Ohio stores. We wound our way through towns with stores he had worked at. One was in St. Mary's, Ohio. Dad worked there when I was born. Since there was no hospital in St. Mary's, I was born in the Celina hospital, 10 miles away. As we drove through the area, Mother recounted the details of my arrival into the world. Dad was transferred to another store soon thereafter and we moved on. That happened again and again. To this day, names of the numerous communities we moved to are very familiar to me. Mother talked about them often. But my memories only go back to Buchanan, Michigan. We lived there when Dad bought the Constantine store.

Our trip turned complicated when my sister reported, "I don't feel good." She had come down with the measles. From that point on we were quarantined in the car and hurried home. On the way, Dad went into restaurants to bring food to the rest of us in the car. These were the days before drive-through windows. Sister claims she still bears emotional scars from the commotion caused by that situation.

Wallpaper Factory and Tom Sawyer Experience
On another occasion we visited wallpaper mills in Joliet, IL. Known as the wallpaper capital of the world, the patterns we sold came from there. Dad was invited to visit the plant and see how they were produced. Our tour began in a large drafting room. A dozen or so artists sat on tall stools at high-top drafting desks drawing flowers, scenes (some with animals or people), and geometric patterns to be printed on roles of wallpaper. The work looked tedious. I wondered how those folks could sit and do that day after day. I also thought the doodles I produced in school notebooks were just as good.

The drawings went to a shop that produced printing rollers. It looked a lot like our school shop classroom, a large room filled with tools and machinery. Wooden cylinders about 6 inches in diameter, the width of a roll of wallpaper, were produced there. Quarter inch wide brass metal strips were fastened on edge onto the rolls in an outline of the artist's designs. The outlines were filled with pieces of heavy felt and became printing surfaces used to produce wallpaper designs. Depending on the complexity of the design, it took several rolls to print one scene. Each one printed just one color and only one portion of the scene or design. The ability to figure all this out impressed me. Years later when engaged in my paper industry career, having seen the wallpaper printing process helped me understand the demands our customers put on the printing papers we produced.

Leaving the wallpaper mills, we traveled onward, reaching the Mississippi River. I was excited to see the famous river I had heard so much about in school. "How do you spell Mississippi?" the girls yelled out on the playground. Invariably, a chorus of young voices erupted, "M-I-S-S-I-S-S-I-P-P-I." In class, we read Mark Twain's Adventures of Tom Sawyer and his friend Huck Finn. I wondered if these places and people had actually existed. We crossed the river at Hannibal, MO and visited the Mark Twain boyhood home and museum. The highlight was the long fence said to be the one Tom was sent out to whitewash, but cajoled friends into doing it for him. I thought, "This guy knew how to get along in the world."

We Always Found a Dime Store
Other non-hunting or fishing outings included trips to the Wisconsin Dells, the 1948 and 1949 Chicago Railroad Fairs, a 1956 trip to Niagara Falls and accompanying long ride along the northern shore of Lake Ontario. We went there to take a boat tour of the St. Lawrence River. Dad wanted to see the 1000 Islands, as he said, "before they disappear when the St. Lawrence Seaway is built." Construction of locks and canals needed to open the river to oceangoing ships began in earnest in 1954. The project was controversial and characterized by some as destructive to this island rich area. Finished in 1958, the 1000 Islands remain a popular tourist spot.

No matter where we traveled, we always sought out dime stores to visit. That kept Dad and Mom up to speed on business trends and activities. Dad also subscribed to a national magazine focused on retail store operations. Generally focused on large stores, it was published by a business association, and required payment of annual membership dues. I asked Dad why he belonged to the group since their coverage seemed unrelated to his business. He replied, "These folks represent businesses in front of state and federal governments. I support them so they can continue lobbying on behalf of the businessman." This helped me learn the value of networking and engagement in civic matters. In my professional career, I became very active in trade association activities.

Sales Promotions and the Discount Store Challenge
The Boss Says
Dad loved running his own store and being the boss. Time and time again he proclaimed, "I'm my own boss." Always even tempered, he almost always seemed to be in a good mood but was definitely "in charge." A second framed sign that hung on the office wall beside his desk proclaimed, *"The boss may not always be right, but he's always the boss."* It helped him maintain quiet authority using a noncombative style.

His "Boss" title appeared in weekly ads that ran in *The Trading Post*, a local shoppers guide. Featuring seasonal goods and weekly specials, they carried the tag line "The Boss Says." A typical ad read, *"The Boss Says: 'A new shipment of fabric remnants has just arrived. – 79 cents each.'"* Or, *"The Boss Says: 'it's back to school time, stock up on school supplies'."* Each ad also carried the slogan "One-half Block of Bargains."

Even his hunting and fishing trips became promotional opportunities. When he took time off for these, Mom usually stayed home "in charge." That led to special promotions proclaiming *"The Boss Is Away. Look at what is now on sale."* They created buzz around town and fun customer conversations.

Promotions and Special Sales
Back to school window displays included stacks of paper tablets and notebooks arranged in artistic circular towers. Fan shaped pencil and artistic crayon, ruler, scissor, and gum eraser arrays attracted attention. Summer fun window displays featured children's sand pails, shovels, inflatable pools, etc. enhanced with "special effect" props like a floor covered with Lake Michigan sand hauled in from the beach. Christmas window displays featured toys, including live action model trains. Giftware and flashing-light decorations enhanced them. However, they didn't go up until the day after Thanksgiving. Mother had a hard and fast rule regarding that.

Special sale packages featured merchandise brought in for promotion and described in full color fliers sent to local mailboxes. The subtle message to residents was they could get about anything needed right there in town. There was no need to travel to discount stores in nearby cities.

Dad checked out the flashy new Topps store in Kalamazoo. It's entrance facade looked like the Hollywood Bowl and caused quite a stir. The inventory was huge, and prices were lower. He found the pricing competition a challenge but remained convinced his more personal customer attention would keep customers coming through his door. But he did hear about pricing from them. When customers looked at a $1.29 item they sometimes said, "It's 99 cents at Topps." He sometimes became philosophical. A favorite story or his was, "A customer came in and asked me for a baking pan. I showed him one for $2.19. He said, 'I saw the same thing at Topps for $1.99.' I asked, 'Why didn't you buy it?' He replied, 'They didn't have any.' I said, 'Hell, if I didn't have any, I'd only ask a dollar and a half.'" Whether or not this conversation ever took place, I don't know. He would have only spoken that way to someone he knew well. Time and time again, he drilled into all of us, "Remember, the customer is always right! Be polite."

The Orange Slices Sale
When summer temperatures became too warm to keep chocolates in the candy case, the inventory was switched to varieties such as gum drops, hard shelled "burnt" peanuts, and orange slices – orange flavored gum candies shaped like orange sections. A special sale accompanied the changeover.

Orange slices normally sold for 19 cents a pound. During the sale Dad offered them for 10 cents. His cost was about 15 cents per pound. Using this "loss leader" to bring customers into the store, his ad read, "**The Boss says, 'Orange slices – 10 cents per pound or two pounds for a Quarter**.'" As anticipated, the two-pound pricing arrangement prompted lots of questions. Some folks recognized the bargain, enjoyed the humor associated with the ruse, and actually paid 25 cents for two pounds. Others became incensed, bought one pound, walked out the door, then turned around, to come back in and buy a second pound - for 10 cents. When asked why the strange pricing, Dad replied, "These things cost me 15 cents a pound. I can't afford to lose that much on a two-pound sale."

Part 3 – The Community Network

Chapter 6

Finding Work and Odd Jobs

For me and my peers, odd jobs available in our community put money into our young pockets and taught us responsibility. Though my dime store jobs provided many "business school" lessons, Dad said they amounted to him taking money from one pocket (his) and putting it in another (mine). He also wanted me to find other jobs so I would learn to work with other people while bringing cash in from outside the family.

I understood the concept, but it was a bit scary for me. I had used the store job as a convenient hiding place when I didn't want to face some outside world societal pressures. For example, one day some of my scouting peers organized a hike around the entire outer perimeter of the community. They were packing lunches, donning backpacks, and striking off on a day-long outing. I liked the idea of the adventure, but all that walking didn't sound good. I asked, "Can we take our bikes?" "No," they shouted, "It's a hike!" I found it easier to say, "No, I've got to work," rather than take a chance on not measuring up to the rigors of the trip.

Similarly, in junior high school years, friend Terry Boynton organized frequent football scrimmages in his back yard. I liked the comradery and wanted to be asked to be a part of the group. But when skill levels required for the game exceeded my abilities and tastes, I lost interest and told the guys, "It's time for me to head to work at the store."

The other advantage of my store job was an ability to quickly check out from it when opportunities that I *did* want to participate in came along. Things like playing music with a group or hanging out with a gang at Armstrong's soda bar. I could quickly set aside "job" duties and headed out to get involved. Dad saw through this and as I got older urged me to get out and find other jobs.

Delivering Show Bills

John Geisler, the older son of funeral director Tom Geisler, was two years ahead of me in school. He had a Saturday morning job delivering Park Theater show bills to local residences. Entering junior high, he wanted to get rid of this responsibility. He recruited me and a few of my fifth and sixth grade friends to go to the theater early one Saturday morning, meet owner Cocky Howard, and hear what the job was all about. Three or four of us agreed to take over portions of his community-wide delivery route.

Show bills were pocket-sized pamphlets that described movies playing at the theater during upcoming days and weeks. Movies shown changed about three times a week. Each edition informed the reader which movies were available on what dates. Our job was to walk our designated routes and leave one show bill on the doorstep of each house along the way.

Our "pay" was free passes to movies. Each week, we earned four free passes to any movie playing at the theater. These were not time sensitive and could be accumulated. We could bring family members to the theater and use accumulated passes for their admittance as well. Records regarding how many passes we had accumulated were kept by Mr. Howard himself, written in pencil on a sheet of paper posted on the wall in the theater box office. I always felt "rich" when I checked-in with him and asked how many passes I had accumulated. The number could get to be quite high, 20, 30 or upwards of 50 passes! I felt important when I took my family to the theater and got all four of us in free.

My route was the entire length of Washington Street, the town's main street. I started at the north village limits across the river and worked my way to the southern limits at "the point" intersection with Canaris Street. Other delivery boys had streets located throughout the community.

While walking the route that first week, John showed me where to place the show bill at each house so the occupant would see the small pamphlet. He offered opinions as to which persons or families were likely to go to the movies. Television was a new thing in those days. If he saw a TV antenna on the roof he concluded, "It's OK to skip this one." He didn't expect anyone with a new TV to go to the movies.

We were given a sizable stack of show bills and expected to deliver all of them. I looked for opportunities to get rid of as many as possible and thought it better to leave extras rather than skip houses. When I walked the route on my own, I left bills at all houses, regardless of whether or not it sported a TV antenna. Some of my peers delivering other routes also sought ways to unload large numbers of bills. They suggested tossing a few in the river as they crossed over the bridge to get to the town's northern neighborhoods. "That would get rid of some," they concluded. I didn't know how many may have been disposed of that way but I didn't follow the practice. I brought extras to the store and put them at the checkout for customers to pick up.

I enjoyed the early Saturday morning outing that this job required and really liked the status associated with accumulating free movie passes. I stuck with it for about a year. It was a good start as my first job outside the store.

The Paper Route

A natural progression from the show bill job was delivering newspapers. This paid real cash. For years, I watched carriers prepare to make daily *South Bend Tribune* route rounds from Lakes Walgreen's Drug Store next door to the dime store. I thought I would like to do that one day. The *South Bend Tribune* was the most popular newspaper in town. Paper bundles arrived daily on the northbound afternoon Indiana Motor Bus Company coach. Carriers gathered in the alleyway next to the store, unpacked and counted out their papers then headed off on their routes. About three or four of these covered the town. They were big routes, each with over 100 customers. The carriers were hired directly by the South Bend head office. It was unclear how to get these prestigious routes. A "word of mouth" thing, it required "connections."

The more sure thing was obtaining a route delivering one of the other papers distributed in town. These were managed by Mr. Lee Smith, the local broker who handled delivery of small papers such as the *Sturgis Journal*, *Three Rivers Commercial*, and *Elkhart Truth*. I was in sixth grade when I obtained one of these routes, delivering about 40 *Sturgis Journal* papers. After proving myself on this small route, I was "promoted" to an 80-plus customer *Three Rivers Commercial* route. I also carried a few (four to six) *Elkhart Truth* papers. These newspapers did not publish a Sunday edition, so I got one day a week off.

Deliveries started from the downtown stock room at Armstrong's Drug Store. I met fellow carriers there right after school each afternoon. In summer, on school vacation days, and on Saturdays, we had more time and often met a little early at Armstrong's soda bar. We ordered cherry Cokes or, in the case of someone trying to flex some muscle, a lime phosphate. We sat at the bar on tall red stools in front of the sink area where we could easily talk with the "Soda Jerk," usually someone we knew well. This was the most prized teenage job in town. They (usually she) mixed soda fountain drinks, prepared ice cream sundaes and sodas, scooped up cones, etc. Their contacts with customers gave them a wealth of information they could share with us to keep us current on latest gossip and important topics of the day.

George Armstrong, the adult son of pharmacist and store owner Ross Armstrong, kept a close eye on us. He monitored our conversations and occasionally added a comment or two, letting us know he was present. We really liked his friendly and affable style.

After hanging out for a while, trading jeers and tall tales, we four to six boys (and an occasional girl) got down to work in the stock room. We unpacked bundles of newspapers thrown from the back of a box truck that rumbled through the alleyway behind the store about the same time each afternoon. Papers in the largest bundles were printed in neighboring communities Three Rivers and Sturgis. Other bundles contained smaller numbers of papers from larger cities, the *Kalamazoo Gazette*, *Grand Rapids Press*, *Elkhart Truth*, *Chicago Daily News*, and even the *Detroit Free Press*.

Each carrier grabbed bundles containing the papers we delivered and carefully counted out the number needed for our respective routes. On some days Lee Smith joined us as we prepared. He arranged for the newspapers to be dropped off at Armstrong's, devised carrier routes, recruited and supervised individual carriers, and handled the business end of things with newspaper companies. If you wanted to become a newspaper carrier of anything other than the *South Bend Tribune,* you had to contact and be interviewed by Lee.

He was an all-business fellow. We were always a sedate group in his presence. Once our canvas newspaper carrying bags were stuffed full, we threw them onto our bicycles and fanned out across town to serve our customers. A middle-aged adult, Lee was single and lived on a family farm across the river at the northern edge of town. He drove a meticulously kept, late model, light green Ford pickup truck. He traded them about every two years, and always bought a new one the same color. He did little farming and worked as a shift operator at the local Michigan Gas and Electric hydro-electric power generation station located just across the main street bridge, a half-block from Armstrong's drug store. When his shift work permitted, he drove through our routes checking on us as we made our rounds. We always kept a keen eye out for that light green pickup.

We were each independent contractors, responsible for delivering papers to customers within our assigned area. We also collected the weekly subscription fee from each one, tracked who was up to date on payments, and "settled up" each week with Lee. We paid him for the papers delivered and kept our share of money collected.

Lee gave us a list of customers when we took on the route, counseled us on how to keep them happy, and expected us to recruit new ones. He instructed us on how to keep track of who owed how much and when it was to be paid. He provided our large canvas newspaper carrying bags (emblazoned with the name of the paper we delivered) and a green-covered five by seven inch paper notebook with a stitched binding for us to record how much each customer owed and paid. He suppled printed punch cards about two and one-half inches wide by four inches long, with payment dates marked along three sides of the perimeter. We gave each customer a new card at the beginning of the calendar year and punched out dates with a heavy-duty paper punch (provided by Lee) when we collected each week's fee. The punches produced a peculiar-shaped hole, not easily duplicated by the customer. This protected us from customers punching their own card to avoid payment. Lee also gave us a small, zipper closed, canvas, First Commercial Savings Bank bag to keep our money in. Collections were made each Saturday morning, meaning that I traveled my route twice that day – once in the morning to collect, then again in late afternoon to deliver that day's edition.

Lee never raised his voice when dealing with us. Always willing to listen if we had a problem or sought advice, he remained firm when it came to the business aspects of our relationship.

Each Tuesday after supper Lee came to my house toting his record book and a manually operated adding machine. He came in, exchanged pleasantries with my parents, and sat down at the dining room table. I dumped the contents of my bank bag on the table and counted the money. Meanwhile, Lee examined my collections notebook and began making 25 cent entries into his adding machine, one at a time for each customer I had delivered papers to that week. I was to have recorded who paid how much, which customers might have requested a vacation hold, note any who stopped delivery all together, and added any new subscribers I had picked up.

Lee made each machine entry with great flourish. He enthusiastically punched the numbers on his keyboard, then with a satisfied nod, pulled the machine handle to enter each one. A long tape emerged from his machine displaying a perfect column of 25s. When finished, he pushed the "total" key and pulled the handle one last time. The number that came up was the amount he was to be paid out of what I had collected.

Lee always got his take first. Anything left over was mine. In theory, five cents from each customer plus money from any tips I received would be left on the table. Most of the time it worked out that way, but if had I made any recording errors, failed to collect from one or more customers, spent some of the money on bubble gum, candy, bean shooter peas, or somehow lost it, the shortages were all on me. Lee got his 25 cents per head regardless of my performance. I got what was left over.

Occasionally, an error resulted in my having more money left over than I was due. I could keep the unexpected windfall. But things always worked themselves out. In the weeks to come, that windfall somehow disappeared and became a lesson learned through experience.

Lawn Mowing

Like many in town, our corner house lot at the intersection of White Pigeon Road and Chestnut Street included a good-sized lawn that required weekly mowing. When I was seven or eight my father thought it was time I started taking on that task. We had an old reel type push mower. If the grass had not grown too long, pushing it across the lawn wasn't too hard and the unique snipping sound made as the reel passed over the machine's blade was satisfying. But in longer grass, push mowing was hard work. Grass blades jammed between the reel and cutting bar, locking up the mower wheels and produced a sharp knocking sound. This made it impossible to push the machine across the lawn without several backward strokes to free the jammed mechanism.

Power lawn mowers had become popular, and I pestered Dad about getting one. I showed him newspaper ads from Sears and Roebuck, Montgomery Wards, Gambles, the local Smith

Hardware, and Perry's Appliances who were all selling them. Prices were in the $100 range. Looking for the best deal, Dad ordered one through a wholesale merchandise supplier.

He chose a Moto-Mower model. It was a reel type mower with a two and one-half horsepower Briggs and Stratton engine mounted over the cutting reel. It arrived at the store a couple of weeks later, packed in a large box. I was anxious to take it home and get it going. It looked simple enough to operate. There were only two controls, a throttle, and a belt tightening lever used to engage the chain, belt, and pulley arrangement that drove the wheels. I was ready to fill the gas tank, wind the starting rope around the crankshaft pulley, and pull on it to get it started. Dad insisted we read the directions first and make sure we did such things as fill the engine with motor oil, grease the drive pulleys, etc.

I was also anxious to show it off to the two Metzlar boys that lived across the street. Always up to date with the latest and greatest equipment, they too had recently acquired a power mower. However, theirs was one of the new rotary style models. It was lighter in weight, a bit less expensive, and according to them, could lop off those buckhorn and other tall stringy weeds that would bend over and not be completely cut by reel mowers. Though I was catching up, I didn't impress them with my heavy conventional style mower.

It turned out that Dad had an ulterior motive for equipping me with the new mower. He thought I should make some money using it to mow lawns for other people. I would not have been excited about that idea had the Metzlar boys not struck off to do the same thing. Game on! It was a contest to see who could line up the most lawns to mow. Separately, we headed off to nearby neighborhoods soliciting lawn mowing services. I quickly signed up three close neighbors. They came up with four. They continued to boast about the superiority of their machine, but as it turned out, I had an advantage. Once word was out that I had gone into the business, I acquired several customers. Folks coming into the store, told Mom or Dad they needed my services, and I was signed up. These lawns were located all over town, much further away from home than those signed up by the Metzlar boys. That meant I had to "walk" the mower up the street to get to the job site. Since my machine was self-propelled, I could start it up and run it up the street under power. They had to manually push theirs between jobs. I did need to be careful to avoid rocks and debris as I moved along, and often got some strange looks as my noisy machine moved along the streets. We lost track of the scorecard and who ended up with the most customers, but we each maintained our clientele and made some money in the process.

Pal Dave Daughtery, the banker's son, also became a lawn mowing contractor, but his father took a different approach. He sent Dave down to Perry's appliance store to purchase a new rotary mower, using borrowed money. Then he had to find his own customers, buy his own gas, keep track of all expenses, and pay down the mower debt. Undaunted, Dave went into this big time, serving over a dozen customers. My arrangements were different. Dad bought the mower and supplied the gas, I just had to do the work and put the proceeds in my pocket.

After two or three seasons, other interests became priorities, and I ended my professional lawn mowing career. Overall, it had been a good experience. I earned some money and it kept me occupied when I wasn't delivering papers, working at the store, or at school.

Church Custodian

The First Congregational Church building located on South Washington Street, just south of the business district, was spectacular. Built in 1888, the building had an impressive bell tower. Three large stained glass "rose windows" made up most of the north, south, and east sanctuary walls. The largest of five church buildings in the community, it had the smallest congregation. Though the sanctuary would seat 300 people, Sunday morning congregations numbered less than 100. However, those of us who attended found it to be a spiritually rewarding place of worship.

My father began taking me to Sunday school there shortly after we moved to town. I was just three and one-half years old. My mother began playing the pipe organ there during my young adolescent years. I spent many hours sitting next to her on the organ bench while she practiced. That produced a lifelong interest in organ music but, for some reason, I was not inspired to make the effort to learn to play. Instead, while Mother played, I wandered around behind the organ facade watching all the moving parts and listening to the sounds coming from the ranks of various sized wooden and metal pipes positioned back there.

Several of my school chums and scouting peers also attended this church. We attended Sunday school classes, formed and sang in a youth choir, and in our junior and senior high school years became an active Pilgrim Fellowship group. We returned to the building on Sunday evenings for meetings and organized group outings that took us to neighboring community movie theaters, skating rinks, and bowling alleys. They provided convenient excuses for us to get out of our respective homes and hang out together.

The expansiveness of the church building was inspiring. We were impressed to learn that the huge windows had been imported from France and the organ had come from Italy. A large ventilation vent covered by a huge scrolled grille centered in the sanctuary ceiling seemed to breath. We felt that God was all around us as we sat in that worship space.

I often served as an usher, distributed Sunday bulletins, and lighted candles at the opening of services. I became an organizer of ushers and acolytes who walked the aisles during the offertory, wielding long handled collection boxes passed into pews as we worked our way through the congregation. Rob Polleys, Tom Flatland and I often performed these duties together. We sat in the back of the church and passed notes, reading materials, or other items brought with us for amusement – or to show off. A small pocket squirt gun or giant bubble gum jaw breaker provided distractions during what we regarded as long boring sermons.

When the church needed a custodian, it seemed natural for me apply for the job. It wouldn't take much of my time. On Saturdays, I got things ready for the next day in a couple of hours. I went in early on Sundays to open the building. This job replaced some of the income I lost when I gave up my paper route during my eighth and ninth grade years.

While performing custodial duties I had the huge building all to myself. I let myself in using the key to the back door I had been entrusted with and went to work sweeping and arranging chairs in the Sunday school room. I dusted pews in the sanctuary and vacuumed carpet runners in the long wooden floor aisles leading to the dais at the front of the sanctuary. The church owned a new Hoover Constellation vacuum cleaner. It was a ball shaped machine, a little larger than a basketball, that had an exhaust port located on the bottom. When operating, the ball floated on the cushion of air exiting the machine. I was impressed by this futuristic marvel. It followed me around as I worked to pick up dust and dirt, dead flies, and other debris. After vacuuming I carried a broom and a couple of large buckets of water out the bell tower door and scrubbed pigeon droppings off the front steps. These pesky birds loved to roost up under bell tower louvers and made a huge mess of the steps. It took nearly as long to clean the steps as it did to do all of the inside tasks. Finally, I retrieved a high step ladder from a closet to wind and set the large pendulum clock that hung on the sanctuary back wall. Prior to becoming custodian, I had organized a youth group project that raised money to have the clock repaired. It had hung inoperable and silent for years. I liked hearing the soft tick-tock sounds reverberate around the room, adding to the spiritual atmosphere experienced in this space.

Fred Davenport, our Sunday school teacher, taught us that our sanctuary space was special, a place we were to treat with reverence each time we entered it. That, he said, would bring us closer to God. Once I finished my work, I usually sat quietly in one of the pews for a few minutes before leaving the church and heading down to Vail's Department Store to report in with Maribeth Stephenson, the church treasurer. I reported completion of my tasks and was ready to receive my pay. She, looking at me over the top of her glasses, asked several times if I was sure I had done all of them. Finally, she reached for her purse and extracted my $1.50 pay.

On Sunday mornings I arrived at church early, unlocked back and front doors, and once again cleaned the front steps. Generally, my mother and I locked up when services were over. As organist, she was usually the last person out the door, leaving just behind the minister. My First Congregational foundation has supported my faith throughout my lifetime.

A Summer Apprenticeship

In my junior high school years my father began to think about remodeling our house. My sister and I had shared a bedroom up until then and he determined that it was time for her to have her own room. Though adding the third bedroom was the primary motivator, he and my mother also identified several other desired changes. The list included excavation of the basement under the rear portion of the house, removal of a wrap-around front porch and replacing it with a new entry vestibule, and adding an extension, with fireplace, to the living room. It was an ambitious project. To visualize his plans, Dad not only drew up floor plans, but produced a scale model of the structure out of cut-up corrugated boxes. He showed the model to contractors, obtained price estimates, then decided the only way he could afford to do the job was to do most of the work himself. This launched a year-long project for both him and me.

Dad started the basement extension in the fall. He dug it by hand throughout the winter. Working nights, after closing the store, he headed down the basement stairs to shovel dirt from under the back half of the house onto home built conveyors, sending it to his trailer parked beside the house. Once the dirt was removed, he laid cement blocks to form the new basement walls. He finished this part of the job in the spring of my eighth-grade year.

He and my mother agreed he would take the summer off from the store, she would run the business, and he would devote full time to the remodeling project. My sister, a rising fifth grader, picked up housekeeping tasks and provided some meals. I became Dad's apprentice.

We started by pouring the floor in the new basement. I mixed the cement in a borrowed cement mixer set up in the yard beside the house and poured each batch down a chute Dad had fashioned out of our backyard slide. He spread it into place. Next, we started on the additions. We tore out old doors, windows, and walls, dug and built new foundations, framed walls and rooflines, then closed in the remodeled house. To finish the job, we put new siding on the entire house and as fall and my freshman year in high school drew near, applied a new maple-tan colored paint job. Dad did hire contractors for some of the work. A local mason built the fireplace and chimney. I served as the mason's apprentice as well, handing him bricks and pieces of stone, while Dad mixed mortar. Interior plastering and wall/ceiling finishing was completed by a professional crew.

That summer job really kept me busy. It was pretty much a sunup to sundown proposition. I learned a lot about masonry work, carpentry, house wiring, roofing, and other building trades. It was hard physical work, but I enjoyed it. Besides strengthening the close relationship I had with my father, I also had many opportunities to interface with the local lumberyard delivery man. He was an interesting and philosophical black man that made daily trips to our job site. I couldn't understand widespread racial questions or animosities that swirled around this real nice fellow. He lived just up the street from us and was always pleasant.

My friends and peers occasionally stopped by to see what progress we were making. Neighbors and friends of Mom and Dad came to look things over and provide comments or advice on how to address challenges encountered. In many ways it became a community project. Such was the way in a 1950s small town.

Painting the Garage
In the summer following my sophomore year, Dad decided it was time for the garage to be painted so it matched the remodeled house. He contracted with Dave Daugherty and me to do the job. It had been a long time since the garage was last painted. The light green paint had peeled on all four sides. Our job was to scrape it down, prime it, and apply the matching maple-tan paint.

It was quite a project. It took heavy scraping to get loose paint off the siding. The white trimmed eaves were not boxed in, so scraping and repainting around the ends of exposed rafters was tedious work. We started on the back wall and worked our way around both sides before starting to work on the front.

It took a couple of weeks to complete the job. But what held our interest turned out to be activities taking place across the street. Farmlands across from our house had been developed into a new housing subdivision. During the time Dad and I were working on the remodeling project, a local contractor built a house on newly developed Cherry Street one block beyond us, but directly within Dave's and my line of sight. A new family from out of town was moving in.

As we painted, we kept an eye on activities over there. We determined that the family included two girls – one of high school age, the other a few years younger. We began to spend a lot more time working on the front of garage, seeking more information about the "new girl in town." My dad began to wonder why painting the front of the garage was taking so long. He asked if it really needed four coats of paint.

Wrapping up the project, we decided to collect some on-site data. Dave was quite the ladies' man and a good looking, very self-assured fellow. He was still delivering the South Bend Tribune newspaper and boasted that he had signed up that house as a new customer. Each day he left our painting project early to go make his delivery rounds. Though he had delivered papers to the new house a few times previously, he had been unaware of "the new girl." Given our discovery, he became more anxious than ever to get going on his paper route. I didn't want him to meet the new girl before I did. After all, she moved into my neighborhood, not his. My Cushman scooter was parked in the garage. After some discussion, I talked Dave into letting me drive him over that portion of his route with him riding on the back seat. Only three houses had been completed in the new neighborhood, so we got to our targeted location, 125 Cherry Street, quickly. As we putted up the drive, out of the front door walked a nice-looking young lady. She took the paper from us. We made self-introductions and learned that her name was Barbara Kolb. We exchanged a few words and left, heading back to my driveway. I had prevailed! Dave had not met her before I did. In the ensuing weeks and months, I kept a close eye on things over there and timed my daily walk to school to coincide with that of she and her neighbor Kathy Bizoe. Six years later, after we both graduated and were attending Western Michigan University, she became my wife – for the next 51 years.

Chapter 7

Other Adventures

I can't cite the reasons or statistics regarding our perceived security during the era in which my generation grew up, but it led to us kids spending more time out running around the community than occurs today. Perils were certainly out there. We were taught to "look both ways when crossing a street." Told, "don't play with fire," and given other basics. Bad things did occasionally happen. However, we didn't have "helicopter parents." (Nor had we seen many helicopters in those days). More often, we were sent outside to play early in the morning and told to be home at mealtime, or by dark. Freedom to roam the community, odd job opportunities, and our in-school experiences combined provided life skills training, an academic education, and some great adventures.

Let's Go Sledding

In winter we sledded at the park in the center of town. Located about three blocks from downtown on Washington street, the park's open grassy area lies at the bottom of a gully. A steep bank on the Washington Street side provided a good sliding hill. With good conditions, we could flop down on our Flexible Flyers, roar down the hill, and glide across the lower lawn all the way to the alley behind the park. There was one hazard, a small fishpond in the middle of the lawn. Sometimes this shallow pond was frozen over, but accumulations of leaves and mild winter weather produced a pool of slushy water rather than solid ice.

One late winter Saturday morning, Mother was loading my sister and me into the car for the usual trip up to the dime store. We had received a fresh snowfall. I talked Mom into letting me take my sled along and be dropped off at the park to join other kids on the sliding hill. She agreed but made sure I was warmly dressed in my woolen snowsuit, bomber style hat, buckle boots, and two pairs of mittens.

It was an active morning at the park. Several grade school friends were already there, including Virginia and Jim Langworthy. Their father ran Read's Market and they lived behind us on South Washington Street just one block from our house. When I arrived, Virginia was in the midst of organizing a snowball fight. I joined in and helped build two snowbank forts. We rolled a dozen two-foot diameter balls of snow and stacked them two rows high for each fort. Behind these we stockpiled many rounds of firmly patted grapefruit sized snowballs. The snow was "packy," perfect for the occasion.

The battlefield was out in front of the large Civil War cannon that still sits in the park atop a stone-faced pedestal. That monument, placed there to honor village soldiers involved in that conflict, had a storied existence. On warm weather days we climbed the stone platform, examined the cannon closely, jumped up onto its large barrel and slid out to the end with our legs dangling from either side. Looking down inside it, we imagined how 30-pound cannonballs came flying out when an explosive charge was ignited back down at the butt end. We studied the filled-in fuse hole and wondered what putting a torch to it would have been

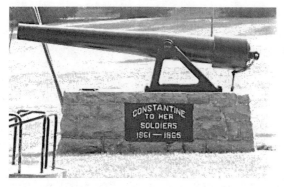

like. A center of attention in the park, vandals from the town of White Pigeon loved to sneak over on the eve of the annual Constantine-White Pigeon high school football game and paint the cannon red and black, their school colors. But on this day, we simply used the monument as the backdrop for our snowball conflict.

Once everything was ready, Virginia declared it time to start the "war." She quickly divided us into two groups of about six kids each. We took positions behind our respective forts and started throwing snowballs. A few hardpacked ones landed on my chest and head. I got off a few good ones that hit the opposing group but carefully picked opponents to aim for verses those to avoid. I didn't want to face retaliation for hitting those likely to come after me when it was all over.

Once our ammo was exhausted, both sides claimed victory and we switched to sliding. We grabbed our sleds, ran up the snow-covered lawn, and climbed the concrete steps located in the middle of the Washington Street hillside. At the top, we lined up and made runs down onto the broad lawn. After successive trips, the snow was packed down and the ride became faster. We were excited to coast across the lawn all the way to the opposite side of the park.

Inevitably, on one of my runs, I couldn't avoid heading straight on into the fishpond. The slushy water grabbed me, and the sled sank into the muck. I quickly jumped off and tried to get out without getting wet, but my heavy snowsuit was already soaked. What to do? I didn't want to leave and miss out on all the fun, so I tried to ignore the situation, grabbed the sled and worked my way back up to the top of the hill for another run. Unbeknown to me, an adult had been observing the action and went directly down to the dime store to report my plight to my mother. She came rushing back to pick me up and take me home for dry clothes, scolding me for not coming to her on my own. Such was the way in our community. It took care of us. We couldn't get away with much. We knew everyone in town. Someone was always watching and rescued or reported on us as needed.

Free Boat Anyone?

The abundance of waterways in and near town provided many watersport opportunities. One of my early adventures involved an attempt to retrieve an old boat from the East Water Street riverbank, down behind the Co-op feed mill. Barry Swartwout lived two blocks from this wet and heavily wooded floodplain. We began exploring the area in about the fourth grade. Trudging around down there we had to be careful and not step into deep water filled holes. Huge carp wallowed in muddy coves along the shoreline. They sucked up corn kernels and other grain washed into the river by the mill. On every chance he could get, Barry was down there with a fishing rod in his hand. One day an adult fisherman, who also spent a lot of time in the area, pointed to a small wooden boat lying on the riverbank and asked Barry if he would like to have it? "It just needs to be fixed up a little to stop a few leaks," the man said. Barry was excited. He dreamed of getting out on the water rather than having to fish from shore. For several days, Barry talked about having his own boat at school, how he was going to fix it up, and where he would go when he got it in the water. But first, he needed to retrieve it and take it home for repairs. One day, after school, he drafted me to go there with him to recover it.

We walked to his house, picked up his express wagon, and struck off for the riverbank. We weren't sure how we would get the boat on the wagon and pull it through the woods, but Barry insisted it could be done. Climbing through the squishy swamp we managed to get the wagon in there. We grabbed the boat and lined it up crosswise over the wagon. When we set it down, Barry's hand got stuck between the boat and the wagon. He yelled, "Get if off my hand, get it off my hand!" I tried lifting it, but it was too heavy. We looked for a stick or something to pry with, but no luck. He screamed, "Go get my mother." I left him there, ran through the woods, up the street, to his house. Fortunately, his mother was home, but that was when I learned that he had not told her about the venture and what we were up to.

After a brief interrogation and some words expressing frustration and worry, she grabbed her coat and ran to the riverbank with me. Working together, we quickly freed Barry from entrapment. Then, she marched us out of there leaving the boat and the wagon where it was. Hustling us back to the house, she asked what we thought we were doing? Whose boat was it? Why did we think we could take it? etc. Barry was not injured but the prospects of retrieving and restoring his boat were put into question. His mom said he would have to take that up with his father when he got home from work.

A few days later Barry and his father completed the retrieval and over several weeks repaired the boat. His garage and the under-repair boat became a gathering place. Several of us frequently checked on the progress. Following repair and reminiscent of river raft adventures of Tom Sawyer and Huck Finn (Mark Twain),

Barry and Jim Smith used the boat to get out on the river after dark to spear redhorse suckers. They came to school the next day talking about those adventures. I didn't participate in them. They took place after my curfew.

A Hut in the Grass

Tony Witek, a year ahead of me in school, lived at the corner of South Washington and Sixth Streets. Like his father, the manager of the local A & P grocery store, Tony was a very active sportsman. He got up very early every morning to run his trapline in the Mill Pond swamps. He caught a wide range of critters, muskrats, now and then a beaver, an occasional raccoon, and was always seeking the elusive mink. I don't recall him ever catching a mink, but when I stopped by his garage while walking to the store after school, I watched him skin and stretch hides from animals he had picked up before school that morning and listened to his tales about seeing mink "sign" near his traps. He described numerous strategies for moving traps on the next Saturday to improve chances of catching one. He waxed eloquently about how much money he could make if he caught mink instead of muskrats. Once the pelts had dried, he loaded them on his wagon and pulled them to Luke Erwin's shop to sell them.

Occasionally, I visited Tony on Sunday afternoons. He was usually holed up in his second-floor bedroom reading adventure series comic books and listening to mysteries on his radio. He loved *The Creaking Door* and *The Shadow Knows* programs. I too listened to dramas on our living room console radio but preferred *The Green Hornet*. The engine in that hero's powerful sounding Black Beauty car raced as he chased down criminals during weekly episodes.

Other chums, including Smith and Swartwout, gathered at Tony's. There was always something interesting going on. A vacant lot across the alleyway behind his back yard attracted us. There were no trees on this flat field. It was covered with tall grasses and scrubby shrubs that were all taller than we were. We tramped down an intricate maze of trails leading to the center of the lot. There, we built a hut out of discarded house doors and a couple of large pieces of corrugated metal siding. The doors were stood sideways on their edge to form the walls. We laid the siding sheets over the top to form our roof. The ceiling was pretty low, forcing us 10- or 11-year-olds to duck down or crawl on hands and knees to enter the hut.

We stocked the hut with comic books and newspaper sports pages containing Detroit and Chicago baseball player stats. From somewhere, Tony came up with an army surplus shortwave radio console. It was huge and (though we didn't use the term back then) a very "hi-tech" looking thing. The black metal outside case was about three feet long, eighteen inches deep, and a foot tall. It had numerous dials, knobs, switches, and meters on the front. We had no power supply, or other accessories needed to make it work, but we sat it up inside the hut on a pair of orange crates then sat cross legged in front of it twisting knobs and using our imaginations to simulate radio transmissions to and from a number of places. We pretended to be on a ship crossing oceans and communicating with other ships. We conjured up visions of serving as a military operations headquarters sending out orders to planes, ships, and ranks of soldiers. We speculated that if a big storm blew in and shut down the town's power and phone systems, we could activate the unit and become an emergency communications center for the community. It was a great place nestled among those tall grasses. Only we knew how to get to it by following the right trails through the maze of weeds. At school, while out on the playground during recess, we passed the word around, "Meet at the hut after school."

Come winter, we found it too cold to sit there and by the next spring our lives and interests had changed. We no longer visited the hut, but it had served us well during that period of our lives.

Nighttime Adventures

In warm weather, evenings after supper were also times when we went out seeking adventure. The compact residential center of town with its network of alleyways provided off-street rendezvous points. One popular spot was behind Jim Noecker's house. His house faced Washington Street, right across from the First Congregational Church. Behind it, an intersection of alleys serving the neighborhood's deep but narrow house lots created an out of the way open space. Much of the area was used by homeowners for backyard gardens. Each was fenced off, but an intricate system of paths and gates provided access between plots and routes out to the alleyways.

Our gatherings were centered at the intersection near telephone and electric utility poles that ran through the area. These were not organized gatherings. The area was just a natural place to cruise through to see if anyone was out-and-about, and when others were there, stop-in to compare notes and catch up. Often games of hide-and-seek were initiated, or a softball game was started in Noecker's back yard. Generally, things went well during these gatherings, and were pretty quiet during the waning light of day. But as darkness drew near, finding unique places to hide out while running through the maze of garden fences became a tempting pursuit. One or more of the neighbors often came out to chase us hoodlums out of the garden spots, enhancing the mystique of the place. In late summer or fall, when garden produce ripened, things got more out of hand.

Some members of the gang couldn't resist picking tomatoes or squash and throwing them at each other. Watermelons or pumpkins became tempting "cannon balls" to loft or "shotput" out onto nearby streets. The cooler and darker the night, the more intense the garden raids became. I was expected to be home by dark so was anxious to leave and avoid curfew infraction troubles. I also knew it was wrong to be raiding gardens. I could hear in my head the voices of my parents telling me, "These people worked hard to produce a nice garden. It isn't your garden or property." I slipped away quietly and went home, hoping no one would notice and brand me a "sissy." The next day, meeting up with the gang, I heard tales of certain victories or heroic acts. I had nothing to boast about so gained no macho status among my peers. That trophy was reserved for those who left the biggest splotches of pumpkin or watermelon "guts" in the middle of main street.

Movie Nights and Skating Parties

Early teen year gatherings became mixed boy–girl events that were less random or ad hoc and more planned. Out of town excursions to see movies or go skating were organized with one of the group's parents tagged to drive us to the venue. By this time, the Park Theater in Constantine had closed. Cocky Howard had shifted his attention to a new theater, the Sun, he had built in the town of White Pigeon, four miles to the south. It and additional theaters in Three Rivers (nine miles to the north) and Sturgis (twenty miles to our east) were also destinations. The local skating rink had been completely shuttered and torn down. But new, modern, skating rinks in Three Rivers, Sturgis, and at Eby's Pines (near Bristol, Indiana, 12 miles south) also attracted us. Our world had expanded substantially.

One Saturday evening, we planned a White Pigeon movie outing. It was one of the latest 3D movies. We wore paper framed, dark, polarized 3D glasses supplied by the theater to view the movie. It was an action thriller. We dodged objects that appeared to fly right at us from the screen.

Besides the usual clan of Polleys, Smith, Swartwout, and me, girls Virginia Langworthy, Molly Zimont, and my sister were included. My mother drove us to the theater, another parent was to pick us up when the movie ended. As we piled out of the crowded car in front of the theater, my mother asked me to find out what time the movie ended. I checked with Cocky Howard who was selling tickets in the box office and relayed the time back through the line of kids to Mother who sat, door open, waiting for the message. She went off to line up our ride home.

After the movie, we gathered in front of the theater expecting to see a vehicle belonging to one of our parents. No luck. No one was there to pick us up. We waited for quite some time. No one came. Using the box office phone, Molly called home. There seemed to be some confusion about who was supposed to come after us. We continued to wait. In the meantime, the boys in the group got anxious and concluded we could walk home. After all, it was only four miles. We took five-mile hikes in scouts. I wasn't in favor of walking that far, especially in the dark. The girls didn't want to do it either. The debate continued and the guys decided to head out. The girls and I stayed behind. A few minutes later our ride arrived. We got in the car and rode home looking for the boys walking along the way. We didn't find them. We traveled along the main highway while they were walking a country road that ran through farmlands leading back towards town, getting home sometime later.

As the story unfolded between mothers, it wasn't clear who had dropped the ball or failed to get the message to come after us. But in their eyes, I was the "hero." They concluded that rather than strike off with the guys and leave the girls standing on the sidewalk all alone in the dark, I had stayed behind to protect them. That surprised me. I had given some thought about looking after my sister, but mostly, I just didn't want to walk that far. I kept quiet about the question and decided to enjoy being tagged "hero" for a change. That didn't happen often.

Home Alone on Saturday Nights

In my early teenage years, my sister and I were no longer expected to be at the store on Saturday nights. We could stay home, do chores around the house, and watch our family's newly acquired TV. Rather than have us all go to a local restaurant, as had been the practice when we were younger, Mom and Dad came home for a quick supper. Returning to the store, they left the clean-up and dish washing tasks to my sister and me. Four years older than she, I assumed the role of "sitter."

Like most in those days, our kitchen didn't have an automatic dishwasher. We washed them by hand in the kitchen sink. I didn't like putting my hands in the sudsy dishwasher, with all the food scraps floating around in it, so I made my sister do the washing while I dried. I also served as inspector, picking up dishes after rinsing and checking to see if she had missed any spots. If I could find the slightest speck or imagined imperfection, I loved sending pieces back for rewash. Loudly, I shouted "reject" and dumped them back into the wash water in front of her with great flourish. This and using the drying towel to give her a snap or two, made for a lively time as we finished the task before finding other things to do during our home alone time.

My sister's friend Sid Messner lived two blocks away and often came over for the evening. They disappeared into my sister's bedroom while I played loud music on my record player. It was a "hi-fidelity" model I had received at Christmas from "Santa."

Usually successful in bothering the girls, they came out yelling for me to "turn it down." If things got too raucous, someone in the neighborhood would notice. If they headed downtown on some errand, they were likely to stop into the store and comment or report on the commotion they heard back at home. We heard about it when Mom and Dad got home.

By this time, I was getting itchy to drive cars. We had two cars, our five-year old 1950 DeSoto two-door sedan, the first new car Dad owned, and a slightly newer Plymouth station wagon Dad used for hauling merchandise and hunting/fishing gear on Sunday outings. Mom and Dad returned to the store in the station wagon leaving the DeSoto parked in the garage.

A spare DeSoto key hung from a hook on the kitchen wall. Once my sister, Sid, and perhaps another friend or two of hers, had gone about their business, I headed for the garage with the key. Initially, I just turned on the ignition and listened to the radio. I scanned the dial to see what far off stations I could lock onto. In those days, car radios often had better reception and sound than radios used in the house. Sitting behind the steering wheel, I checked out the vehicle controls and fantasized about driving down the road while listening to stations in Chicago, Fort Wayne, Indiana, or WWVA in Wheeling, West Virginia. Later, I got a bit braver and tried starting the engine. Visits to my grandfather's farm during harvest season had given me opportunities to drive his tractor in the fields. That had taught me to be careful using the clutch and make sure the car was out of gear during my experiments. At first, I just sat in the car with it running. I kept the shift lever in neutral with the handbrake securely set. Revving the engine, I continued my fantasies.

One evening, I found myself putting the shifter in reverse and slowly backing out of the garage. The car was equipped with

"Fluid Drive," an early semi-automatic transmission. Though I had to push down the clutch peddle to get it into gear, it didn't lurch or jump when I let out the clutch. Once out of the garage, I stopped, waited a minute, shifted into forward and drove back in. Careful to stay in the same track, I didn't scrape the sides of the car or outside mirror on the garage as I entered. Impressed with this first success, I repeated the experiment a few times. Our driveway was over 100 feet long, so I made quite a trip going back and forth several times.

But the open street was calling. Just north of our driveway, White Pigeon Street veered off White Pigeon Road at a "Y" shaped intersection. About a half-block from the intersection, Clinton Street cut across both streets, providing a pie shaped route that seemed to be a good place to test street driving talents. On my next outing, I boldly backed out of the driveway, headed up the short distance to White Pigeon Street, bore left, drove the few more feet to Clinton Street, turned right onto Clinton, crossed over to White Pigeon Road, turned right again, then headed back to the driveway. I parked in the driveway for a few minutes replaying the trip in my mind. It had gone well I thought. No mishaps, no traffic, all seemed in order. I tried it again – and again – a few more times before putting the car back in the garage. I returned to the house quite satisfied with myself.

Later, when Mom and Dad got home, I learned that someone in the neighborhood witnessed my adventure, stopped into the store, and spilled the beans. "Who do you think you are?" "How did you think you would get away with that?" my mother asked. The key disappeared from the kitchen hook, and further adventures were banned.

In my defense, my practice of driving on neighborhood streets had been established years earlier. At about eight my father built me a little race car. It had a wooden chassis, sheet metal body, and even an engine bay in the rear where he installed his two-cycle Maytag washing machine engine. It made me a very popular kid in the neighborhood. Youngsters from blocks around flocked to our driveway to see and drive my race car. With no knowledge of NASCAR, I named it car number 3. My Cub Scout den was Den 3 and I had always regarded three as my "lucky number." It took some assistance from my father to kick-start the engine, but once it was putt-putting, my friends and even my sister took turns driving up and down the driveway.

Eventually we sought longer trips. On the other side of our house, White Pigeon Road intersected with East Chestnut Street. It connected White Pigeon Road with South Washington Street and was used primarily by neighbors accessing their driveways. There wasn't much traffic on it. Without kicking up much fuss from my parents, we started running up and down that street. In addition, my dad and I had taught my sister to ride a bicycle on that street. He got her seated on the bike, gave her a shove, and she peddled to where I stood to catch her. I turned her around and she peddled back. After several of these sessions she was on her own.

When quizzed about why I thought my DeSoto excursions were appropriate, I argued that they weren't much different from these precedents. Nonetheless, the key stayed off the hook.

Scouting Builds Character

I became a member of Cub Scout Den 3 when I was about seven. It was one of 4 or 5 Dens in our Cub Scout Pack. Other Den 3 members included cohorts Barry Swartwout and Jim Smith. We were an early trio that found numerous ways to get into mischief together.

Barry's mother was our Den Mother. We met weekly at their house, Barry and I walking the half-mile or so to get there after school. We learned scouting ideals, litanies, skills, and worked on badge requirements, putting us on a path for climbing future Boy Scout ranks. After our Den meeting, we enjoyed a round of Kool-Aid and cookies while waiting for parents to pick us up. We also checked out Barry's father's new toy, a television set. It was one of the first sets to arrive in our town. We watched Captain Video and his Video Rangers. The signal was broadcast from WKZO, channel 3, the one available TV station located in Kalamazoo. Space Cadettes traveled interplanetary space in their rocket ship, Galaxy, stamping out evil forces and bringing harmony to civilizations inhabiting earth's neighboring planets – including Pluto. Among us earthlings of the day, there was much uncertainty about the nature of the planets. In some of our minds, the existence of "Martians" was not totally ruled out. Episodes also included short messages urging us "Video Rangers" to follow the Golden Rule and treat all people equally regardless of race or color. This new media form was already working to build a positive image and blunt charges from critics that it was an evil media that would degenerate society.

Monthly Cub Scout Pack Meetings, held in the Methodist Church basement, included potluck dinners and opportunities for Scouts to display work products that satisfied requirements for working through Bobcat, Wolf, Bear, and Lion Cub Scout ranks. Our parents were an important part of the process. They signed off on paperwork confirming we had completed requirements and stood with us when we were awarded rank patches. We learned responsibility and accountability through the process.

The meetings included speakers who talked to us about good citizenship, respectful behavior, and life skills. One evening an out-of-town speaker described threats associated with the growing use of a substance called marijuana. He said use of it became addictive, made us crave even stronger drugs, and would ruin our lives. He burned some there in the church basement and told us to remember the pungent odor. He instructed us to run as fast as we could in the opposite direction If we ever encountered the odor. I was impressed. My father was impressed. He talked about that meeting often.

Becoming Weblos Scouts and earning our Arrow of Light awards, we entered Boy Scouts and began the quest for our Tenderfoot rank. The Boy Scout troop was a larger group with a much broader range of ages. We were assigned to Patrols, led by older Scouts. The troop met evenings at "Headquarters," upstairs over the fire station. Activities included local camping trips and regional camporees that included troops from other communities. Patrols performed "good deed" service projects in our community and held fund=raising events to earn money for troop equipment. We learned to work together, help one another, and discovered that advancement through ranks required individual effort.

My Patrol leader, Clarence Wenzel, had a brilliant mind and adventuresome spirit. He and his parents lived out on the western edge of town in a small house on a deep lot abutting the river. We held Patrol meetings at his house in early evenings or on Saturdays. We used these meetings to plan for troop camping trips and other activities. He and I had a lot of common interests. He appointed me Patrol Scribe, essentially his assistant. Smith, Swartwout, and two or three others from our Cub Scout Den were also Patrol members. We learned fire building skills and developed knife, axe, and shovel talents. We experienced tent erecting and other outdoor-life comfort successes and failures. Open-fire cooking and dreaded (sometimes penal) KP duties were part of the mix. Scrubbing cooking pots to make the outside as shiny as the inside after they had been used over an open fire, was strenuous. Despite having been liberally "soaped" on the outside before using them, they were always blackened by the fire.

Clarence and I usually shared a pup tent. Initially we used army surplus tents made up of two halves joined together by buttons along the top ridge. They had no floor. We used canvas ground cloths for that. We put one down before erecting the tent over it and trenched the perimeter, using our folding handle Army surplus shovels to encourage water to run away from our tent. As hard as we tried, it was impossible to make things watertight. It often rained on these outings and our sleeping bags always got wet. After a few successful fund-raising events, the troop purchased new all-in-one canvas tents that included a sewn-in floor. They worked much better. Unless we touched the inside of the canvas while it was wet, we were able to stay reasonably dry. However, a mere brush of the fabric broke the surface tension on water mist droplets that accumulated on the inside, and drip–drip, we had a leak.

We packed a good supply of comic books in our knapsacks so we could share them. Evenings we read by flashlight for as long as our batteries held out. Our official Boy Scout flashlights had a 90-degree bend at the head end and a belt clip on the back of the battery tube. We clipped the lights to a string, or boot lace stretched between tent poles to illuminate our reading materials. Our tastes in comics differed. Clarence was into superhero/action figure comics. I favored Donald Duck or Bugs Bunny stories. Sharing broadened each of our experiences somewhat.

When air mattresses under our sleeping bags stayed inflated, we were in fine tenting luxury. However, that rarely happened. We always had to blow them back up a time or two during the night only to find them soon flat again. Rocks poking us in the back made it tough to sleep through the night.

Our troop age group was fairly wide. Some older scouts were more worldly than we younger ones. As a result, conversations covered a wide variety of topics. Older boys knew more about differences between human sexes and intersexual behavior. Many of us heard about this for the first time on camping trips. Our parents didn't talk to us about these things in those days. Older boys also brought reading materials with them, but they weren't comic books. Girly magazines circulated from tent to tent until confiscated by adult leaders.

Scoutmaster Fred Davenport, the village Postmaster (and for some of us also our Sunday school teacher) befriended, coached, and plodded us along on our scouting journey. Given our Weblos experience, we quickly earned our Tenderfoot badge. From there on we had to produce on our own. Fred mentored us, holding evening merit badge workshops at his home. My father, also a good mentor, helped me with many projects. A Sea Scout in his youth, he didn't get the opportunity for much advancement since his family moved a lot. He pushed me to work on merit badges, reminding me that obtaining the Eagle rank was a target I needed to shoot for. However, the 1952 national Presidential election, won by Eisenhower, changed political party control of government offices. Postmaster Fred was replaced and had to find another job. He no longer had time to serve as Scoutmaster. Others made efforts to keep the troop together, but the blow to leadership along with actions of some troop members on evenings following troop meetings, resulted in troop dissolution. Rumors had it that an attractive young lady was providing entertainment from behind a picture window in her home while scouts gathered outside on the lawn to watch. I was not a participant so can't attest to the authenticity of the rumor. However, the opportunity for others and me to continue climbing scout ranks closed. The troop was reestablished a year or so later, but by that time many of us were busy doing other things and didn't return to scouting.

Girls in the community had a better experience. My sister and many of her cohorts were able to work through all Brownie and Girl Scout ranks, obtaining their Curved Bar, the rank equivalent to Eagle.

Woodsmen and Aviators

Clarence and I continued our adventures. The lot behind his house was undeveloped, wooded, and extended back to the St. Joseph River. He camped out back there, but in a mode different from our Scouting experiences. He liked to imagine, and portray, the lifestyle of the American Indian. He asked me to help build a Teepee and stay the night with him. I headed over one Saturday morning to start the project. When I arrived, he was dressed in a loin cloth, had a hatchet lashed to his waist with a rope, and was standing over canvas materials he had laid out, ready to get to work. This shocked me a bit. I didn't expect this and wasn't into wearing a loin cloth. But I went to work, helping him find and cut poles needed to support the teepee and stretch the canvas around them. Clarence pointed out that we were simulating the use of buffalo hides. He spent some nights in the structure, but I never wanted to. I had a small umbrella tent that I pitched in my back yard on warm summer nights. I preferred using a cot and sleeping bag rather than laying on the hard ground wrapped in a blanket, as Clarence did. We did our sleepout nights independently, each in our own back yard, and compared notes the next day, describing stars we could see, and the imagined wild animal sounds we heard on dark nights.

Clarence also loved to build and fly model airplanes. I too had an interest in building models. His were meticulously built "stick models." Using detailed plans printed in model building magazines, he constructed the frame using balsa wood sticks, covered it with tissue paper, then "doped" the tissue skin with a lacquer finish. It was an art form, and he was good at it. Mine were Struct-O-Speed models assembled from stamped balsa wood panels and plastic parts that came in a kit ready to assemble. I only needed a tube of model cement, some model paint, and modest skills to build my planes. I had an endless supply of kits. My father stocked and sold them at the store. Both types of models would fly. Mine flew under rubber band power using a long heavy rubber band and plastic propeller that came packed in each box. Though Clarence's models could also be powered by rubber bands, he preferred using model airplane engines. His larger and more sophisticated planes had working ailerons, tail flaps, and rudders. Glow-plug-fuel powered engines, wooden props he carved out of balsa wood blocks, and control lines made them fly. We each built our models independently at home, then met at the school baseball field for flying sessions.

I didn't like to start his glow-plug engines. We had to snap the props over using our fingers. The engines were finicky. They often backfired, throwing the propeller backwards, stinging the finger. We developed a two-person approach to cranking up his planes. I held onto the back of the model and let him prop the engine, then he ran to pick up the U-shaped handle and control lines previously laid out on the ballfield. On his signal, I picked up the plane and launched it while he stood at the center of the circular flight path and put it through its paces. He made it climb and dive, then as the fuel ran out tried to bring it in for a soft landing. Now and then he was successful. Other times the plane crashed causing damage that had to be repaired before the next flight. Clarence let me take the controls and fly the plane, but I didn't like getting dizzy while twirling around in that small circle. I also didn't want to be responsible for crashing his plane and smashing it. I preferred to wind up my rubber band model, let it go off on its own, then retrieve it from wherever it landed – sometimes in a tree.

Poker Games on Sundays

Reaching high school age, our desires for comradery only strengthened and our adventures became more worldly. Reminiscent of the show *Guys and Dolls* (Frank Loesser), all we needed was a place to gather in an adult accepted location, and our peers would show up. The Daughtery house was one of those.

Bank President Foster, his wife, Jean, and their five kids lived on East Second Street just a half block from downtown. Middle child, Dave, was one of our social-circle ringleaders. A large screened in porch across the front of the house provided a place to hang out in good weather. Groups sat there watching for passers-by and accumulated participants through yells or jeers.

A single wall mounted telephone in the main hallway inside the house had a long handset cord that could be passed all the way out to and around the front porch. It provided an important communication link that could also be used to collect participants.

Their finished basement contained a billiards table, an authentic juke box loaded with popular tunes of the day, a large poker table, and other amenities. We loved to hang out there on Sunday afternoons but needed to make sure we had a pocket full of pennies when we arrived.

Once critical mass had gathered, we headed for the poker table. Dave broke out the cards and rounds of five-card stud began. Daughtery, Swartwout, and Smith were masters of the game. Some of the rest of us, Polleys, Flatland, me, and others not so much. Sometimes the "pros" mentored slower players. Other times they enjoyed seeing how quickly they could clean us out. Four to six players sat at the table and were "in" the game. Additional people formed a gallery behind the players. When one or more players got wiped out, they were replaced by someone from the gallery. The conversations, jukebox music, and supply of Cokes from a vending machine in a corner of the room, complete with a supply of nickels in the coin return slot used to secure one of the glass-bottled drinks, kept everyone occupied.

Swartwout occasionally provided formal instruction. He showed examples of card combinations that constituted various game ranks and pointed out which was higher and would win a hand. He demonstrated the royal flush, a straight, four of a kind, the ranks of various pairs, etc. During the game, he served as referee when questions regarding who won the hand came up. He, Smith, and George Wortinger were intense players. They professed to know how things were done in "Vegas." They demonstrated their visions of how cards were dealt, held, and played there.

This smaller group met at George's house after school for more serious sessions and became quite absorbed with multiple games of chance. Later, taking mother Wortinger's car, they struck off on their own seeking their fortunes. It was a big scandal in our small community. "They've run away from home!" "Where did they go?" "Are they ever coming back?" The rest of us were astounded! Collective groups of parents asked lots of questions of many of us. "What did we know about these plans?" "Where did they go?" But we knew nothing. The "runaways" had not confided with any of the rest of us. It was a surprise to all. Many speculated that they were headed for Vegas. After all, this was all they talked about. But, as it turned out, about 10 days after their odyssey began, George Wortinger became ill. It was apparently quite serious and forced the group to call home. They had made it to Florida. Parents went down and brought them back. George was bedridden for a time once they returned. All three returned to school. The rest of us were told not to talk to them about their adventure. "Let things blow over and return to normal," we were instructed. A general opinion among most of us was that it had been an ill-conceived act from the start. For me, the comforts of home seemed pretty good compared to the outcome of such a high-flying adventure. I was, as usual, the conservative.

Chapter 8

School Days

Our school grounds and the building itself were a huge center of activity. School population was pretty stable. Most of us attended classes in the same building from the time we entered kindergarten until we became high school seniors and graduated. During the school year, we spent at least six hours per day in that building. Grades kindergarten through eight classrooms were on the first floor, high school classes on the second. In summer, community recreation programs took place on schoolyard ball fields.

The kindergarten room in the back southwest corner seemed spacious. It had features designed to make the first school year comfortable. A large tan brick fireplace stood at the front of the room flanked by a good-sized sandbox located between it and windows that lined the west wall. Chalkboards lined remaining walls. Student-sized tables and chairs stood in the center of the room. Our very friendly teacher packed half-day sessions with alphabet, numbers, and vocabulary lessons. Story times took place in front of the fireplace, where I wondered why there was never a fire. Sandbox play periods, outdoor playground recess, a rest period during which we laid our heads on the desk, and one day per week of music instruction rounded out school half-days. My music interests were peaked when we listened to recordings such as *Tubby the Tuba (*Paul Tripp*)* and *Peter and the Wolf (*Sergei Prokofiev).

Kindergarten was fun. But reality hit us head-on in first grade with a curriculum geared strictly towards "reading, writing, and arithmetic." From then on, teachers were more somber, class sessions stern, and assignments robust. In addition, life lessons forced onto us by peers (especially bullies) out on the playground, in the restroom, or on streets and sidewalks while walking to/from school were strenuous. This is not to say that school experiences were bleak. We just had to understand hierarchies within society and begin to find our place in it.

Mostly, we liked our teachers but quickly learned which were more personable (or strict) than others and began to form opinions about which grade was likely to be more fun (or difficult) than others. The expectation of respect for teachers was unquestionable. It grew quickly from the process and was reinforced by our parents at home.

As we entered the building each day, teachers stood in the hallway beside their classroom door with eyes and ears fixed on the masses walking the hallway. Entering our classroom, we hung our hats and coats in a long shallow closet that stretched along the inner wall, then took assigned seats among rows of floor mounted benches and desks. We stored textbooks, pencils, papers, and other personal belongings in our desks under hinged desktops. We had to be careful not to let the heavy top slam down on our hands as we opened it. We didn't have individual lockers for coats or other belongings until we reached eighth grade. We were expected to be orderly during the arrival period. Once the bell in the hallway rang, teachers came inside, closed the door, and the school day began.

Should any discipline issues develop, teachers quickly asked a peer in an adjacent classroom to keep an eye/ear on things, left the door open, and walked offending students down to the

Superintendent's office where he took charge. We all knew this was serious business and aware that he kept a long leather strap in a bottom drawer of his desk. If the infraction was severe enough, he used it to apply a few smacks to our backsides. It didn't happen often, but we all knew this level of corporal punishment was available. And most of us had been informed by our parents that if we did something prompting this action at school, we would get a more strenuous follow-up dose when we got home. There was no question who was in charge, who deserved respect, or how we were to behave.

Two grade-school teachers I most remember are Mrs. Fellows (first grade) and Mrs. Smith (fourth grade). In first grade, we began to learn to write. I was left-handed. In those days, a common practice was to force left-handed students to switch and use the right hand. Fortunately, Mrs. Fellows was also left-handed. She understood the need for students to utilize natural tendencies. She stood up for me and resisted calls from traditionalists to force me to switch. I remained a lefty.

For me at least, fourth grade was all about arithmetic. We began multiplication tables and long division. I struggled with this, especially memorizing the multiplication tables. Mrs. Smith was a tough taskmaster. We were drilled and tested on the tables daily. No number line or mathematical theory was provided, just a requirement to memorize the multiplication tables published in the back of our arithmetic textbook. Tables for sixes' and sevens' were most difficult for me. I could visualize how the other tables made sense. Multiples of twos', through fives's were easy, but it was difficult for me to deal with mid-level, especially odd, numbers. Each daily quiz included some of those. I was always frustrated. Mrs. Smith just shook her head when I couldn't come up with right answers. At home evenings, while washing supper dishes, my mother made me sit in a kitchen corner rocking chair and drilled me on multiplication tables. She moved up and down through the tables, forward and backwards, trying to get them fixed in my head. It was always an unpleasant scene. Mother was frustrated with my wrong answers and disinterest. Mrs. Smith's stern face always came to my mind while I struggled.

On The Playground

School began at 9:00 a.m. and adjourned for lunch at noon. There was no school lunch program. We either walked home for lunch, returning for classes that resumed at 1:00 p.m., or brought lunch from home in a brown bag or colorful cartoon character emblazoned metal lunch box. Since my sister and I lived only two blocks from school, we and most of the other neighborhood kids, walked home for lunch. Those who stayed ate their lunch in an assigned room where a lunch-duty teacher was in charge, then were excused to go out to the playground until the bell range a few minutes before class time. Those who walked home and back arrived a few minutes prior to bell time and joined the crowd in the playground. We couldn't re-enter the building until the bell rang.

During recess, at lunchtime and after school, the playground was where additional life-skill lessons emerged. No teachers or other school personnel patrolled the playground. A wooden bicycle shed stood near the grade school entrance. Many kids, especially those from neighborhoods further away, rode bikes to school. A front wheel resting parking rack ran down the middle of the shed, dividing it into two halves. One side was designated, by mob-rule, as the "little kid" area. Bikes belonging to younger students were parked there. The other side was used by older, third through fifth grade, students. The shed was a hang-out place for boisterous older boys, the bullies and bully wannabees. They climbed the parking rack and sat amongst roof trusses awaiting arrival of other kids. Yelling nasty words and insults down to them, they focused on the meek and younger ones. During winter they grabbed hats and mittens from their prey and hung these items from roof trusses where it was hard for smaller kids to retrieve them. Some kids were targeted for additional harassment. Air was let out of their bike tires.

I liked the idea of riding my bike to school, but soon learned doing so called more attention to me than I desired. I walked. But that didn't isolate me from the bullies. They often jumped down from their perches and patrolled the playground. In winter, we wore "buckle boots." Any buckles left unfastened jangled together as we walked, producing a chink-chink metal hitting metal sound. Not buckling boots and walking around jangling them conveyed toughness for the bullies. It was a defensive thing for the rest of us. When we heard the sound growing closer, we knew they were coming up behind us. We tried to move out of the way or huddled up with others, bracing for the onslaught.

Some of us avoided the bike shed when we entered the playground and headed to the opposite corner of the playground. A tall slide, swings, and a newly installed set of "monkey bars" stood in this area. The girls tended to hang out there. This egged-on the bullies. As they patrolled the playground, they yelled "look at the sissies," (meaning us boys hanging out with the girls) as they jangled by.

As social groups among students began to form, separate playground areas served as gathering places where stories and tales were swapped. As we got older, vocabularies developed, and facts-of-life topics not covered in classrooms, textbooks, or at home emerged. The playground was a tough and enlightening place. One that helped us develop both social and survival skills.

Summer Recreation

In summer, school was out, and the playground and adjoining baseball fields were used for community recreation programs. Geared for pre-teen adolescents, these provided an organized opportunity for mixed age groups of primarily boys to gather daily to play baseball or softball. The program varied. Some days we played baseball, others, softball. Run by a man teacher or college student, half-day morning sessions met Monday through Friday for a period of about six weeks.

My parents thought it would be good experience for me to attend, and it got me out of their hair for a portion of the day. I liked spending time with my peers but was not at all into athletics. I lacked muscle coordination, was a chunky little guy, and no matter how much I wanted to conform to the jock models exhibited by many in the group, my body and interests just wouldn't comply. But I wanted to be part of the group, so I gave it a try.

Every day started out the same. We gathered at the playground and waited for our leader to arrive. He drove into the schoolyard and unloaded canvas bags from his car trunk containing bats and balls we were to use that day. After greeting and chatting with us for a while he selected two persons, usually the most able athletes in the group, to serve as team captains. Certainly, I was never selected to hold that coveted position. Next, we headed to the ball diamond where the captains lined us up along the first base line. They stepped out into the infield and, alternatively, began picking their team members. One by one, players were beckoned by each captain to join their ranks. Left standing in line after each choice, there were always just two of us remaining, Howard (Howd) Bush and me. One of the captains was then forced to decide which would join his team and said, "Oh, come on over" to one of us. By default, the other became the final member of the opposing team. Like me, Howd had coordination and athletic ability deficits. But we were both pleased to be part of whichever team we ended up on and tried to make contributions to their success.

I liked being at bat best. Standing at the plate, I had a chance to look like a member of the team. Though there was little chance I would actually hit the ball, by being at the plate there was some action involved and a reasonably good chance that I would draw a walk to first base. On rare occasions, I hit grounders and if the ball happened to go through the right spot between infield players I might actually get on base by running. Making it around the bases to home plate was also unlikely, but if enough fielding errors were made, I occasionally came in and scored a run. These rare occasions provided enough sense of accomplishment to make me stick with the program. But they were always accompanied by time to head for the outfield.

I hated playing outfield. Only occasionally was I assigned an infield position. Once in a while I was put in as shortstop, especially if there were enough players that day to use two shortstops, one between second and third base, the second between first and second. This "extra" spot is where I could end up. But mostly, I was sent out to centerfield. Few of our young players could hit the ball that far, so I had little to do out there. Returning balls that did end up there required a bit of a relay. Throwing the ball to the 2nd baseman was the most assured thing I could do. Teammates would yell for me to get the ball back to the pitcher or all the way to home plate, in the case of an advancing runner. I could try, but the probability was that the ball would end up short or wide of its mark.

I've always tended to let my mind wander. So, when standing in center field I was easily distracted. I found gopher holes in the turf that needed to be checked out. Birds flew past that I tried to identify. Better yet, perhaps an airplane flew over. These things always shifted my attention away from action at home plate. Suddenly, I would hear a plop as a ball dropped down right beside me. Then I had to wake up and spring into action, generally after cries and screams from fellow players. Catching a fly ball to center field was a rare event for me.

The refreshment stand was another draw to the recreation program. Recognizing the popularity of the program, the Carey family, who lived just one block away from the school, established a simple refreshment stand business in the schoolyard. One of their older kids stood inside a small roofless plywood enclosure selling soda pop and candy bars. During mid-morning ball game breaks, we dug into our pockets for the nickels and dimes we were sure to bring with us and selected a "bottle of pop" from an ice water filled blue Pepsi Cola emblazoned cooler. Several soda flavors were offered. Coca Cola, Pepsi Cola, Nehi grape, orange, and cream soda. But at this venue, we rugged gamesmen needed something stronger. Royal Crown Cola became the "official" drink of the summer recreation program. I loved those time out periods. We sat in the shade of school yard towering maples, sipped our RC, swapped tales, and poked fun at one another. Leaving the yells and frustrations of missed plays and strikeouts behind, we focused on the fun of being together.

Our Second Home – The School Building

The school building itself was a quirky place. This huge brick building was situated on a plot of ground about the same size as a village block and occupied the entire length of that space. The formal entrance, in the middle of the long building, was set back in an alcove that sheltered doors opening onto the main first floor hallway. Only teachers and visitors used this entrance.

Students used side doors located at each end of the building. In our early school days, classrooms to the left of the formal entrance accommodated grades K through 6. Rooms to the right housed school offices, our junior high classrooms (grades six, seven and eight) and the home economics classroom. The gymnasium sat Immediately across from the main entrance on the back side if the building. It was just large enough for a full-sized, hardwood basketball floor and narrow perimeter that accommodated three-row-high roll-out bleachers along the sides of the two-stories high room. Basketball backboards and hoops hung at each end. A raised stage area on the north end was flanked by small backstage areas. Two locker rooms were also tucked into each end of the heavily used gym. Boys to the north, girls to the south.

Besides in-season school basketball games, gym classes, school assemblies, pep rallies, and after-game dances were held in the gym, along with basketball team practice, pick-up basketball or volleyball games, concerts, school plays, and community events. The town Rotary Club held variety shows there. A minstrel style show featured a men's chorus and a group of four "End Men" who interacted to tell jokes and poke fun at each other. My father (a Rotary Club Charter Member) demonstrated how he could play *Turkey in the Straw* (American Folksong) on his violin "five different ways." He stood on one foot, held and played the instrument behind his back, held and played it under one leg propped up on a chair, etc. He and one other "End Man," our neighbor Art Whittington, stretched a rope off of the stage down the length of the audience asking them to hold onto the rope. When asked what they were doing by the interlocutor, my father responded, "We wanted to see what a string of suckers this long would look like." Once a year, junior and senior classes performed plays there. During my junior year I had a role as a detective in the play *January Thaw* (William Roos).

On occasion, some of us boys had reason or opportunity to enter the girls locker room. Of course, no girls were in there at the time. We found it curious that the girls had individual shower stalls in their area, whereas the shower on the boys side was one big room with several shower heads spaced out around the walls.

Fire Drills

The schoolhouse feature that caused me great angst during grade school years was the fire alarm system. Large bright-red horns were located at two places along the long downstairs hallway and two locations upstairs. On the wall immediately below each, a red rectangular box with a circular glass window on the front displayed the words "In case of fire break glass." A small metal hammer attached to the box by a short metal chain was to be used to break the glass when needed to activate the alarm. These, and the horns above them, looked menacing to me. I always walked way out around them, not touching the wall as I went by, fearing I might brush against the switch and set off the alarm.

I hated the sound of those horns. Six times a year, once in each marking period on unannounced days, fire drills were held. Sitting at our classroom desks the alarm suddenly went off. We had been previously told by teachers what to do. "Get up from your desks, walk quietly out the classroom door, exit the building though your assigned doorway, and meet your class at the designated spot out on the school grounds. Take nothing with you, no coat, boots, or books." The entire procedure was scary, but for me the worst part was the sound of those horns. They were very LOUD. Their low-pitched, piercing, buzz tone hurt my ears! In lower grades I dreaded the experience so much I began to try to guess when a fire drill might be sprung upon us. I counted the marking period days. When we reached the mid-point within that six-week timeframe I got anxious. I just knew it was time for a drill. On a few occasions, I faked sickness so I could stay home on days I expected fire drills. But alas I didn't ever pick the right day or avoid a fire drill experience. In the third grade, I missed the class picture. It was taken on a day I chose for my sick out, but no fire drill was held.

Memorable Junior High Teachers

While the building was central to our learning experience, it was our teachers who made lasting impressions and provided knowledge that helped mold us into the adults we became.

Mr. Richmond

As we moved through the school system, the first man to teach our class was Mr. Vincent Richmond. Our seventh-grade year was his first year in the system. He taught us that year, then moved up to the eighth grade with us. He lived on a farm up near Flowerfield Township north of Three Rivers and drove to school each day. He always appeared freshly scrubbed. He appeared to have worn the exact same suit and tie for the entire two-year period. A very conservative individual, he brought his ideals to school with him.

Often critical of U.S. government actions and organizational structure, he lectured us not only on what that structure was, but how he thought it should be run and how the country was headed in the wrong direction. To highlight these points, he started each seventh-grade class day by reading to us portions of the books, *Animal Farm* and *1984* (George Orwell).

His academic lectures were detailed and could be boring, but he often took sidetracks into daily societal affairs, adding his beliefs and critiques on subjects that happened to come up. He was a tough grader and didn't consider his views the correct answers to test questions, so it became our job to sort through the classroom conversations and our textbooks to pick out correct answers. Some of his commentary was entertaining, so a common tactic was for one of us to deliberately ask a question or make a comment that would launch him into a tirade. This made class time go by much faster than sitting through textbook lectures.

Mr. Riipa
A single floor wing on the northwest corner of the building adjacent to the eighth grade classroom, housed the school shop and band room. The shop had a class seating area near the front. Tall drafting tables, with backless stools, served as student desks and seating. An adjacent tool cage held a collection of hand tools. Saws, planes, hammers, screw drivers, pliers, etc., were neatly hung on the wall in front of black painted outlines of each tool. A lumber rack stood in the back of this locked area. The shop's center area was outfitted with a large bench saw, a couple of drill presses, pair of wood lathes, jointer, thickness planer, and a newly added radial arm saw that had been manufactured by a company started in town by one of my neighbors, Hugh Fisher. The rear portion of the shop included metal working and auto repair areas. Metal working tools included a small forge, metal lathe, and welding equipment – an oxy-acetylene torch for brazing and a primitive electric arc welder. A 1939 Buick sedan was kept in the auto repair area. High school students took it apart to learn how automotive systems worked.

Boys could take shop in both junior high and high school years. Girls took Home Economics classes. My shop days occurred during junior high years. Our teacher, Mr. Riipa (pronounced Re-pa), taught us to use elementary drafting tools to draw project plans. In seventh grade we learned woodworking skills for cutting, milling, sanding, finishing, and producing woodworking joints. Our eighth grade class included elementary metal working skills such as sheet metal forming, steel machining, and tool hardening. Mr. Riipa was originally from Finland and had a strong accent. Though very friendly, he had a "down-to-business" personality. Shop safety and good work ethics were his priorities. Standing erectly in the shop in his starched gray colored shop coat, he lectured us constantly on these points, always using his staccato accent. We respected him greatly but behind his back imitated his accent and referred to him as Mr. Leepa. In particular, we enjoyed getting him excited so we could watch him spit out his words distinctly.

I chose building a desk as my seventh-grade project. Having left elementary school, I had more demanding homework assignments and needed a desk in my bedroom. My father and I worked up the design. The simple one pedestal (left side) three drawer design appeared easy enough. The top was to be made from a flush door purchased from the local lumber yard and supported on the right side by a single mail-ordered wrought iron leg.

Mr. Riipa had never seen a project design quite like this. He thought it was an ambitious first project but agreed to let me try it. Other students chose smaller projects. They built lamps out of discarded bowling pins, simple magazine racks, or stepstools. The plan was for Dad and me to each build a desk. His, to be built at home, was for my sister to use. He procured the flush door and cut it in half lengthwise, producing tops for each. We purchased the two wrought iron legs from the Sears catalog. I labored in shop class each day producing the pedestal and its drawers. Dad was in no hurry to start his.

It took most of my first semester to build the pedestal. Its three drawers took the second semester. Once I completed that, I only needed to combine the pedestal with the premanufactured top, add the leg, and apply a clear varnish finish to the entire desk. Mr. Riipa kept a close eye on my efforts, inspecting each dado, rabbit, and lap joint. We agreed that I shouldn't attempt to join drawer backs and sides using butterfly joints. That would have been a high school shop requirement. My drawers were made using lap joints. It all finally came together the day before the spring school open house when projects were put on display. During that last class period I applied the varnish and moved the desk into Mr. Riipa's office where it was to be displayed. It looked nice. I was proud of it. I thought it more impressive than the bowling pin lamps and magazine racks. Early in the morning on open house day I went in to again admire my handywork. I was stunned and horrified by what I found. Someone had taken a pencil and scribed a big figure eight mark across the top of my desk! Astounded, Mr. Rippa launched an investigation, but I never heard who might have done it. I had to quickly sand out the mark and refinish the top. There was barely enough time for it to dry before the evening open house. I guess it was payback for having built the most impressive project of the class.

I got an A on the desk, took it home and put it in my room. I asked Dad where his was? He hadn't started it yet. He went to work that weekend and produced his version in two days. It was a bit more professional looking than mine, but both served their purpose. Mine still sets in my basement shop. In eighth grade shop I built a wooden desk lamp using a laminated block that I made from alternating walnut and pine boards. I cut the lamp base from that block. The lamp stem and fluorescent bulb shade were also made from walnut, all of which came from a tree that had grown in our back yard. During that year I also did some metal work, turning and tempering a centerpunch cut from a length of steel bar. I also produced a plum bob on the lathe.

These projects and skills learned from my father produced "handyman" abilities that have served me well over the years.

Unforgettable High School Teachers
Miss Harvey

Miss Dorothy Harvey, our mathematics teacher, was most infamous. She had taught in the system longer than anyone else and served as Principal in years prior to our high school days. No student working their way through the system could avoid classes from her. Miss Harvey's teaching methods were memorable and scary but effective. Once out of school, former students credited her as one of the most effective teachers they had. However, in-class encounters with her were frightening.

She sought to make us think and derive answers to questions on our own. She never spoon-fed us problem solutions that we would easily forget. Her classroom was ringed with enough black slate chalkboards to accommodate the entire class at the same time. Most class periods included sessions for all students at the chalkboard. She wrote a math problem on her section of the chalkboard and asked each student to do the same. If it involved new concepts she worked through the problem and had students duplicate the work. Then she assigned each student a different problem and asked us to write out the solutions. She walked along behind everyone examining their work. When she came to someone struggling, she stopped and waited for them to ask for help. If we asked, "How do I do this?" or said, "I don't get it," she would say, "What do you mean?" The student stammered, "I don't know how to do the problem." That was just what she was looking for. She asked, "What don't you understand about it?" After a silent moment, in a quaky voice, the student repeated "I don't know how to do the problem." Sternly, she replied, "You see, you haven't learned." Shaking her head, she continued, "If you don't understand what you don't know about it, I can't help you." As uncomfortable as it was, it made us learn to think before asking a question. If we made an honest effort to work through the problem and explained it to her step by step, she helped us. For her, the learning process was an all-business matter. She wasted little classroom time on trivia or chit chat. Once we had completed her classes, we grudgingly admitted she had taught us a lot.

I struggled in algebra. It took half of my freshman year to catch on and become comfortable with her teaching style. I did better in sophomore geometry. I only heard the dreaded "You see you haven't learned" statement a time or two that year. In my junior year, advanced algebra was a challenge, but solid geometry and trigonometry were easier in my senior year. However, memorizing trig functions was a struggle. I developed an unorthodox study method. I wrote out trig function formulas (Sine = Side Opposite/Hypotenuse) on scraps of paper and placed them facing downward under the top mattress of my bunk bed. Each morning when I woke up, lying in the bottom bunk, I read through them. I never told Miss Harvey about my technique but imagined she would have liked it.

Miss Harvey also served as senior class advisor. We gained new perspectives of her in this role. She loved helping students work through questions about what they would do after graduation. She spoke blissfully about our available options and characterized the doorways each of us would step through as exciting, exclaiming how she longed to be standing in those doorways with us.

I struggled with college algebra and when home on weekends called her and asked for tutoring time. She graciously agreed and invited me to her house. We sat at her antique Queen Anne styled dining room table and worked through challenging problems. Her demeanor and methods were completely different. She too had to think about what she didn't understand. Together, we worked our way through the problems. She and her sister were an anomaly in the community. They lived together on Centerville Road, in the middle of town in a stately Greek Revival styled home. Sister Josephine was an insurance agent. She drove a new Dodge car every year. Dorothy had an older Plymouth. Neither ever married. The common rumor was that the house, built by their father, would be given to whichever one of them was not married when he died. Since neither were when that occurred, they owned the house jointly. It was beautiful, but not many people ever saw the inside.

Prior to my time in Miss Harvey's classroom, I delivered their newspaper. Knocking on their big, tall, front doors on Saturdays to collect was an eerie experience. They seemed to know who was there, opened the door a crack, and quickly paid me. They always gave me a small tip, but the mystique made it uncomfortable. This was all dispelled during my college math tutoring sessions. Both were welcoming, and Josephine offered me freshly baked cookies.

Mr. Freeland and Mr. Hammond
General science, biology, chemistry, and physics were taught in the science classroom and laboratory located in the southeast corner of the building. Mr. Kent Freeland taught us the first three of these sequential subjects. He left the system after our junior year. Mr. Martin Hammond replaced him and taught my class physics during my senior year.

Mr. Freeland was a fun teacher and peaked my long-standing interest in science. General science, a broad-brush introduction to all science areas, took us beyond what we had learned in lower grades. We did our first science fair project that year. Finding electricity interesting, I rewired a small primitive battery-operated electric motor from my father's childhood erector set and turned it into a generator. To power my generator I connected my own erector set motor to it using a rubber band as a belt. I hooked a small socket and light bulb borrowed from my electric train set to the generator demonstrate that I had produced electricity. The prize I won surprised my skeptical mother and pleased my father.

During one general science class period Mr. Freeland said, "The products of combustion are always heat energy, carbon dioxide and water." That prompted me to think about atmospheric carbon dioxide levels. While looking out classroom windows at the snow-covered landscape I asked, "Since we burn lots of fuel to heat our houses, won't that increase carbon dioxide levels in the atmosphere?" He replied "No, the atmosphere is so vast, we'll never notice it." I had an uncomfortable feeling about that answer. Decades later, working as an environmental specialist, I spent a lot of time on this question.

During sophomore biology class, a student brought an owl to school. It had been hit and killed by a car. Mr. Freeland thought it would be great to recover and assemble the owl's skeleton. A class project was begun. Working in small groups we took turns plucking feathers, boiling the carcass, and removing flesh from the bones. It turned out to be an arduous process. Most class members, including me, lost interest when strong odors emerged. It got so bad that students in all classes didn't want to enter the room. The project ended and the specimen was disposed of.

Mr. Freeland's humorous teaching style included rhymes and anecdotes recited while explaining science principles. When teaching us the chemical formula for sulfuric acid he quipped,

"Little Willy used to drink but he don't drink no more, for what he thought was H_2O was H_2SO_4." During a chemistry lab experiment we generated hydrogen by placing zinc metal pieces in a jar containing hydrochloric acid. We collected the hydrogen gas produced using inverted water-bath bottles. Mr. Freeland didn't want us to dispose of leftover zinc metal by putting it down the sink drain. He walked the room reciting over and over again, "Don't put the zinc in the sink, don't put the zinc in the sink." Once, the entire class did poorly on an exam. He lectured us about studying harder then said, "Even a sponge sitting in this room could absorb more knowledge than you did." He placed a sponge on a chair at the front of the classroom and said, "I'm going to give it a test at the end of the next unit to prove the point." The sponge sat there for several class periods, with him occasionally acknowledging it.

I did well in chemistry class. Mr. Freeland's hands-on approach included lots of lab time and I loved it. He started a "photography club." We met one evening per week. He converted a small closet into a dark room. We took pictures outside of class and brought the exposed film to club meetings. We mixed chemicals for developing negatives and, working only by feel in the dark room, bathed them in the solutions. Not having an enlarger, we produced contact prints while working under a red "safelight." After laying dried negatives on top of photopaper sheets we flicked on the white closet light for one second then bathed the exposed paper in its developing chemicals. Watching our images develop was great fun. We learned the hard way to only open photographic paper packages under the red safelight to avoid exposing it.

Things changed when Mr. Hammond became science teacher. He and his wife had recently moved to town. Both were very serious people. She, Dr. Jacoby, was our wiry new veterinarian.

He was very academically focused and had a no-nonsense teaching style. I struggled in his physics class. His tests were tough. I sat next to my friend Al Hyde. Al was brilliant, got all As, and flourished under Mr. Hammond's teaching. My papers and tests came back with Cs on best days. I studied hard but couldn't match Al's all As results. Remembering Mr. Freeland's style, I postulated that the problem wasn't my abilities. Al's name started with the letter A and mine the lowly D, therefore it made sense that my grades were lower than his. In college, I learned that though I had enjoyed Mr. Freeland's classes, he failed to teach us many chemistry basics. I lacked knowledge expected by college freshman chemistry instructors. Fortunately, an older roommate enrolled in the pharmacy program tutored me and helped get me through my first year of college chemistry.

Miss Sebring
Across the hall from the science classroom, Miss Sebring taught business subjects. They included typing, bookkeeping, shorthand, and business math. My father had an old Remington typewriter in his office. He had purchased the antique at an auction sale. Frequently attending auctions, he often came home with items that made my mother shake her head. He thought the typewriter would be useful for the occasional business letter he needed to write. The only problem was, he had no typing skills. He used one finger on each hand to "hunt and peck" the letters. I liked the idea of being able to produce typed documents and, along with some of my classmates, thought being able to type college papers would be a necessity. We signed up for the beginning level typing class during our junior year.

Miss Sebring's classroom was outfitted with two dozen Royal Standard, manual typewriters. Each day, we filed into the typing room and took seats behind the machines. She presented a brief lecture on the skill she was focusing on that day, then turned us loose to practice what she had presented. The noise from all the typing was intense but produced an atmosphere of action more invigorating than quiet study sessions typical of other classes. Near the end of the period, Miss Sebring stopped us to give speed and accuracy tests. I turned out to be an OK typist with modest speed and accuracy skills. I mastered "touch typing" for letters and elementary punctuation, but numbers typing was beyond me. For those, I resorted to the "hunt and peck" method. Near the end of our one-semester class, Miss Sebring introduced us to the electric typewriter. She had two of them in the back corner of the classroom. They were impressive. Quieter, they produced neater looking characters, and had a keyboard button for paper carriage returns. The typing speed obtainable was significantly higher, she said. Our exposure to them was for demonstration only. Learning to use them was an advanced class.

Though friendly, Miss Sebring regarded students, especially the boys, to be a crude unpolished bunch. Always impeccably dressed, her friendly smile quickly turned to stern expressions when she sought orderly classroom decorum. She worked acceptable decorum, social practices, and attire into classroom lectures. One day, as we filed into her classroom, she stood at the typing room doorway as usual. As I approached, I noticed a gum wrapper laying on the floor in the center of the doorway. I stopped and picked it up. She held out her hand and took it from me. As I passed by, she said, "I put that there to see how long it would be before someone stopped to pick it up." Pleased with myself and thinking this was a test I had passed with high regards, she continued, "You are the first person through the door and ruined my experiment." She expected the entire class to ignore the wrapper and had planned to lecture the class on slovenly performance. I ruined that for her.

Study Hall Teachers

The school's second floor high school classes were accessed using stair wells located near each end of the building. Math, science, and business classrooms were on the south end. English, the library, and social studies classes were held on the north. The space between consisted of a hallway connecting both ends and a long narrow room used as a study hall. The hallway had a very squeaky wooden floor. Doors between the study hall and hallway were always left open. Unless we had permission, and a written pass allowing us to be somewhere else in the building, we were expected to be in study hall when we didn't have a class. Teachers took turns keeping study hall order. We were to work on homework, read books available in the adjacent library, or quietly sit and daydream. The mood or sound level in study hall depended on which teacher was on duty and what they would allow, or prompt. Students often tested the system. Someone in the back of the room would rustle papers, tap on a desk, clear their throat, or utter some other sound. Another student usually responded with similar or alternative sounds. That triggered additional responses until the teacher gave-in and called for order. Then, all was quiet until someone repeated the act. The squeaky hallway floor also prompted reactions. Whenever anyone walked by, each footstep produced loud squeaks. Some sort of acknowledgment, the growling of the student's nickname or production of other sounds was assured.

One study hall teacher had more trouble keeping order than others. Miss Vanderbeek, the Home Economics teacher, got flustered easily. She seemed odd to students. When someone started making noises, she avoided reaction for several minutes but as the frequency and sound level rose, she proclaimed in her squeaky voice, "All right, enough of the jungle noises." That was exactly what the perpetrators were looking for. Someone in the room kept track of how often they could rile her during the period. Hallway discussions that followed recounted her reactions and acknowledged the perpetrators involved.

Mrs. Whitworth, Miss Johns and Coach Turka

Teachers at the English and social studies end of the building included Mrs. Whitworth (freshman/sophomore English), Miss Johns (junior/senior English and literature), and Coach Turka (history/civics/economics). English and literature were my least favorite classes. Grammar had come to me easily in grade school, but I found sentence diagraming and other English basics extremely boring and difficult. When my mother fussed about my low freshman English grade, I argued, "All the time Mrs. Whitworth spends making us diagram sentences is unnecessary. Using proper grammar just makes sense." Mother retorted that pursuing this logic didn't help my grades. I dug in and brought my grade up a little, but Mrs. Whitworth could sense my disdain and didn't cut me any slack.

Similarly, I loved to read but Miss Johns insisted we read classical literature. I preferred stories relating to adventures of bush pilots in the Yukon, tales about hero Alaskan sled dogs saving their masters, or articles describing cars, motorcycles, and airplanes. I tried sneaking these into book report assignments but was rebuffed by Miss Johns. She forced me to read classics, but she couldn't make me like them.

Coach Turka's history class was interesting but required lots of study to memorize the dates and facts he tested us on. I liked his economics class and thought the concepts regarding business success needed to be understood by all. His classes were laid-back and featured open discussion periods always more interesting than textbook derived lectures. In one of these he mentioned he liked to wear dresses. This caused a stir among classmates. I just sat back and smiled.

Our junior class year didn't include the usual language requirement. Latin teacher, Miss Troutman, had retired at the end of our sophomore year so we didn't have a language teacher. Mr. Glass, a Spanish teacher, joined the faculty for our senior year. Though I could have, I didn't join that class.

Principals Mr. Johns and Mr. Olson
The principal's office at the end of the upstairs hall was regarded as the discipline ward. Offenders ended up there. In my junior year Mr. David Olson replaced the stern Mr. H. Richard Johns. Mr. Olson was a welcome change. Projecting an air of both friendliness and authority at the same time, we couldn't help but like him. We respected his corrective outcomes from misbehavior and appreciated the hours he spent as our guidance counselor. During individual sessions in his office, we looked at job placement potential, colleges, and military service options. He explained what it took to succeed on each of those paths.

Our teachers played important roles in preparing us to meet the world when graduation day finally arrived. If we didn't understand or appreciate this at the time, we did so once we experienced life's realities. We were fortunate to have received the knowledge and character guidance they provided.

Extracurricular Activities
Team Manager
The summer recreation program served an early tryout role for high school athletic activities. As freshmen, my buddies, Swartwout, Smith, and others (including Howd) went on to play football, basketball, baseball, and participate in track events. Having demonstrated my athletic inabilities and disinterest, I was

terribly conflicted. I wanted to be a part of the gang participating in these programs but knew my chance of seeing my name appear on team rosters when they were posted on the first-floor hallway trophy display case was meager. I didn't bother with the in-school tryout events. Instead, I sought football and basketball team manager positions. I figured my peers might get to be high-flying jocks, racking up impressive statistics while winning games, but if not for the team manager, they wouldn't even be able to take the field. To get the job, I had to be interviewed by Coach Whitworth. He, a friendly man with a big voice, also served as our gym class teacher. Having observed my athletic performance in that venue, he agreed that team manager was a good fit for me. I went to work, and we hit it off right away. When the team was out on the practice field, he knew better than to ask me to throw him a football. Instead, he said, "Bring me the football." I mustered up as much hustle as I could and carried it to him.

I assembled team uniforms and equipment, kept the gear in good order, organized the locker room storage cage, served as Coach's "gofer" on the sidelines, kept records on who had been assigned what equipment, tracked jersey numbers, performed helmet fittings, and kept on-field statistics during games. After games, I reported stats and scores to local news media by calling newspapers (*Three Rivers Commercial, Sturgis Journal,* and *South Bend Tribune*) as well as the Kalamazoo TV station, WKZO.

The reporting responsibility netted me two distinctions. I got paid to report game stats to the *South Bend Tribune* and, in order to file reports immediately following each home game, I was entrusted with a key to the Superintendent's office. This was a huge responsibility. I was to tell no one that I had the key. I went into the office after games to make the calls but was to take no one with me. I was not to touch anything on the

Superintendent's desk except the phone, and I was to leave behind no trace of my visit.

As "heady" as all this responsibility was, it had one significant drawback. After games, team players quickly changed out of uniforms, showered, and headed to school dances for the evening afterglow. My work had just begun. I had to gather official game record books from scorekeepers, pick-up smelly uniforms and stuff them into laundry bags, police the locker room, then head to the Superintendent's office to make my calls. This meant I arrived at the dance later than everyone else and had to work my way into groups already assembled in the darkened gymnasium. The more popular girls at the dance had pretty much been paired up with heroic jocks by the time I got there.

But it made me a member of the team. I rode the team bus to away games and on home game days got out of study hall to put line markers on the football field. Heading down to the locker room, I grabbed the key to the stadium refreshment stand/storage building and got to work. Using a device similar to a lawn spreader, I applied fresh lime to white yard marking lines crossing the playing field. I worked to keep them straight and "professional looking." I marked goal and out-of-bounds lines and put yard marker signs on both sides of the field. Our football complex was a bowl-style stadium. It had a sunken playing field encircled by an earthen berm about 10 feet high. We were proud of it and thought it was the best looking of all the schools in our Class "C" league. After marking lines, I quickly checked bleacher areas and picked up any trash lying about. I worked diligently to complete most of this before Coach finished teaching for the day and came to "help." I preferred having him inspect and critique my work, rather than "help" me by providing detailed instructions for each task. I considered the complex "my field" and took pride in readying it for Friday night games. Years earlier, my father had a role in improving the field. He led a Rotary Club project that raised money for lighting the stadium. Prior to that, games were played after school or on Saturdays during daylight hours. Being able to play Friday night games under the lights greatly enhanced the status of the school and community. I wanted to continue that objective.

Playing in the Band
Being team manager rather than a player also meant I could play in the band on game nights. I had been a band member since we were invited to join beginners' band in the fifth grade. Similar to Harold Hill in the show *The Music Man* (Meredith Wilson), an instrument salesman accompanied by band director Robert Smith came into our classroom. Since kindergarten, music had been a part of our grade school curriculum. During visits to our classroom, our vocal music teacher taught us songs and simple music theory elements. In fifth grade we had the opportunity to start playing an instrument.

I enjoyed singing. There was always lots of music in my family's home. Mother played piano and Dad played violin, mandolin, and the harmonica. Both could also sing, though neither did much of that outside of the house. At age three or four, I sat next to the piano in a child's rocking chair that once belonged to Grandfather Ernest and sang while Mother played. *Bellbottomed Trousers* (Moe Jaffey) and *Swinging on a Star* (Jimmy Van Heusen and Johnny Burke) were my favorites. When I was in the third grade, Mother sent me to piano lessons from Mrs. Chrisman who lived several blocks from our home. I rode my bicycle to and from lessons and liked having connections with a music teacher. I was really impressed by her baby grand piano but didn't enjoy the practicing mandated by my mother.

Listening to the musical instrument salesman, the idea of playing trumpet appealed to me. When the band director asked who would like to "try out," my hand was one of the first to go up, but we couldn't just "sign up." We had to be tested to assess our natural music skills. One by one, we joined the instrument salesman at a piano on the gymnasium stage. He played a few notes and asked which were higher or lower on the scale. He asked us to sing pitches back to him. If we passed these tests, he examined our teeth to determine if our mouth was best shaped for playing reed or brass instruments. Then, a note was sent to our parents offering opportunities to rent or purchase instruments.

I was thrilled with the prospect of playing trumpet. In my mind that was a lot more interesting than trying to play piano. My mother was OK with the idea but hated to see me give up the piano. When I broke the news to Mrs. Chrisman she said, "Playing trumpet is fine, but one day you'll be sorry you didn't stick with piano." She was right. I did stick with the trumpet. Playing in bands has been a life-long pursuit. But I wish I could also play piano.

During home football games while performing team manager duties, I wore my band uniform pants, a white shirt and a black tie under my team jacket. During pre-game and halftime shows, I quickly switched to my band uniform jacket and took the field with the marching band. Band peers who also wanted an athletic career didn't have this advantage. Jim Smith gave up playing trumpet and stuck with playing sports. Al Hyde, a tall lanky fellow who could run really fast, left band ranks on game days to play football. During basketball season I kept my team manager duties, but during game halftimes I led a small pep band I had recruited, playing tunes to entertain game fans. We received great feedback, some saying they came just to hear the pep-band.

This wasn't the first small band I had organized. Back in junior high days, Curt Fisher, one of my younger neighbors was a talented drummer. When he was in sixth grade, he was invited to play in the high school band. He and I often sat in front of his family's nice console "hi-fi" system listening to big band music. We played records by all the greats – Benny Goodman, Glenn Miller, Buddy Morrow, Count Basie, and of course drummers like Gene Krupa and Buddy Rich. In those days our music teachers did not encourage us to play this music. Not considered "legitimate music," they schooled us in classical and traditional band music. However, I found some popular music books and put together a small group that included Curt on drums, Rob Polleys on trombone, Dave Daughtery on tuba, and me on trumpet. It wasn't quite the swing we were listening to, but we played semi-Dixieland style and other popular tunes, including some performed by a new artist named Elvis Presley. We wailed on *Blue Suede Shoes* (Carl Perkins) and *When the Saints Go Marching In* (James M. Black and Katherine E. Purvis). We played them during a band variety show to great acclaim. Curt, Dave and I were good sized kids. Rob was tall. When we were asked to name the group, we called ourselves, "The Famished Four."

I did all right playing trumpet but wasn't a prodigy. I worked my way through the ranks in junior and high school trumpet sections. As seventh graders, we who mastered the basics were invited to join the high school band. We were placed at the bottom of the band hierarchy in "last chair," but could "challenge" people above us, regardless of grade level, and move up through the chairs. I moved up fairly quickly and played the coveted first trumpet part, from second chair, by the time I was a sophomore. Judy Cox, a year ahead of me played first chair. I came close to beating her, but she hung on until graduation. I played first chair in my senior year.

Band membership did include one bit of trauma. When I was issued my first high school band uniform, I had problems finding pants that fit. After several trials, the only pair that worked was a pair of girl's pants. They were plain in front, with no fly. They had a zipper on the side. How humiliating! I found the situation embarrassing but was not going to let it keep me from playing in the band. To hide the front of the pants, I always kept my uniform coat fully buttoned. It worked most of the time, except on warm days when we marched without jackets, or when I had to use the restroom. Rather than jostle up to the urinals with the hot-shot boys who raced to get into the restroom first, I hung back and waited until all urinal positions were filled then stepped quietly into a stall to take care of my needs. All of this got me by during my first year, but when Roger Daughtery (Dave's older brother) graduated, I got to wear his pants sparing me continued embarrassment.

I was invited to play in the All-State band several times, attended summer band camps, and took private lessons. Each week, my father drove me to Elkhart, Indiana for advanced lessons with Mr. McDermott. I practiced a lot. During warm weather months, with no air conditioning in the house, we left the front door open. Neighbor Art Whittington and his wife, Berniece, lived directly across the street. Sitting in their screened-in breezeway trying to deal with the heat, they had to endure the sounds of my practicing in our living room. Besides the scales and exercises required by my teacher, I also liked to play popular tunes, some while being accompanied by phonograph records played loudly on my hi-fi system. A favorite was *The Tennessee Waltz* (Red Stewart and Pee Wee King). It has a high note in the first phrase that was a challenge for me to hit. My horn squawked each time

I tried to play it. I went over that passage time after time trying to hit that high note. Most of the time, I missed it. One day when Art and my dad were out in the front yard engaged in neighborly conversation, Art asked, "Is that kid ever going to learn to play that song?" Today, the swing band I play in performs this tune. Each time it comes up I always think to myself, "This one is for Art Whittington."

Much of my horn playing enthusiasm came from encouragement and beginning lessons taken from band director Robert Smith (he asked us to call him Smitty). We all really liked him. Young and fresh out of college, he guided us from our first days in beginning band through our sophomore year. That summer he announced he would be leaving to lead the music program at Three Rivers High School, the larger community nine miles to our north. We were devastated. We had to pick up the pieces and carry on. Successor Mr. Ivan Kell came to fill the void. Recognizing the hole Smitty had left behind, he wisely asked older students to take leadership positions to "help him," hoping that would partially fill the void.

In the meantime, my father told me that when I could learn to play the tune *The Trumpeter's Lullaby* (Leroy Anderson), he would consider me "a trumpet player." He loved that tune. Smitty had brought it out back in my eighth grade year, when Roger Daughtery was playing first chair. Though Roger played well and worked hard, the piece turned out to be too much for him. At concert time, Director Smitty, stepped in to play the solo. That's when my father first threw the challenge to me. I vowed I was going to play it and during my senior year I convinced Mr. Kell to let me take it on.

I started practicing in September. I worked on it constantly over the next three months. The goal was to play the piece during the annual Christmas concert. Throughout my preparation, I didn't tell my father what I was up to. At home, I practiced when he was away. I did let my mother in on the plan, asking her not to tell him. She complied. Finally, the big concert night came. I was very nervous and went off to school way ahead of concert time. When Mom and Dad arrived and took their seats, he looked over the program and saw the title with my name next to it. He asked my mom, "Did you know he was going to do that?" She, with satisfaction, nodded that she did. We had pulled off the first part of the prank and he was indeed surprised. But I still had to play it. My performance wasn't flawless. I think I missed a note or two, but it was a respectable rendition of the tune. When I got home after the concert, Dad greeted me by saying "Hello, Mr. Trumpet player." Mission accomplished.

Chapter 9

Scooter Boys

Spreading our Wings

In our junior high years, the urge to expand horizons into the outer world became strong for me and my peers. Though the school system had not officially branded them as such, it felt good to refer to ourselves as junior high students. We felt older, and our teacher, Mr. Richmond, provided a classroom atmosphere that had a more grown-up character. When we gathered outside the school building before doors opened for classes, we did so at the north end of the building. This was where the high school students hung out. We no longer frequented the south entrance with the grade school students and young bullies. Some older high schoolers, especially those that lived out of town, drove cars to school. They parked adjacent to the north entrance along Lafayette Street.

Older in-town kids walked to school. Bicycles were no longer considered "cool." Only those living near the outskirts of town peddled in, out of necessity. A small bike rack near the Lafayette and Canaris Street intersection provided parking space for them. In this same area, parking for another transportation mode emerged. One for motor scooters. Ron Stears and Richard Carter, both a year ahead of me, arrived daily on their Cushman scooters. My buddy and oldest classmate Jim Smith soon joined them. Now that was cool! Scooters were a huge step above bikes. Not only could riders cruise town streets on one, but the scooters also expanded their range out onto country roads. I imagined the feel of breeze on their faces as they putted along.

There also were a few motorcycles in town. Now and then we got a close-up look at one when an older out of school fellow showed up at one of our hangout places. They proudly put their Indian or Harley Davidson bikes on display. These loud, heavy, and expensive machines looked interesting but were out-of-reach for us schoolboys. They also had a reputation of being dangerous and, in the eyes of our mothers, more likely to be ridden by "tough crowd" fellows. We were given stern instructions not to go off riding with one of these folks, sitting of the back of their large saddle style leather seats.

I gazed at those monster machines with fringed streamers hanging from their handlebars and checked out gear shift leavers that stuck up beside the center mounted gas tank. I surveyed the foot silhouette shaped peddles used for the brake and "suicide clutch." I thought I would be scared to ride one, especially since numbers on the speedometer dial read upwards to 120 mph. One of the leather jacket clad fellows who stopped by to show off his bike boasted that he hadn't yet made it to 120 since the machine "Began to vibrate a little at 106."

Motorized bicycles were also an option, and there were a few of those in town. Whizzer bikes were of special interest. Neighbor Maurice Metzelaars, the oldest of the three boys in that household, had one. It was flashy and had chrome fenders just like those on my Schwinn Black Phantom bicycle. In fact, it was built on the same model Schwinn frame. Powered by its small pancake shaped engine, snuggly bolted into the center of the bike's frame, it could go 25 or 30 miles per hour. A flat leather belt connected the engine to a large diameter pully attached to rear wheel spokes. For me, the primary disadvantage was the cost of the bike. They sold for about $200. That was beyond my means. Used ones were available but high priced as well. You could buy Whizzer motors and other parts needed to assemble your own, and a couple of bicycles in town had been outfitted with alternative motor kits mounted over their front wheels. Eddy Loomis, son of The Mens Shop owner Vernie Loomis (three years ahead of me in school) mounted a lawnmower engine on the rear luggage rack of his bike and utilized a Whizzer style rear wheel drive mechanism. I studied these options and concluded that a Cushman scooter was the most plausible way for me to put myself on the road under power.

But first I had to convince my mother that I needed to do so. This became a scenario akin to the "You'll shoot your eye out" arguments portrayed by adults in the movie *A Christmas Story* (Bob Clark and Jean Shepherd). Mom rebuffed every argument I presented about getting a scooter with similar responses. "You'll get hurt riding in the streets with all that car and truck traffic," or "You'll be off running around far away from home, and I won't know where you are or what you're up to." Dad was a bit more supportive, but only on a one-on-one basis. When I approached him with the question, he merely said, "You'll have to talk with your mother."

Seizing the Opportunity

It all came to a head one spring day while I was out riding my bicycle around town. Checking things out to see what was going on, I stopped in at Tracy's downtown Shell station next to the Co-op feed mill. Lee Tracy's son Walter (three years ahead of me in school) was working at the station changing a muffler on a car up on the hoist. I watched him cut away rusted muffler clamps using a hacksaw, then work to get the burned-through muffler off the car. Following several hammer and cold chisel blows, it came crashing down onto the floor. We chatted about what else he had been working on and his plans for fixing up his own car. He had a sharp looking two-door 1949 Chevy Club Coupe. Black in color, it had chrome hubcaps, red wheels, and whitewall tires.

He kept it immaculately clean. He said he was saving up to get new seat covers for it. During the conversation, he said he probably could pay for them if he could find a buyer for his Cushman scooter. My antennas shot right up! "Selling your Cushman?" I asked. He replied, "Yeah, I don't ride it anymore." That was the first time I knew he had one. I didn't remember seeing him ride it around town. I had only linked him to his Chevy. Nonetheless, a serious conversation was quickly underway. I asked, "What year is the scooter?" "What color?" "Does it run?" "How much do you want for it?" He replied that it was a 1948 model, red in color, yes it ran well, and, "It just needs a little loving care." Then, knowing he had a fish on the hook added, "Fifty dollars would be my best price." I could handle that! I had that and more in my bank account. I said, "Don't sell it to anyone else, I'll go talk to my folks."

I went off to the dime store for a quick chat with my dad. "Walter Tracey is selling his Cushman for 50 dollars," I said. Dad said, "Well, you'd have to get your mother to agree first." Hmm, she was coming to the store in a bit, so I found something to do to fill the time while awaiting her arrival. As I puttered around on various stockroom projects, I ran all my best arguments through my mind. I was certain she would not want to agree and was counting on support from my dad to gain approval.

When she arrived, the banter began. I rambled through each of my arguments and heard, again, all her worries and concerns. But then without agreeing, she stopped and simply said, "I don't want anyone to get hurt so you've got to be careful." I was ecstatic! I hustled down to the bank, withdrew 50 dollars from my savings account, and rushed over to the Shell station to hand Walter the money. The deal was done, I had bought the scooter, sight unseen.

A day later, Dad drove me to the Tracy home to pick up my prize. It was stashed in their garage with a stack of old rags and
blankets piled on top of it. Walter removed the pile and pushed the Cushman out onto the driveway into the daylight. It looked a little rough. The red paint was faded. Instead of the trim metal cover on the rear of the body that provided access to the small trunk and gas tank (like the other scooters in town) it had an upholstered rear seat with a floppy latch that no longer snapped together to keep the seat in place. The driver's seat fabric was worn through on both sides with internal coil springs showing. The factory installed center taillight on the back of the body had no glass lens in it. Walter said the bulb socket was defective, so the light didn't work. In its place two add-on lights had been installed, one on either side of the non-working one. They were loose and flopping around on their mounting brackets. Closer inspection revealed some cracks in the sheet metal near louvers stamped into the body that provided engine-cooling air circulation. As I looked over these defects, Walter said, "That's what I meant by it needing some tender loving care." Then he put some gas in the tank and stomped down on the kick-starter. The engine coughed a bit, then on a second kick, started up. Some blue smoke emerged from the tail pipes. Yes, there were two of them. An unusual but cool thing about the scooter was its set of dual exhaust pipes. No one else had those. That, the fact that it was running, and the realization that the other items could be fixed, were enough to boost my excitement over the purchase. We shut it down and the three of us picked it up, turned it on its side and slid it into the back of Dad's station wagon for the trip home. Upon unloading and examining it

further, Dad remarked, "Your mother will be pleased. You won't be riding this too far for a while. It will take a lot of work to get it roadworthy."

A Restoration Project

I went right to work on it. I removed the two seats from the body and using some vinyl upholstery fabric obtained from the dime store wrapped and stapled new seat covers right over the old ones. Word quickly spread about my purchase and other scooter boys came put-putting over to check things out. They advised me to drill small holes at the end of each crack in the sheet metal body. This would keep them from spreading. The front fender had a heavy chrome trim piece affixed to its leading edge. We all agreed the scooter would look better without that, so it was removed. I determined that there wasn't much I could do with the floppy taillights at the back of the body. They had to come off. But it was evident that I couldn't repair the factory installed center one either. I went shopping at Gambles' auto accessory department and found two round taillights that could be flush mounted on the body. It meant drilling larger holes in the body to accommodate the mounting stems, but they looked a lot better. Then, after sanding and painting the body (using spray cans available at the dime store) the entire rig looked a lot better. My two-tone paint job was similar to what was showing up on new cars in the mid-1950s.

I painted the front fender red and the front fork white. I painted the main portion of the body red but masked off a section under the seats and painted that white. I used a dart shaped design similar to what I had seen in pictures of the 1955 Fords due to come out that fall. I painted the metal cage surrounding the non-working taillight and rear seat passenger foot rails white. The scooter was beginning to look good and seemed to be "roadworthy."

Hitting the Road

The next order of business was to get it registered and obtain a license plate. There was no such thing as a title for scooters. We simply went to the Secretary of State's Office in Centerville (the County Seat) filled out a registration form, paid the fee, and received a plate. Besides the registration, I also should have had a driver's license. But most of us were only 14 or 15 years old. We had to be 16 to get a license. Hence, we ignored this requirement, hopped on our scooters, and rode off as we pleased. There seemed to be an understanding among local authorities that as long as we behaved ourselves and abided by the rules of the road, they wouldn't bother us. No one had insurance either. Things were simple in those days.

However, there was a time when I inadvertently tested the system. One evening, after dark, while riding along Riverside Drive, I got pulled over by local cop Charlie Gould. He approached me and asked, "Do you know how fast you were going?" Since the scooter had no speedometer I said, "No." He said, "You were doing 37 miles an hour. The speed limit out here is 25." Surprised, I said, "37? I didn't know this thing would go that fast." I really did think that 35 was about top speed. He didn't ask to see my license or registration, he just said, "Try to keep it down."

Lessons in Mechanics

As important as cosmetics were, the scooter also had to run reliably if I was going to keep up with the scooter boys' pack. I quickly learned that my unit had some mechanical faults.

It started easily, if I didn't flood it by over-choking the carburetor. But it was sluggish when I tried to get it up to speed. At "high" speed it had a loud engine knock. My scooter buddies listened to it carefully and diagnosed the problem as "piston slap." They explained that the engine cylinder was worn such that its diameter was larger than the piston. When combustion took place and the piston was forced down the cylinder, it rattled around in there on the way down causing the knocking sound. They said the remedy was to have the cylinder "bored out" then install a new "oversized" piston that exactly fit the bore. This required an engine tear down and expenses that I wasn't prepared to support. I ignored the problem and rode on, trying to keep engine RPM low enough to avoid the loud knocking sound.

The next problem couldn't be ignored or put off. The scooter was chain driven. A small sprocket on the back of the clutch was connected to a rear wheel sprocket by a heavy-duty bicycle-style chain. Increasing engine RPMs by twisting the left handlebar grip engaged the clutch. As the scooter began moving forward a loud and jarring "clunk-clunk" sound occurred. Investigation showed that the clutch sprocket was worn out and slipped on the chain when getting underway. I had to quickly get acquainted with the mechanics of the machine and find a source for parts.

Scooter pals came to the rescue. They were already familiar with the Kalamazoo Michigan Cushman dealership located 30 miles to our north. When one or more of us needed parts, the word went out within our network and we talked one of our parents into driving us, as a pack, up to Ray Ellis Cushman Sales. It was an exciting place to visit. He sold new and used scooters and other Cushman products, including the small service vehicles used by industrial plants, golf courses, farms, etc. During these visits, we checked out the latest scooter models and dreamed of being able to afford one of the beauties on display. Ray's parts department was well stocked, personnel knew exactly what we needed, and instructed us on how to make repairs.

Most of us were riding 1948 or 1949 model-year scooters. My 1948 Pacemaker was a low-end model. Most of my pals had Eagles. The primary difference was the drive train. Mine was a single speed system with a simple "automatic" clutch. The Eagles had a manual clutch and two-speed transmission. They pressed down on a clutch peddle with their left foot then shifted into low gear for takeoff. Once under way, they depressed the clutch again and pushed the gear shift lever (protruding from the left side of the scooter below the driver's seat) backwards to shift into second or high gear. When I wanted to get my scooter moving, I simply twisted the left handlebar grip to make the engine race causing clutch shoes contact the lining of a round baking pan shaped drum and move the scooter forward. Both worked, but the sound was different. With mine, the initial racing sound gradually quieted as I came up to speed. Their takeoff was initially quieter followed by a pause in sound as they shifted gears. This sound difference was a dead give-away that my machine was of less prestigious design. I learned to fake it by getting underway as quickly as possible, throttling back to silence the high-rev sound, then quickly throttle up again to maintain speed. It sounded like I too had shifted gears. Definitely a face-saving move.

Another difference between models was engine horsepower. My scooter had a four-horsepower engine. Theirs used the same engine block but had a high compression head that increased horsepower to almost five. Perhaps they gained a bit of top speed from this, but mostly the difference was only visual. Anytime the driver's seat was lifted to check-out or display the engine, that difference was obvious. My spark plug protruded horizontally out of the front of the engine head. Theirs had the plug sticking up vertically out of the center of engine head. We debated the difference and the merits of the upright spark plug. I learned I could convert mine if I replaced the head with a high-compression model. Ray Ellis would gladly sell me one. I put this on my list of improvements to make, but never did. I had plenty of other reasons to spend money at the Ray Ellis shop. We all experienced frequent breakdowns so there was always something to fix. Getting through an entire week without having to remove the scooter body to make driveline, braking system, suspension, engine, or rear wheel flat tire repairs was rare. We celebrated and boasted about those occasions.

Another difference between the scooter models was tire size. Mine had 4.00 X 8 size tires. The Eagles had 6.00 X 6 tires. Their tires were wider and squatter than mine, another dead giveaway that my machine was different. I could do nothing about this visual. It just set me apart from the others. In either case, flat tires were frequent events. Removing wheels to fix a flat was especially involved when it occurred on the back. The entire driveline had to be disassembled to remove the rear wheel. Once off the scooter, two halves of split-rims had to be disassembled to remove the tire and innertube then patch the hole. The split rims did make it easier than having to stretch tire beads over small diameter rims. But we had to be careful not to pinch the tube between the two halves when putting them back together.

My first repair, replacing the worn drive sprocket, was the first of many learning experiences. The sprocket was riveted to the clutch drum. I had to use a hammer and cold chisel to cut away old rivets then fasten the new sprocket to the drum by pounding new rivets flat. In the process of making this repair, I discovered another issue. A keyway slot machined into the engine crankshaft had been worn into a V shape. This allowed the clutch assembly to rock back and forth rather than fit snugly on the crankshaft. There was nothing I could do to fix this other than to replace the crankshaft. That was a major and expensive undertaking. I chose to ignore the problem, hoping it wouldn't get worse. Fortunately, it didn't. Front drive sprockets wore out often. We all could plan on replacing them at least annually.

Besides flat tires, other frequent repairs included replacing drive chain master links brake and clutch linings, suspension system coil springs, and maintaining visual appearance – often through new paint schemes. We learned to carry spare chain master links, and tools to change them, in our trunk compartment. It was often necessary to perform repairs at roadside.

My most tedious repair was replacement of coil springs. There was one on either side of the front wheel and two more on the rear wheel suspension. The coils often broke causing the wheel involved to tilt to one side rather than sit upright, making steering and balancing tricky. Removing broken springs was easy. The two halves made access to the nuts and washers that secured the springs easy. Putting things back together was another matter. We had to slip washers and nuts through the new tight coils, get them threaded onto their studs, then use an open-end wrench forced between the coils to tighten them. Lots of patience, a bit of skill, and good luck was required. We always ended up with bruised fingers and needed an hour or two to accomplish the task.

Major Overhaul Needed

One afternoon, late in my first summer with the scooter, I headed off on a ride seeking relief from thoughts of school reopening. I headed up White Pigeon Road towards the five points intersection. About one and one-half blocks away from the house, the engine suddenly stopped running. I quietly coasted to a stop. When I kicked over the engine to try and restart it, I found that it freely turned over. There was no compression whatsoever. Uh-oh, the piston slap problem had just caught up with me. I pushed the scooter home and started to tear things down to see what had happened.

Removing the engine head, I saw that the top of the piston had broken off. The only solution was to completely disassemble the engine and take the block up to Ray Ellis to have it bored out and a new oversized piston installed. I had to ask Dad for help paying for this repair.

That would have been a good time to replace the engine head with that coveted high compression model. But, since I needed the financial help just to get it going again, I decided to not bring up the subject. It was a couple of weeks before the repaired engine was ready for pick up and I could put things back together again. Once I did, I was anxious to kick the starter, hear it run, and enjoy a perceived increase in power resulting from the slightly oversized piston.

Typical of Cushman engines, that overhaul didn't last long. A year or so later, it was already time for new piston rings. That time, I did all the work myself, only needing to make a trip to the Ray Ellis shop to obtain parts.

Not all the tinkering and fussing with tools, grease, and oil was prompted by mechanical failure. We were always changing things to "improve" at least in our mind's eye, performance. We made sure we kept our spark plug clean. We removed it from the engine and took it to a local gas station for cleaning. A device we could use ourselves sandblasted carbon off the plug. By looking through a small window in the cleaning machine, we could track progress and observe the spark pattern produced by our plug. We carefully examined plug porcelain and reset the gap to exactly 30 thousandths of an inch. At the first sign of pitting or other wear we bought a new plug. After putting a plug back into the engine, we struck off on a test ride, looking for performance improvements.

Riding Out and About

Cruising streets and rural roadways was what our scooters were all about. The high maintenance required could be frustrating, but even these experiences were interesting and certainly instructive. We felt a sense of accomplishment each time we brought the scooter back to life, hit the road once again, and felt the breeze hit our faces. We did so both individually and also as a group. My father cautioned us about riding as a pack, especially through the downtown area. He was concerned that the noise and commotion would draw the attention of local authorities. He reminded us we didn't have drivers' licenses. "So, keep a low profile," he advised.

The noise level from individual scooters, and most definitely the pack, depended on the exhaust system configuration of the day. We changed these frequently. They ranged from quiet stock mufflers bought from Ray Ellis, louder dual exhaust systems like I had inherited on my scooter, to "straight pipes" that we just had to try out to see what they sounded like. Jim Smith had an advantage over the rest of us. He created all sorts of exhaust system configurations from the endless supply of piping parts he had access to at his father's hardware store.

Outing participants depended upon who was available and were usually organized on an ad hoc basis. Often one of us instigated a mission by running past another's house to see if they were available. One by one, we picked up participants while riding around town. Sometimes we found companions at one of the gas stations. The Standard Oil station north of town and Pure Oil station on the southside, one block from my house, were likely gathering spots. We cruised in, pulled up to the pumps, and opened the rear lid (or rear seat in my case) to expose and fill our two and one-half gallon tanks. Usually, 50 cents worth of gas did the trick.

Collecting four or five members of the pack, we cruised through downtown (despite my father's admonitions) then headed off to some out-of-town destination. The Tumble Dam was a favored one. Located northeast of town, we rode a mile or so out Old 131 to the railroad track crossing, turned onto a dirt lane alongside the tracks and rode a half-mile to the dam.

In winter we ice skated on the opposite in-town side of the pond created by this dam. It also maintained water levels in a series of in-town small canals that we called raceways. These supplied hydromechanical or hydroelectric energy to the creamery, Drake Casket Company, Williams Manufacturing Company, and a village public water supply pumping station. All were located on East Water Street. Besides watching water "tumble" through the main dam gate, we liked to walk out on an adjoining concrete retaining wall to look for fish. In our younger years we had ridden our bicycles out there, toting fishing poles, and tried to catch whatever swam there. When I was much younger, my father took me there to fish for bullheads. We usually caught several. They didn't have scales. He used a sharp knife and a pair of pliers to pull the skin from them and produce filets. He had to be careful to avoid being stuck by their sharp barbed fins. We didn't stay long or bother with fishing on scooter trips. We had other places to go.

We continued by riding a mile or so up Old 131 to Constantine Street. There, we had a choice. We could turn south and loop back into town, or head north towards Three Rivers, six or seven miles up the road. We often turned north, riding all the way into Three Rivers. We used quiet in-town surface streets to get back onto Old 131 and cruise back to Constantine. This route took us through farmlands, light Three Rivers traffic, across the Prairie River, and past the Sauganash County Club. It was a favorite route of mine, one I often traveled on my own.

One day as I rode the route alone, I did so in reverse. I took Old 131 all the way into Three Rivers, crossed the St. Joseph River on east Broadway, then turned south on Constantine Street to head home. All was going well. I made it nearly all the way back to Old 131 when a car roared past me. It was a black Kaiser Henry J. We laughed at these strange looking, 1950s "economy" cars. Front end styling was odd. The grill looked something like a Studebaker with a round nose but had no bullet stuck in it. In addition, the front bumper was recessed back from the nose, making it look as though the car had hit something that pushed the lower half of its front beneath the grill. It also sported small tail fins that we thought were borrowed from late 1940s model Cadillacs. Given their small engines, we boys concluded they wouldn't go very fast, so I was surprised to be passed so quickly by one. As it went around me and out of sight, I putted along. Rounding a curve, I was again surprised. The Henry J was off on the left side of the road piled up against a large tree. The driver's door was open, and he was rolling out of the car onto the road shoulder when I arrived. I stopped and went over to him. He muttered something that I didn't understand then just laid there. No blood was flowing, he seemed to be breathing but had passed out for sure. What to do? I needed help. A few hundred feet away, a small house was situated some distance back off the road. I hopped on the scooter and drove up the long driveway to the house. A woman came to the door. I explained that there had been an accident out on the road, and we needed to call police and an ambulance. She rushed off to do so and I returned to the vehicle. The driver was still lying in the road unconscious but breathing. I was amazed at how quickly a county Sheriff's Deputy arrived. He must have been nearby. We didn't have cell phones in those days, but police cars did have two-way radios. I gave the Deputy what details I had regarding the mishap and asked if an ambulance would be coming. He replied, "Naw, I think he'll come around, he's just drunk." He told me I would no longer be needed and could be on my way. I left, relieved that no questions were asked about my having or not having a drivers' license.

The flat fertile prairie lands surrounding town were formed by ancient glacial melt outwash. Agricultural development produced an extensive roadway system that intersect in one-mile blocks throughout the area. These provided an excellent grid for our rides. Main arteries were paved but many crossroads remained graveled. The flatness of the area provided excellent visibility, making navigation easy. We could always find our way home by scanning the horizon for smokestacks or water towers. However, they were quiet places. There was not much traffic on these roads. One risk was limited opportunity for rescue should we have a mechanical breakdown. In a worst-case scenario, we pushed the scooter home.

But there were white knights out there. As I was riding along by myself on another day, I ran out of gas. Being a little short of cash, I had elected not to fill up before leaving town. I was certain I had enough gas for a short ride. However, about a mile and a half outside of town I came to a sputtering stop. I started pushing towards home. Before I had gone very far, a truck pulled up beside me. It was Pete Brown, father of a girl I had been keeping an eye on. He was driving his Pure Oil gasoline and fuel oil delivery truck. He serviced farms in the area, filling tanks used to fuel tractors and heat houses. He stopped and asked what the problem was. I explained I had run out of gas. He said, "Do you want regular or ethyl?" I replied, "Either will do." Pete hopped out of the cab, pulled the hose out of the back of the truck, and filled my tank. I was thankful, but embarrassed since I didn't have money to pay him. He just smiled and said, "No problem, I didn't want to see you push that thing all the way home." He drove off headed towards town.

One nice summer Saturday evening, I cruised by Dave Daugherty's house. There didn't seem to be much going on, so he hopped onto my rear seat, and we struck off on a Three Rivers route ride. All had gone well on the way up. Stopping at the Windmill drive-in, we enjoyed a malt then headed back. Just leaving Three Rivers on the Old 131 route, we were climbing a small hill near the Sauganash Country Club when we heard and felt a loud thump under the scooter. We skidded to a stop. Investigating, we found that bolts holding the rear rim to the hub had sheared off. What to do? We hadn't fallen over, and no one was hurt, but we couldn't push the scooter, and we were about eight miles from home. Being a Saturday evening, my folks were both working at the store. Since there was no telephone there, I couldn't call them. Dave said he could call his dad. We walked to the club house and used their phone. Dave's dad came out, driving his new 1954 DeSoto. We picked up the scooter, laid it on its side, and drove home with it sticking out of the back of the trunk.

I had known for a while that those bolts were weak. Apparently, sometime in the scooter's previous life, they had become loose. When starting and stopping, the rim worked back and forth cutting their holes into slots and forming grooves on each of the bolts. I had been trying to keep the bolts tight enough to prevent the movement, but that had not done the trick. In their worn condition the bolts snapped off under stress from the two-person load. The fix was a trip to the Ray Ellis shop to buy a new rim and bolts. I should have done it sooner.

An in-town ride that provided a bit of adventure was on a set of trails in a sandy-soiled, sparsely wooded area at the southwest edge of town, out behind the school building. The place may have had a different name, but we kids called it Paris Lane. It was vacant, a few acres in size, and no one seemed to know who owned the land. The trails, barely negotiable by car, meandered through the area and led diagonally across the parcel out onto Riverside Drive. When riding through there, we had to move swiftly, or our wheels would bog down in the sand.

There was considerable mystique associated with the area. Older teens frequently told stories about cars that parked back there and the things that went on in them. It was one of those places that our parents told us we were to stay out of, but we didn't really understand the fuss. For the scooter boys pack, it was a challenging place to ride and carried with it the thrill of doing something we were told not to do. We ventured into the area often.

One summer Saturday evening, I decided the take a ride through there on my own. I rode down the access lane off Canaris Street and entered the wooded area that encircled the sand banks. Since I was about to encounter the sandy trails, I was traveling at a pretty high rate of speed. Suddenly, a strand of heavy barbed wire appeared, stretched across the trail right in front of me. I slammed on the brake trying to stop but was going too fast. The barbed wire caught me on the upper chest, just below my neck. The scooter tipped on its side, and I was dumped on the ground. I lay there dazed for a moment or two, then went about righting the scooter and checking out the wire.

I had no idea where it had come from or who put it there. It had never been there before. I was concerned that someone else might encounter it, so I unwrapped the wire from the trees on either side of the trail that it was wrapped around and threw it off into the woods. Then I turned around and headed home to clean up and examine my cuts and scrapes. Fortunately, no one was home when I arrived. My parents were at the store and my sister was off with her friends. Both my shirt and undershirt had been torn to shreds by the barbed wire and I had several large, bloody, scratches on my chest and neck. The chest scratches could be covered by a clean shirt, but the neck scratches could not be hidden. I worried about having to explain where I had been and how this happened.

I decided my best defense was a bold offense, so after getting cleaned up, I hopped on the scooter and headed downtown to the store. Approaching my mother, she said, "What happened to you, are you OK?" I said I was fine and that I had encountered a piece of barbed wire someone had stretched between two trees, "out behind the school." I didn't mention that it was on the Paris Lane trail. She and my father checked me over, shook their heads, and went about their business. Whew "Better than I thought," I said to myself. But I still worried about having to explain the scratches to others.

Within minutes, I was standing at the front of the store when Paul Geisler, son of the local funeral director (three years behind me in school), walked in. Both of his forearms were bandaged up. I said, "What happened to you, Paul." He said, "Oh, I ran into a barbed wire fence while riding my bicycle." I said "Really, where?" He casually said, "Oh, out behind the school." I showed him my scratches. Suddenly, we were kindred spirits. Neither of us had to explain exactly where we had been. Comparing notes, I asked when his incident occurred. It was earlier that afternoon. I said, "Why didn't you take the wire down?" He replied, "I was too scared, I just wanted to get out of there. I wasn't supposed to be there."

I don't think either of us ever said much to others about the experience. For me that was easy. The next day, Sunday, I left town to attend music camp at Western Michigan University. I was away for two weeks. By the time I returned, my scratches had disappeared.

The Michigan State Plowing Contest

Our little town didn't have many festivals or other hallmark events to draw people into the community. For a few years, the local Rotary Club held an annual summer wrestling match event, outdoors at the high school football field. Second-line wrestling professionals, accompanied by a couple of "headliners" created a bit of a stir and brought a few hundred people into town to view their one-night stand. "Headliners" included big-name, TV star wrestlers such as Gorgeous George, The Strangler, and Don Eagle assured good gate receipts. But just for that one night.

Sidewalk Days held by local merchants in the downtown area created some stir. On one fall weekend, merchants put merchandise displays on sidewalks in front of their stores and tended them dressed in old-fashioned costumes. Though these events were popular and imparted a festive downtown atmosphere, customers lining the streets were mostly local folks. The events didn't provide much outward reach.

To "put the town on the map," village officials worked to get the area established as the site for the annual Michigan State Plowing Contest. During this event, competitors came to the area from all over Michigan and the adjoining states of Indiana and Ohio. They sought to determine who could plow the straightest, most even, uniformly deep, and well-shaped furrow (a narrow trench made in the ground by plow) on several local farm fields.

It was a big deal. Anyone in the tri-state area could get involved in this three- or four-day event. Local stores ran special sales, vendors set up displays (both in-town and out at competition sites). A parade took place in the downtown business area, and a contest was established to name the "Queen of the Furrow." The competition and selection process for choosing the Queen was not a beauty or talent pageant, but purely an economic one. Candidates were given an opportunity to "sign-up." During a designated timeframe, customers of local stores were given one "ballot" for each dollar they spent. They wrote the name of their favorite candidate on each ballot and stuck them in the box posted in the stores. The competition started several weeks before the event. That gave candidate advocates a significant period of time to seek and cast votes.

For the scooter boys, the event was also a big deal. On each day of the festival, there were activities both in-town and at farms out in the country. We could take all of this in by running between venues on our scooters. We worked out plans in advance to maximize our coverage and riding opportunities. This required us to make sure our scooters were in good condition and fit for the occasion. Not wanting to be left out because of some mechanical failure, we installed new chain master links, adjusted chain tension, and inspected coil springs to make sure none were broken. We checked brake linings and brake pedal linkages. In anticipation of some nighttime riding opportunities, we made sure our generators were functioning so we could run lights. A couple of us needed parts so we had to find a ride to the Kalamazoo Ray Ellis shop.

My inspection revealed that I needed to adjust my brake linkage. The pedal was connected to the rear wheel brake by a long rod that ran through the scooter frame from front to back. The rod was connected to the pedal by a special yoke and bolt arrangement. After adjusting it, I decided to use a new bolt. Digging through my toolbox I found a stove bolt that fit perfectly. With the parts back together, it was time for a test ride. I hopped on the scooter, headed out the driveway, and drove around the corner onto Clinton Street. I crossed the main highway (Washington Street) and rode over to the schoolyard on Canaris. Turning the corner onto Lafayette I head back home. When I got back to Washington Street, I hit the brake pedal at the stop sign. It hesitated for a second then slammed all the way to the floor. The scooter kept going. I had no brakes! Washington Street traffic was heavy, and I was headed right across the intersection. Quickly, I turned up the sidewalk running along the street. There, I was able to slow down and come to a stop. Whew! What a shock that had been. Slowly I drove home and crawled under the scooter to see what had gone wrong. My stove bolt, made of soft steel, had sheared off. I needed to use a hardened steel bolt for that connection. Lesson learned, I walked downtown to get one at the hardware store.

Off and on throughout plowing contest days, the pack rode to and from various venues. We always turned heads when we arrived. We parked, walked the grounds looking at equipment displays, and watched individual plowing trials. After staying for what we determined was the appropriate length of time, we returned to the scooters, kicked over the foot starters, and rode off to the next venue. We thought we were pretty big stuff.

Moving On

Growing older (approaching the age of 16) our interests began to change. I was among the youngest of the pack. Dick Carter was one of the first to start driving cars rather than his scooter. Ron Stears and Jim Smith were still riding scooters, but both were spending time visiting a house out on Riverside Drive where sisters Pat and Judy Milhahn lived. Ron and Pat were the older of the foursome. Since they spent so much time there, our scooter rendezvous point shifted from gas stations to the Milhahn home. Often, we all just sat in lawn chairs in the front yard with the Milhahn parents, joined conversations, drank an endless supply of root beers, and didn't go riding together much anymore. I was also spending more time cruising around my own end of town. My friend Ken Spade had acquired a scooter. His family had just built a new house right across the street from me. Ken's scooter, also an Eagle model, was in much better condition than mine. It required few repairs. He had painted it black with a whIte trim patch at the back of the body below the trunk lid. It looked really sharp. When we headed out on rides, he always questioned whether mine would survive the trip. It usually did, but he was frequently amused when he looked across the street and saw me crawling under my machine to address the latest issue.

The other new focus for me in our neighborhood was the Kolb home over on Cherry Street. Cruising the streets in that new subdivision, I hoped to find Barb Kolb out in her yard. If I did, I stopped to invite her to go for a ride with me. She generally declined. Her father had told her she was not to ride on that contraption. But, one afternoon she hopped on the back seat and agreed to a short ride. We headed out Mintdale Road. As we turned around at Lutz Road to come back into town, the drive chain broke and came flying off. It barely missed hitting Barb in the leg as it flew out from under the machine. We stopped and I picked up the pieces. Searching through my toolbox I couldn't come up with the master-links needed to put the chain back together. We pushed the scooter back to her house. Concluding that this was what she got for taking a ride she had been told not to, she hoped no one had seen us. After that, she liked it when I stopped to visit, but was never comfortable with me parking the scooter in her driveway. She worried about "what the neighbors would think." I started walking over for my steadily increasing visits.

I kept the scooter though my first couple of years of college. Near the end of my second year at Ferris Institute (now Ferris State University) in Big Rapids, Michigan, I came home one weekend and Dad told me that someone had come into the store inquiring about my scooter and whether I wanted to sell it. I thought about it for a while then agreed I could put the money to good use. The scooter was in much better shape than when I bought it. It ran well and looked pretty good in its 1949 Mercury blue metallic paint job. A couple of years earlier, I had talked Ford Garage body shop man Harry Ware into spray painting it using left over car paint.

I decided I would sell it if I could get $75 for it. That evening, the interested party, whom I didn't know came over, paid me the $75, hopped on the scooter, and drove it out the driveway. My mother watched from the kitchen window. When I returned to the house she said, "It was really sad to see it leave."

Part 4 – Advanced Lessons

Chapter 10

Learning to Drive

Just like today, getting a driver's license on the exact date of our 16th birthday was an assumed birthright. In addition, growing up in an agricultural region produced multiple opportunities to start driving earlier. By age 16, peers that lived on farms had been driving tractors and trucks in fields as well as back and forth between the farm and the co-op grain elevator for two or three years. We "town kids" had a myriad of country roads to practice driving on whenever we could talk our parents into letting us give it a try.

My opportunities came when Dad took me on trips into the woods to go mushroom hunting in the spring or pheasant hunting in the fall. Areas to the north and west of town included parcels of state-owned, wooded, Conservation Land open to the public. We drove through them on narrow dirt roads seeking best spots to find whatever we were looking for. Dad occasionally let me drive on straight ones.

However, I had really started "driving" when I was three years old. I had a peddle car when we lived in Buchanan, Michigan. When a bit older, I took to the wheel of the Maytag washing machine engine powered race car Dad had built for me. Then of course, there were those home alone on Saturday night excursions when I backed the car out of the garage and tooled around neighborhood streets.

Experiences with Farming and Tractors

I also had opportunities to drive my paternal grandfather's tractor when visiting his farm. Each summer, our parents sent my sister and me off to visit Dad's parents on their southeast Michigan farm near Adrian. We got there by riding the train between White Pigeon (four miles south of Constantine) and Wauseon Ohio, located just South of Adrian. Our parents took us to the depot, bought our tickets, and put us on the train in the custody of the conductor. The train stopped several times enroute. When we finally got to Wauseon, 100 miles away, he helped us get off and find our grandparents. We stayed a week before Mom and Dad drove over to bring us home.

During these visits I shadowed my grandfather as he worked the fields, tended the cows, and slopped the hogs. We both shadowed Grandma as she worked in her large garden, tended the chickens, gathered eggs, and cooked on her wood fired kitchen cookstove. With no running water, we hand pumped water from indoor and outdoor wells to fill buckets used in the house, barn, and animal drinking troughs. We used the outhouse located near the chicken coop.

Grandpa never owned the land he tilled. He rented and sharecropped on two different farmsteads in my time. The first was a small farm where he kept just four cows. He maintained a passel of hogs, perhaps as many as two dozen head, and Grandma tended a couple of good-sized chicken flocks, as many as 40 or 50 birds in a mix of Leghorns and (her favorite) Rhode Island Reds. In my early days, Grandpa tended the fields with horses. He kept two large draft horses in the same barn as his cows. We sat together on T-shaped milking stools while he hand milked the cows, but he never let me go near the horses. He said they were too skittish for me to be around. A few years later on one of our winter visits, Grandpa asked if I wanted to see his horses. Excited, I said, "Yes." Rather than head for the barn, he reached under the couch and smiled as he pulled out his wallet. In it were several twenty-dollar bills. He had sold the horses.

That spring, he bought a brand new 1951 Case tractor. When my sister and I went for our next weeklong visit, my tractor driving lessons began. I found the clutch a bit hard to operate. With its stiff spring, letting it out slowly was really hard. My starts were pretty jerky. That summer, I only drove around the yard in front of the barn. I advanced to pulling wagons in the field during wheat combining operations the following year.

When Grandpa moved from the four-cow farm to a larger one, he acquired a herd of 16. He advanced from milking by hand to using a Surge milking machine and piped milk directly to water bath cooled 10-gallon cans. I studied the milking machine apparatus. That gave me knowledge I thought would help me understand and try to converse with my cousins on Mother's side of the family. Her five brothers (my uncles) were all dairy farmers who kept large herds of registered Holstein cows. During visits I joined my cousins out in the barn where they discussed farming topics, including the merits of different brands of milking machines. The uncles all used DeVilbiss systems set up to serve their large herds. They piped milk directly from the cows into large, refrigerated storage tanks. I tried to join the conversations but quickly demonstrated (and they reminded me) I was a "town kid" and would never master their lingo. Taking this difference further, they all drove John Deere tractors. I liked standing around the tractors and crawling up on them. We talked about which control lever performed what function. But I didn't dare brag about my newfound skill of handling a Case tractor. Like the Surge milker, in their minds it was an inferior machine.

Grandpa's wheat fields were still located next to his old four-cow farm. That summer when I went with him to combine wheat, I looked forward to pulling wagons loaded with freshly harvested grain through the fields. He drove us there on his tractor. I sat beside him, seated on the fender that covered the large left wheel. There wasn't much for me to hang on to. There was no such thing as seat belts or a passenger seat. I just tightly held on to that fender as  we bumped along gravel roads at a top speed of 10 miles per hour. We had almost reached the field where we would meet the hired combining crew when there was a LOUD snapping sound. The next thing I knew, I was lying in a ditch alongside the road. My grandfather was crouched beside me and very worried. He insisted that the tractor had run over me! I remembered nothing past that loud snapping noise. Under the stress of my bouncing around on it, the bolts that fastened the fender to the tractor had broken off. According to Grandpa's account, the fender fell onto the large tractor wheel, pushing it and me to the ground right in front of that giant tire. He claimed that it ran right over the middle of my body. He and some others who had gathered told me not to try to stand up. "Just lie there," they said. Someone had gone to a nearby house and called an ambulance. I was taken to the hospital where they found nothing wrong with me. It was a big concern at the time. My parents were notified and rushed over, finding me still in the hospital when they arrived that afternoon. I was not allowed to eat anything. The doctors were still examining me, but I was telling them I was fine and not hurt. I just wanted to get out of there. I was finally released from the hospital late in the day. The following day my folks drove me home, ending my tractor driving career.

The news of my experience traveled around town quickly. For me, the worst part of the whole thing, as I went about my business, was people asking me how I was doing. Not sure I had actually been run over, I just wanted to forget the whole thing. Granddad insisted that the tractor did run over me. I wasn't so sure but was glad all had ended well.

Cousin Rex the Trucker

The son of my mother's sister and my oldest cousin, Rex Reed, was a truck driver. I was first introduced to his driving skills during one of my rare summer visits to my maternal grandfather's farm. For a couple of years, this grandpa grew some sugar beets. At harvest time, a machine dug beets out of the ground and a conveyor dumped them into a truck that Rex drove alongside the harvester. This occurred during my visit. To keep me out of the way, given my history around farm equipment, nervous Grandpa Silas put me in the truck cab with Rex.

Rex was always a lot of fun. He explained how he drove the truck, what gear he shifted into to match the harvester speed, etc. I was impressed with the long floor mounted shift lever that he moved between about six speeds. In the field, we were in low gear. Rex called it "grandma gear." When the truck became full, we headed out of the field to a nearby grain elevator to dump the beets. He shifted upwards through the gears on the way. In the process, Rex asked me to grab a wooden stick lying on the seat next to me. It had a notch cut into one end. As I did, he said, "When I shift into high gear you put the notch in that stick up against the shifter and jam the other end against the dashboard. This thing won't stay in gear unless you do that." That made us a team. As we went down the road, he steered and shifted, while I handled the stick when he changed gears. That was my first truck driving lesson.

Rex's day job was driving a car-hauler. He picked up brand new Buicks from the factory in Flint, Michigan, where he lived at the time, and delivered them to various places, including a large new-car storage lot in Chicago. On his way between Flint and Chicago, he occasionally stopped into the Constantine dime store. On arrival, he walked in the front door, stopped at the candy counter, reached into the back of the case and grabbed a handful of candy. Munching on the chocolates, he walked through the store looking for my parents, his Uncle Walt and Aunt Gertrude. During summer, if I was available, he asked, "Do you want to ride into Chicago with me?"

I jumped at the chance. It was always late in the day when he arrived. We headed off towards Chicago after supper, driving into the night. However, there was one issue. Due to insurance regulations, Rex was not supposed to have riders in the truck cab with him. Before leaving our house, he hung a pair of coveralls from the truck ceiling, extending them down behind my seat, blocking the view through the window in the back of the cab. No one could see me sitting in the passenger seat by looking into the back window. When we approached an intersection or another place where people had congregated, he asked me to lie down on the seat so I couldn't be spotted. He said insurance company inspectors sat around in these places watching trucks go by, checking compliance with the rules. As we drove along, I bobbed up and down whenever he spotted a potential inspection point.

The truck carried four brand new shiny Buicks. Rex described in detail what he had to do to keep the long trailer and heavy load moving along the road. Shifting gears often and making wide swings around corners in the days before expressways and superhighways, he navigated the 120 miles on two-lane roads. Midway through the trip we pulled into a truck stop for fuel, a restroom break, coffee for Rex, and a bottle of soda pop for me. I was impressed by the truckers I saw there. They sat eating big meals, swapping tales about road conditions and their trucks, all while guzzling large mugs of coffee.

When we reached the storage lot, we pulled up behind a long line of trucks, each offloading their batch of new cars. When our turn came, Rex made me sit in the truck while he backed the cars off his long trailer. I was disappointed that I couldn't go out to watch that operation, but I didn't want to cause any trouble for Rex. It was about midnight when he finished unloading. He returned to the cab, put the truck in gear, pulled us back onto the roadway, and we headed back to Constantine. My job on the way back was to keep talking to Rex, "to keep me awake," he said. We swapped tales, talked about fishing, and searched for "good" music on the truck's radio. We pulled up next to my house about 3 a.m. I went in to go to bed. Rex said he would take a nap in the truck, then be on his way back to Flint. When I awoke later in the morning, the truck was gone.

I made three or four of those Chicago Buick trips with Rex. A couple of years later, he stopped driving the car hauler and bought a truck he used to haul grain. This rig was not the typical semi-truck, but a large stake truck that towed a four-wheeled heavy-duty trailer. Both the truck body and the trailer were open, rack-sided vehicles. The truck chassis was a Chevrolet with a large V-8 engine, but one not quite big enough to haul the loads Rex put on the rig. He had gone into independent trucking and continued to make runs from central Michigan into Chicago. When he arrived in Constantine, he was empty, heading into Chicago to pick up loads. Again, he stopped at the store, raided the candy counter, and asked if I wanted to ride into Chicago with him. Of course I did, I loved the adventure. This time there was no restriction about having passengers in the truck. I sat upright the entire trip. We drove to an animal feed distribution warehouse and stood by while warehouse workers loaded the truck and trailer. Rex asked them to "Put seven tons on the truck and 10 on the trailer." We pulled out, heading back to Michigan with the truck straining under the 17-ton load. Rex again provided a complete description of how he handled the truck, when he shifted gears, how to plan routes with fewer hills to climb, etc. Then he said, "When you get your license, I'll show you how to drive this thing." Suddenly, I began paying a lot more attention to the details. I had just another year to go to get that license.

However, Rex encountered several difficulties. He burned out a couple of engines trying to haul big loads with a rig not designed for the task. Tire problems were also an issue. As a result, he went bankrupt and gave up trucking before I got my license. So much for my truck driving career.

Drivers Education

Coach Richard Whitworth came to our high school in the fall of 1954. He was a friendly outgoing individual that all students reacted favorably to. He coached baseball, football, basketball, and track, and taught gym classes. By the time I was a high school junior, he added teaching drivers education to his schedule. It was a one semester class that met during the regular school day. Two days per week were devoted to classroom instruction. On the other three days we drove the drivers education car. Taking the class was optional. Though my chums and I were sure we already knew the driving basics, we thought taking it would speed us towards obtaining that coveted driver's license. Also, it was considered an easy class and gave us more time to spend with Coach Whitworth. Though we were not on a ballfield or in the gym, we didn't address him as Mr. Whitworth in this more formal setting. He was always, and preferred to be, called Coach.

It was the first semester of our junior year. Half of our class members took the course in the fall the other half during the spring semester. Once assembled, we were split into groups of three or four students for driving sessions. My driving group consisted of buddies, Jim Smith, Barry Swarthout, and me. Coach regarded us as "quite the crew" and grimaced when he first encountered us, but with his good nature said, "Come on guys, let's go do it."

The drivers education car was loaned to the school by the local Ford dealership. It was a new 1956 Ford Customline four-door, in an odd light gray and almost pink two-tone paint scheme. The official names for the colors were Platinum Gray and Mandarin Orange, but the orange had a pink cast to it, at least to my eye. To us 1950s era car enthusiasts and analysts, we assumed this combination was Ford's response to the striking and popular 1955 Chevy Bel Aire art deco two-tone color scheme, Charcoal and Coral. But, we concluded, the Ford version didn't quite work. It didn't have the same snap. I concluded that the dealership selected that car to be the school department loaner because no one would want to buy it. However, it was the engine that really attracted our attention. It was Ford's new "Thunderbird Special V8"! We had enthusiastically read about this new 200 horsepower engine and couldn't wait to try it out. Standard engines of the day were likely to max out at a little more than 100 horsepower. Even the new small block Chevy V8s only produced 180 hp. The drivers education engine was coupled to a three-speed manual transmission in a "three on the tree" shifter setup. We were impressed!

Coach cut no corners with our "experienced" driving group. We started, like all other students, driving around the football field track. It was "paved" with coal ash cinders hauled in from the local paper mill boiler plant. Emphasis was on smooth starts. Though we were tempted to do otherwise, given the Thunderbird V8 tucked under the hood, we worked on letting the clutch out easily, not racing the engine, and certainly not making the track cinders fly on take-off. We were also instructed on how to change a tire, check engine oil, and perform a daily walk around the car, checking to see that all lights were working before we got into the car. Coach did give us some latitude by letting us make contests out of tasks we were convinced we already knew how to do. "Who can change a tire the fastest?" became a challenge. Smith won, after I dropped one of the lug nuts while mounting the spare tire onto the bumper-jacked rear wheel. Coach even pulled a stopwatch out of his pocket and refereed the event. Popping wheel covers off using the flattened end of the jack handle and pounding them back on with bear hands made our palms sore.

Finally getting on the road, we drove town streets through many of the tricky intersections. We were instructed on how to proceed through standard two-way stop signs, four-way stops, intersections with yield signs, those with more than four corners like the "Five Points" intersection near my home, and like many in our town – those with no signs at all. We were taught how to make proper left turns, coming to the center of an intersection before turning rather than cutting corners and proceeding diagonally across intersections. The diagonal practice was often favored by our parents. My father fussed each time he was with me and I turned square corners. He thought it unnecessary and likely to "wear out the tires and steering gear." Coach counseled us on staying within speed limits, taught us to anticipate what oncoming traffic was likely to do, and how to properly parallel park. He demonstrated right vs. wrong from behind the wheel before we took over. During our driving sessions, he sat in the righthand seat with his foot resting on a secondary brake pedal, ready to stomp on it and bring the car to a stop if needed. The two of us not driving sat in the back seat quietly nodding and smirking when the driver made some mistake. Each person drove for about 15 minutes before being instructed to pull over to the side of the road and change drivers. At the end of our driving sessions, we pulled up beside the school building and Coach verbally critiqued each of our performances. He read from notes he had taken when we were each behind the wheel.

Once we got through most rudiments while driving in-town, we headed out onto the open road, first on country roads familiar to us from our scooter rides, then onto U.S. 131, the main highway. There, traffic was heavier, speeds higher, and trucks abounded. I found my first highway driving experience quite challenging. Staying in lane, maintaining a constant speed while watching other cars and trucks coming towards and around us, was unnerving. I was relieved when my shift ended halfway up "the big hill" on our way to Three Rivers. Coach motioned for me to "pull over" at a place where I could get well off the road and let one of the other guys take it from there. As we practiced, we got better. On subsequent classes we drove into neighboring communities. Three Rivers, White Pigeon, Mottville, and Centerville were destinations. Occasionally, Coach worked in some of his errands on these trips. We dropped off a bag of balls left at our school by a White Pigeon team after a recent scrimmage. We picked up tickets for an up-coming game that had been printed in Sturgis, etc. We students sat in the car waiting while Coach went inside to quickly conduct his business.

On one of these occasions, Coach said he had a meeting with a Three Rivers coach. We made our way up there by switching off on the driving as usual. As we sat in the car while Coach was in the school, we became somewhat concerned. He was taking longer than anticipated. We needed to be back at our school for the next class. When he rushed out, he came to the driver's door and said, "I'll take it. We've got to get you guys back." He jumped in, adjusted his seat and mirrors, then quickly headed out of town taking the Old 131 route. With less traffic on this country road, he punched the Thunderbird V8 gas pedal and down the road we went. On the many straight stretches we were reaching speeds of nearly 100 miles per hour. He slowed for the curves and finally throttled back as we approached our village limits. It was quite the performance. As he pulled up to the school building and let us out, he said, "I don't want to hear of any stories circulated about this ride." We all understood, nodded, and regarded it as a story we could enjoy only between ourselves.

Getting Our Own Four Wheels

Jim Smith was the oldest of our threesome. He went off to Centerville to take his driver's license exams while still completing our drivers ed class. He easily passed and proudly displayed his license when we gathered for our next session in the '56 Ford. Barry and I had to wait until later in the year for our turns. Jim's family car was a 1948 Plymouth Special Deluxe four-door sedan. Drab green in color, it was a large and hulky looking thing with its sloping back end. The redeeming features were a spotlight mounted on the driver's door pillar next to the windshield, a radio, and the fact that Jim had his own key to the car. He got to drive it just about any time he wanted. He drove to school early and sat in the car parked in a space at the north end of the building. During our social time, we gathered in and around it waiting for the bell to ring.

As proud as Jim was of his personal key, he also boasted about what was to come his way. It was 1956. He had an uncle who lived in Detroit and worked for General Motors. One of his job perks was the ability to drive a new Chevrolet each year. At the end of the year when GM provided the uncle with a new one, he could buy the "old" car at a price said to be much lower than the price of the same car at a dealership. That year, Jim's uncle was driving a 1955 Chevy Bel Air two-door hardtop finished in the coveted charcoal and coral color scheme. For months, Jim claimed that arrangements had been made for his dad to buy that car from the uncle when it became available. The rest of us wondered if this was really a "done deal." We were especially skeptical of Jim's insistence that once the "new" car arrived, he would get to keep the Plymouth as his personal vehicle. In the meantime, he alternated driving to school in either the Plymouth or on his scooter.

After school when Jim had the car, he picked up some of the rest of us as he cruised around town. We rode with the radio blasting. Barry was the designated "radio man." He had a talent for suggesting a particular pop tune then dialing in a random station. More often than not, the sought-for-tune would be playing.

Towards spring, the big day arrived. Jim reported that he and his family had just returned from Detroit with the '55 Chevy. It was home in the garage. After school we all rushed over to check it out. Yes, the prophecy had come true. There it was, charcoal and coral, two-door hardtop, V8 engine, and it was a beauty!

Barry was the next one to get his license. His dad worked in Three Rivers and rode to and from work each day with other drivers. His mother was a teacher who used their car to get to school each day, so he didn't get much opportunity to drive the family vehicle. However, his grandmother lived just down the street from them and had a nice black and white 1956 Ford Customline Victoria two-door hardtop. It was a sharp looking car. She was a very nice older lady whom we all liked. Since she was also a member of the local school board, we were sure to be on our best behavior around her. We weren't sure just what that job entailed but thought she could have an undesirable impact on us if we misbehaved or were impolite. When he had reason to do so, Barry could drive her car. He loved to show it off and we were very impressed when we had the opportunity to get a short ride in it. One condition of his permission to use the car was to always take it back clean. So, Barry drove around town, picked up one or two of us, took us for a ride, all windows down and the radio blasting, then pulled up to his house where we had to help him wash and vacuum out the car so he could return it. Besides the labor, the additional price we paid for these jaunts was to have to walk home. I walked to the dime store two blocks away, rather than the seven blocks back to our house.

As the youngest boy in my class, my time for getting my license came late in December. My family was a two-car household. Back in 1944, we moved to Constantine in Dad's 1937 Pontiac. When the engine failed during WW II years, cars were very hard to come by, so the replacement became a 1936 Buick Roadmaster. When the war was over and things loosened up, Dad traded it for a used 1946 DeSoto four-door sedan. He kept that car for just a couple of years, then bought his first new car, a 1950 DeSoto two-door sedan. Though Mother had driven in her youth while living on the family dairy farm, she had not driven during my early years. Dad tried to teach her to drive the Roadmaster, but she found the floor mounted manual transmission unwieldly and the big clumsy car hard to handle. The DeSotos had Fluid Drive semiautomatic transmissions. They were much easier to manage. She obtained a license and started driving again after we obtained the 1950 model. In 1953, with her driving and an increased need to haul merchandise for the dime store, Dad bought a used 1949 Plymouth station wagon. At the end of the 1955 model year, he traded it for a new "close out" Plymouth wagon at the Low Overhead Jordan dealership in Mishawaka, Indiana. It had a V8 engine and a "three on the tree" manual transmission. The transaction took a few days to complete and resulted in considerable conversation around our evening supper table. Mother agreed that Dad could use a new station wagon. His old one had mechanical issues. But she didn't see the need for the V8 engine. She was leery of "all that power." Dad and I argued that this was just what was needed to safely merge into traffic. I could contribute significantly to the debate since I was learning to drive in the school's Thunderbird-V8 powered Ford. Though the issue was never really settled, the new wagon found a home in our garage.

Later that year, as I was looking forward to obtaining my license, Mom and Dad went shopping for a replacement for the 1950 DeSoto. The 1957 models had just come out. They were flashy. Lots of chrome, V8 engines galore, two-tone paint schemes, and huge tail fins. I provided consulting services by showing them newspaper and magazine ad pictures of various models. They shopped at the DeSoto-Plymouth dealership in Elkhart, Indiana. I expected them to buy a Plymouth. I was really surprised when they brought home a 1957 DeSoto! Much bigger and flashier than the Plymouth, the red behemoth sported white dart shaped side panels, tall tail fins, "shot glass" styled taillights, a pushbutton automatic transmission, and other features.

Flashy as it was, I noticed one anomaly right away. 1957 was the first year for four-light car headlight systems. DeSoto's had them on Fireflight models. Mom and Dad had bought a Firesweep, entry level, model. It had just two headlights. There were other more subtle differences, such as vinyl floor coverings rather than carpet, chrome rather than gold nameplate lettering, and more muted side marking medallions. Those differences were only noticed by the most critical observers. Two headlights rather than four, that was a biggie. Dad was proud of his purchase, but sure enough, when showing it off people immediately asked why it didn't have four headlights. He simply said, "Because I only paid for two."

To some extent, I actually preferred the two-headlight styling. I thought the heavy chrome trim pieces used around the headlights on the two light models looked better than the thin "eyelash" chrome moldings on the quad setup. But visuals were important, and we seemed to have a major one. I quickly came up with a solution. As sold, the car was not equipped with a radio. Dad had ordered one and needed to take the car back to the dealership to have it installed. I said, "Have them install dual antennas on the back of the tail fins. That will make the car look a lot better and draw attention away from the headlights." I'm not sure Dad agreed there was anything wrong with the way the car looked but did honor my request. I was proud of the tall antennas sprouting from the back of those huge tail fins.

Hitting the Road

My drivers ed class was winding down, my 16th birthday had arrived, and I was anxious to head to the Centerville, Michigan Secretary of State office to take my driver's license test. I hadn't yet driven the new DeSoto and Dad was not anxious for me to do so. Despite my bugging to try it out, he held firm that I would go for my driving test in his station wagon. I came to agree that this was the better option. The wagon had a manual transmission that I had mastered in drivers education. The real challenge was passing the parallel parking test. We learned how to do this in drivers education, but I had not practiced that in the boxy station wagon. I agreed it would be easier than trying to do it in the tail finned DeSoto. It was late in the day when we got underway with Dad driving me to Centerville. I had suggested that I drive so I could get more familiar with the wagon, but he reminded me that I didn't have a license. He didn't want to prejudice my chances of getting one by having me pull up in front of the examiner's office without one.

Except for one trick question, the written test was a snap. Coach Whitworth had prepared us well. That one question had something to do with approaching a railroad track with no crossing signals. The correct answer among the five possible was

"All of the above." I had checked what I thought was the most important among the options provided. Consequently, I didn't "ace" the test but easily passed. The failure point was a minus three on the questions. Next came the driving test. The examiner and I headed out the door, leaving Dad sitting in the office. It was already getting dark. I started doing my around the car inspection and he said, "That's OK, we can skip that." We got into the car and off we went, heading passed the courthouse, through the small downtown area, and out onto Covered Bridge Road. The first test was stopping and starting on an uphill grade. The clutch pedal on the Plymouth wasn't as firm as the one on the drivers ed car. We jerked forward as we started up the grade. But we hadn't rolled backward, and I didn't stall the car. Next came crossing a railroad track. Sure enough, there were no signal lights. I made sure to remember the "all of the above" written test answers, came to a stop, looked in both directions and ticked off "all" of the answers in my mind. After two right turns we were back in town. On Main Street, I was asked to parallel park. I pulled up beside the front vehicle and began backing into the space. About halfway through the task, easing into the space, the examiner said, "OK, you've got it, lets go back to the office." Whew! Around the block we went and parked diagonally in front of his office. I had passed! The examiner finished the paperwork, handed me my freshly signed temporary license, started turning out the office lights, and we were out the door.

Of course, I expected to drive home. But it was completely dark by then, so I agreed to let Dad handle the dark country roads. The next morning, I greeted the gauntlet of peers standing outside the school building door, waving my signed license at them and reporting on my experience with the examiner. The girls in the crowd said, "Humph, you got off easy, he would have made us complete the parallel parking test."

It's not if, but when – Especially in the '57 DeSoto

As I learned decades later when my own kids started to drive, it was inevitable that my early driving experiences would include a few mishaps. And the DeSoto's hulk had a lot to do with what took place.

My new driver's license was burning a hole in my pocket, and I was itching to get into that flashy car and cruise the streets. Dad limited me to driving the station wagon for a time but eased up as spring approached. He had concluded that my ability to drive was a convenience for Mom and him as well. They could send me on long-distance errands, and I could help get my sister from place to place. I ended up having personal keys to both cars. Proudly, I always carried them in my pants pocket. This supported their position that since I had been so entrusted, I didn't need to have my own car. Some of my peers were acquiring theirs.

My visits to the Kolb house over on Cherry Street had increased and time had come for my first "car date" with Miss Barbara. Despite her father's misgivings, I picked her up in the DeSoto and we headed up to Three Rivers to see a movie. I drove back roads and we arrived at the theater safely. Coming home everything went well until I turned into her driveway. When we left, I failed to notice that the village maintenance crew had dug a storm drain hole at the edge of the street, right next their driveway apron. A heavy crown-shaped sewer grate had been placed over the hole, but there were no signs, flares, or other markers that called attention to the obstacle, especially after dark. As I turned to drive into the driveway, I swung a bit wide. We heard a loud CLUNK and felt a jolt inside the car! Getting out and looking, I was horrified to see that the righthand side of the DeSoto's huge low-slung chrome bumper had hit the grate, leaving behind a big dent. I was faced with the task of going home and reporting the problem. Dad was not one to raise his voice very loudly. He often became quite quiet when something troubled him. I pulled into the garage, checked over the damage, then went in the house to face the music. Dad came out, looked it over, and didn't have much to say about it. I pinned most of the blame on the village maintenance crew. He shook his head and nodded.

Word spread quickly that I had dinged the bumper. The dent couldn't be removed. The only fix was to replace the entire chromed mass. Since the car was so new, the replacement part had to be special ordered. It was a couple of weeks before the repair could be made, and evidence of my driving incompetence removed. The price tag on the new bumper was $90 ($900 in today's dollars). Though the incident had nothing to do with the tail fins, it was just the first of several that plagued my family while driving this tall-finned monster.

On another dating occasion, I took Miss Barbara to a drive-in movie. I pulled into the movie viewing spot and put the pole mounted speaker on the left rear door window. When the movie ended, I started to drive off without removing the speaker. Realizing the error, I quickly stopped, removed the speaker and hung it back on the pole. However, when pulling away, I didn't swing wide enough to get away from the pole and scraped the side of the left tail fin. That left a scratch. The following day, without reporting the incident, I got out the rubbing compound and worked on the scratch, removing most of it.

One day my mother was backing out of the garage when the fins obstructed her view. We had a long-standing purple martin house mounted on a tall pole in the yard adjacent to the driveway. Veering off the drive into the yard, Mom struck the martin house pole. The house came loose from the top and crashed down onto the wide DeSoto trunk lid. That left a small dent and set of scratches. Experienced, I assured her I could make these nearly disappear using my can of rubbing compound.

Once my sister began driving, she experienced the fin blind spot when she attempted to pass a vehicle out on the open road. She didn't see that another car had pulled out from behind to pass her. Once again, a minor scrape appeared on the left fin.

After high school graduation I entered a two-year-degree program in Industrial Chemistry Technology at Ferris Institute. To finish that program in 1960 and move on to the Western Michigan University Paper Technology program, I attended the Ferris summer term. Since rides back and forth were less assured during the summer term, I took the DeSoto with me. Having a car on campus made me popular. One afternoon a group of guys and gals organized a beach outing at a lake located a few miles from campus. I was tapped as one of the group's drivers.

A second driver had a 1959 Buick, with its own prominent rear tail fenders. We packed everyone into the two cars and headed off. On our return trip the Buick driver was feeling frisky and took the lead. I dutifully followed. We were driving on paved country roads with little or no traffic. He began playing around in front of me by speeding up then slowing down, way down – almost to a crawl. The group in my car started urging me to pass him. I didn't want to do it. I was certain that if I started around him, he would speed up. I didn't want to get involved in that. But the challenges from the Buick continued and the "pass him, pass him" chant in my car grew. I started around. Sure enough, the Buick sped up and began to veer towards me. I veered off into the left shoulder and backed off the gas trying to keep the car under control. As I did, I spotted a huge roadside mailbox right in front of me. To avoid it, I quickly swerved back up onto the roadway. Gravel from the roadside flew in all directions, the car rocked back and forth violently, but I managed to keep the car somewhat under control. Whew! Back up on the pavement, we were OK. The atmosphere in the car was suddenly very quiet and the Buick continued on its way at normal speed. Back on campus I dropped off my passengers, parked in my designated lot, and got out of the car. Walking to the back of the vehicle, I discovered that the antenna on the left tail fin was bent over pointing straight backwards. Apparently, that tail fin had passed under the mailbox as I pulled the car back onto the roadway. What a sobering sight. Quietly, I bent the antenna back upright and let out a great sigh of relief.

That wasn't the only DeSoto incident that occurred when I had the car on campus. I played in the Ferris band. A year earlier, at the end of my first year after most students had left, I stayed on campus with other band members to play for graduation ceremonies. On a previous trip home, I had brought the DeSoto to campus to move my belongings home for the summer. For that week-long period, it was nice not having to go to class or be buried in studies. During the day we had rehearsals, evenings we used the car to visit off campus hang-out spots. The A&W Root Beer Stand was a popular one. Located on the opposite (north) end of town, we only went there when we could find someone with a car. One evening, a group asked me to drive them up there. We piled into the car, headed off, and enjoyed a couple of rounds of root beer floats and other treats. After wearing out our welcome with the "car hop" gals, I started backing out of our serving spot. Mindful of a tall A&W signpost located right behind the car, I backed slowly. However, as I looked out the rear window over the high trunk lid between the tall tail fins, I couldn't see the base of that signpost. It was a solid block of concrete about three feet square, several inches high. As I backed, the left large, infamous, chromed bumper mounted exhaust extension (fake on our model) struck the cement base. That bent both the extension and the left tail fin side panel.

A day later, I had a long ride home wondering how I was going to explain this one. Again, I concluded that my best defense was a good offense, so I simply told Dad that someone had hit the car in the parking lot. His response was more head nodding. It also meant another trip to the body shop for the DeSoto. When I asked Ford garage body man Harry Ware for the repair cost estimate, I gave him the same story. He simply looked at me and said, "Yeah, right. What did you back into?"

The summer that my sister had obtained her driver's license she began her stint of driving only Dad's station wagon. It was a Sunday afternoon and I, had parked the DeSoto in the driveway up near the garage and was washing and waxing it. Getting it all shined up, I thought it was time for a test drive. I knew that my sister had taken the station wagon to run some errands, but being deeply involved in my detailing, I was unaware that she had returned. Not wanting to get too close to me and the DeSoto standing with all four doors, hood and trunk lid open, and radio blasting, she decided to park the wagon in the very end of the driveway, out at the edge of the street. After parking, she used the front door to enter the house. I never saw her. Satisfied I was finished, I closed up the car, jumped in, and started backing out of the driveway. It didn't occur to me to look in the mirror, or out of the back window. I just swiftly backed out towards the street. Suddenly BAM, I stopped with a jolt! Then, as I looked in the rearview mirror, I saw the front of the Plymouth jammed into the back of the DeSoto. What a sickening feeling. Where did that come from? I had to go into the house and report the mishap.

Dad was standing in the bathroom shaving, his face covered with shaving cream. When I reported the mishap, he put down his razor and walked out into the yard, still lathered up, to assess the damage. I pulled the DeSoto away from the station wagon. The back of the Desoto had faired pretty well. It had just a small scratch on the rear bumper and suffered only one broken "shot glass" taillight lens. The front of the Plymouth was a different matter. The grill and front of the hood were pushed back several inches. Fortunately, the radiator behind the grill was not damaged. However, the hood latch didn't work. Dad, after using a towel wrapped around his neck to wipe the shaving cream off his face, and with some quiet head nodding, went into the garage, grabbed a long chain and wrapped one end around a big maple tree that stood next to the driveway entrance. He hooked the other end to the crushed front end of the Plymouth, got into the car and backed it up. This pulled the grill out far enough that the latch could be used to secure the hood.

The next day, I headed back to college, the Plymouth went to the body shop. Before leaving, I took care of the minor DeSoto damage by visiting the DeSoto–Plymouth dealership, purchasing, then installing, a new taillight lens.

The DeSoto agony finally ended one dark evening as Mother was driving home from the store. It was very unusual for cars to be parked along Washington Street in the residential area. But on this night, a 1959 Ford Edsel had been parked in front of a house about two blocks from where Mother would turn to return home. Suddenly, looming out of the darkness rose the tail end of that Edsel. She didn't see it in time to stop. BAM! She rear-ended it. Fortunately, she wasn't injured, and no one was in the parked Edsel. However, both cars were totaled. Dad had the DeSoto towed home and put in it the garage then started looking for way to get rid of and replace it. The replacement turned out to be a used 1959 Mercury, black and white in color. Its boxy style had subdued rear fins and never attracted mishaps like the DeSoto.

Perhaps that was also due to the fact that both my sister and I were pretty much out of the house by that time.

A Run-in with the Law

My high school peers in the class immediately behind mine went through their drivers education and licensing experiences the year after me. Rob Polleys' mother had purchased a new 1955 Chevy Bel Aire, two-door hardtop. It was stunning. He enjoyed showing it off. We agreed he looked really good sitting behind the wheel. Tom Flatland's mom drove Cadillacs. She was a small, short lady who could barely see over the top of the steering wheel of those big 1950s era Caddys. Tom was a bit taller than she, but a '59 caddy was a huge hulk to handle. We were all proud to be out and about plying the streets whenever we could come up with a good excuse to do so and strived to keep up with older peers who had obtained their own cars.

Willie Harder had a Model A Ford coupe with a rumble seat. It was really popular with the girls. Dick Carter drove around in his nice-looking '46 Ford coupe. Jim Smith had his '48 Plymouth daily driver, as well as access to the classy '55 Chevy for special occasions. Marlin Outman lived on a farm just outside of town, was a year ahead of me in school, and an extremely popular super jock. He had his own red and white '55 Chevy hardtop. It was a real nice-looking ride, equipped with Chevy's new V8 engine, and Marlin had installed two really nice sounding glasspack mufflers on it. He dated Sonja Vanzile, one year behind me. She was one of the most popular attendants working behind the soda fountain at Armstrong's Drug Store. We loved heading into Amstrong's, sitting on the fountain stools, sipping Cokes and chatting with Sonja. She heard all the teen-news and could keep us up on latest happenings.

One early spring 1957 evening, Coach Whitworth called a meeting of the Varsity Club. It was a mixed age group. Any student playing on varsity level sports teams, regardless of grade level, was a member. I, as manager of the football and basketball teams, was also one. Tom Flatland, a scrappy basketball player, was a member. He and I, as well as Marlin, attended the meeting at the school gym.

I had driven Dad's station wagon to the school. When the meeting ended, Marlin approached Tom and me and asked if we would do him a favor. He said Sonja was working at Armstrong's and would not be off duty until 9:00 p.m. It was just past 8:00 p.m., so he was going to stay at the school gym to "shoot some baskets." He asked us to take his car down and drop it off so she could come and pick him up when she got out of work. We agreed. Tom would drive the Chevy and I would follow along to bring him back to his home, one block from school.

Tom was thrilled to get the chance to drive that Chevy. He started it up and began gunning the engine, listening to the loud rumble coming from those glasspacks. I pulled up behind him and we headed up Canaris Street towards downtown. Canaris had stop signs at all intersecting cross streets between school and downtown. There were six in all. Each time Tom came to one, he stopped and revved the engine producing loud deep throated rumbles that reverberated throughout adjacent neighborhoods. Upon leaving one stop sign he roared off to the next one at speeds above the limit. I followed but was getting worried. I knew that the town cop, Charlie Gould, was likely be out patrolling the streets. Sooner or later, he was bound to hear the noise and come looking for us. I was astounded that Tom had even made this racket at the corner of Canaris and Sixth Streets. Charlie lived in a house located at that intersection. Onward we went. When we got to Fourth Street, I decided that the risk of getting picked up was too high. I turned off and drove over to Washington Street to finish the trip.

It was about 8:20 p.m. when I pulled up and parked across the street from Armstrong's. I walked over to the drugstore and took a seat at the soda fountain. I explained to Sonja that Tom was bringing Marlin's car down to her and I was surprised that he hadn't already arrived. I sat and waited for several minutes. Tom still didn't show up. We didn't know if Tom was off joy riding or what, but I was getting uncomfortable sitting there. I was expected to be home by now. I went outside and looked up and down the street but saw no sign of Tom. I got into the station wagon and heading home turned onto East Water Street. About halfway along the block, I saw Tom walking on the sidewalk. He had a piece of paper in his hand. I stopped to pick him up. "What happened, where's the car?" I asked. He waived the paper at me and said, "I got a ticket." I started to chuckle, and he said, "Don't laugh, you got one too?" I didn't know how that could be. I hadn't been stopped by the cop. Tom explained, "Charlie pulled me over down by the fire station and wrote me a ticket. I parked the car and walked back." I said, "How did I get a ticket too?" I had broken off from Tom's noisy excursion several blocks away. He said, "Charlie asked who was following me and I told him. He said I was to tell you to come find him." I said, "Thanks Tom!"

Oh, what to do? First, I drove Tom back to Armstrong's so he could give the car keys to Sonja and explain where to find Marlin's car. Then, I drove him home. I considered just going on home myself and hope this whole thing would blow over. But I knew my dad would be down on the main street at 8:00 a.m. the next morning and figured Charlie would show up at the dime store to deliver the ticket to my father. That would be something I needed to avoid. So, I went back downtown, keeping an eye out all along the way for Charlie and the town's green '55 Ford sedan patrol car. As I drove past the fire station, I saw the patrol car sitting on the station apron. I stopped, got out, and walked over to it. Charlie was sitting in the car shuffling through papers. He rolled down the window, and asked, "Yes, can I help you?" I said, "Tom Flatland told me I was to come and talk to you?" He seemed a bit surprised and replied, "Oh, yes, come sit in the car." I walked around the car, opened the passenger side front door and got in. Charlie asked, "What were you and ol' Tom trying to prove?" I gave him my side of the story and said that I didn't want to get caught, so had broken off from the run. Charlie, just nodded, reached for his ticket pad and started writing out one for me.

Climbing back into the station wagon to head home, I now had the unpleasant task of explaining the incident and showing the ticket to my father. Not wanting to face him and my mother at the same time, I called Dad out to the kitchen when I got home. I told him the story. He listened, nodded, and when I finished my tale said, "What the hell did you go find him for?" I was surprised and recited my fear that he would hear about the incident from Charlie himself rather than me. He nodded agreement and said, "Yeah, you did the right thing. But you're on your own for paying the ticket."

The next morning Tom and I had to head back to school. When I dropped him off the evening before, we wondered how this story would circulate among the clan and what razing or other harassment we would face. We agreed that we wouldn't initiate conversations about the incident, hoping it would blow over quickly. Walking to school that day, as always, I met up with Barbara Kolb and Kathy Bizoe at the corner of White Pigeon Road and Clinton Street. Fearing what they might hear about the incident once we got to school, I gave them my version of the story. They wished me luck and Barbara expressed concern that if her father heard about it, she would be banned from riding with me. Entering the school building, I quickly found Tom. We acknowledged mutual feelings that everyone was looking at us. We expected to be branded as the official "number one school criminals of the day." We agreed to keep our heads down and try to not call attention to ourselves. That all worked pretty well. Only Sonja waived her finger at us as she passed us in the hallway. When I saw Coach Whitworth later in the day, he asked, "Did I hear something about you and Tom getting in some trouble with the police department?" He kept up with his students and provided guidance as needed. But he didn't have much more to say about the incident and I went back to organizing basketball team uniforms in the locker room cage.

My next step was to take care of paying the ticket. This was when I learned what the Justice of the Peace did. I walked across the street from the dime store to Justice Seylaz's office. As I entered, he recognized me immediately and motioned for me to sit in the straight-backed chair in front of his desk. He sorted through his papers, selected one and, peering over his glasses, began to read the charges against me. He quoted violations of certain village ordinances and read off a long list fines that could apply. Finally, getting down to the specifics of my case, he said sternly, "The fine will be $10 with court costs of $4.30 cents. That brings the total to $14.30." Court costs? I was shocked. I didn't know what those were, but to add another $4.30 to the fine seemed awful strict to me. However, I wasn't in a position to question or argue. I dug into my wallet and came up with the cash. When I went back to the store, I questioned Mom and Dad about the "court costs." They laughed and said, "That's just the cut that Seylaz gets for doing all the paperwork." I had been saving up to order a second phonograph amplifier kit from the Allied Radio catalog. It was what I needed to convert my homemade hi-fi system to stereophonic sound. The price of the kit was $19.95. When I complained to my mother about the fine wiping out what I had saved for the project, she merely said, "Well, I guess that purchase will just have to wait for a bit." Lesson learned.

My First Car

When I was born, back in 1940, my father took out a life insurance policy on me that would pay $500 when I reached 18 years of age. While I was growing up, he frequently told me that the objective of the policy was to provide cash that would either pay for my first year of college or buy me a new Ford. When I turned 18, inflation had seen to it that $500 wouldn't do either. But the prospect of using it to buy a used car became my goal. Since my access to the family vehicles had suppressed my urge to spend the money, I left the policy in force to build dividends and interest until the Spring of 1961. By that time, I was finishing my first year at Western Michigan University and thought it was time I had my own set of wheels. Cashing in the policy, I had $600 to make the purchase. I began perusing used car lots in Kalamazoo and, when home on weekends, in Constantine. I didn't find much of interest for that amount of money. One lot on Portage Street in Kalamazoo had a green 1956 Ford sedan that looked good. I test drove it a couple of times. But it had a lot of miles on it and made a few strange noises. It didn't feel like a good investment. A dealership downtown on West Michigan Avenue had a very low mileage used Peugeot that could be purchased for the money I had. I looked it over carefully. The car was built in France. I had seen Peugeot ads in issues of *Scientific American* magazine, a journal I read monthly since junior high school days. "One of the World's 10 Best Cars," those ads read. But we rarely saw one on the street. They weren't popular and no one knew much about them. Even the salesman I spoke to didn't understand the car. When I climbed in to check it out, I found very few knobs or switches on the dashboard. Controls for lights, windshield wipers, etc. were all located on a single steering column stalk. U.S. cars were not built that way in those days. The salesman had no clue how to operate the controls but insisted that it was a really good car. Tempting as it was, I decided to follow my father's advice, "Don't buy a foreign car."

On a weekend home, Dad suggested that he and I go car shopping at dealerships in South Bend, Indiana. We spent the entire Saturday cruising Ford, Chevy, and Chrysler/Plymouth lots and not coming up with anything. On the way home we passed a Studebaker dealership on the outskirts of Elkhart. Dad said, "Let's stop-in here to see what they might have." I thought, "Oh, no – not a Studebaker!" Among my peers, Studebakers were anything but cool. They were odd looking and built next door in South Bend. Only in South Bend did you ever see a Studebaker police car. Beyond this, the only Studebaker I was aware of on the entire Western Michigan University campus was driven by a strange little fellow who lived in my dorm that we called Dougie. He lived on the same floor and roomed with Bruce, a cool fellow who became my best friend. Dougie's car

> **Planned Obsolescence**
> Dad pined for the utility of the Model A Fords. He often complained that 1950s new car makers used the concept of planned obsolescence to make sure that cars didn't last longer than a few years – "So they can get you to buy a new one", he said. Complaining about their styling he said, "They're also too low. A man has to be able to get into a car without the low-slung top knocking off your hat."

didn't run well. He often had Bruce and me standing outside in the cold peering into the engine bay trying to diagnose his latest problem.

I just couldn't see myself coming up with a "Stewdee," but here I was standing in a lot full of them. We got off to what I considered entirely the wrong start when my dad said to the salesman, "Kid here is shopping for a car and has $600 to spend. What have you got?" I whispered back to dad, "That's the wrong thing to say. You never tell them how much you want to spend." But as we walked down a long line of used cars, mostly Studebakers, the salesman finally said, "We also own the Buick dealership in downtown Elkhart. We just took in a car down there that you might be interested in." He continued, "It's a '55 Plymouth with only 18,000 miles on it." He added that it had been owned by a local doctor and "It was his wife's car that she didn't drive much." He thought the car could be purchased for something close to my budget. We agreed to drive downtown and meet him there.

The car was a red and white two-door hardtop. It looked really sharp with its whitewall tires and full wheel covers. The only downsides were a six-cylinder engine and an automatic transmission. Not exactly the macho V8 standard shift machine I had envisioned. Nonetheless, despite being six years old, it only had 18,000 miles on it, looked great, and almost fit my budget. The salesman said the price was "$695." He and my father dickered a bit and agreed to a price of $645. Dad came up with the additional $45. An obvious repair needed was a tear in the driver's seat covering. The seats were upholstered with a combination of gray fabric and red leather trim. A driver's seat seam between the fabric and leather had worn through. The dealer agreed to have that repaired at a nearby upholstery shop. All I needed to do was make an appointment and have the work done.

The deal was struck. I had my first car. Proudly, I drove it home, showed it to my mother and drove it over to Barbara Kolb's house to

show it off there. She also attended Western Michigan University and lived in a dorm on the east campus. My dorm was on the west campus. No more would I have to walk the one-mile distance between my dorm and hers. And, we now also had convenient transportation between campus and home.

I worked hard at detailing that car and kept it looking really sharp. Its slow performance made it a less than exhilarating drive, but it got me where I needed to go throughout the next summer. As part of the pulp and paper technology degree program I was enrolled in, I was assigned a summer job at Kalamazoo Paper Company. I lived at home all summer and drove back and forth to Kalamazoo every day. Traveling the same route on a constant schedule put me at a particular stoplight a short distance from the paper mill at about the same time each morning. Often, a fellow driving a tiny DKW sedan pulled up beside me at that stoplight. The DKW was a small car built in West Germany that had a motorcycle derived, three-cylinder, two-cycle engine. It produced between 40 and 50 horsepower, and had an automatic clutch style transmission, not unlike the one on my old Cushman scooter. My car had a 117 horsepower flat head six, coupled with a two-speed automatic "Fluid Drive" transmission. When the light changed, we both "floored it." With engines racing and blue smoke pouring out of the DKW tailpipe, their automatic drive trains spooled up and got us underway. His smoked due to its two-cycle oil burning engine. Our contest only lasted for a block or two, but invariably he beat me. At the time, I didn't know that in Europe, those light-weight little cars were considered quite sporty. They frequently won competitions over there.

Sadly, my first ride ended abruptly the next winter. One evening while returning to my dorm (Ellsworth Hall), after taking a Bridge lesson with Barbara at her dorm (Spindler Hall), there had been a fresh snowfall. Plows were out clearing the streets. As I approached my dorm, a city snowplow pulled out from a side street right in front of me. I had no place to go and couldn't stop in time. I "T-boned" the plow truck right behind the cab. With its dump body full of sand, I don't believe I moved that truck much, but the collision totaled my Plymouth. The back of my front seat broke off, sending me into the back seat with the steering wheel horn rim dangling from my neck. The sharp metal from the horn rim cut my chin. I needed stitches. I was taken to the hospital for treatment and returned to my dorm through the courtesy of the Kalamazoo Police Department. Of course, my next duty was to call home and report my misfortune. Dad answered the phone. When I told him what had happened, he said, "Oh no, not you too?" Then he explained that Mother had rear-ended an Edsel with the DeSoto earlier that same evening. Even over the phone, I could visualize his quiet nodding.

Chapter 11

Coming of Age

As important as getting our drivers license was to our coming of age, that process began decades earlier while we were all, as the title and lyrics from a song in the show *Annie Get Your Gun,* (Irving Berlin, Dorothy and Herbert Fields) says, *"Doin' What Comes Natur'lly."*

In spite of all our parents taught us, one thing that didn't occur often within families in those days was "the talk." We were pretty much left on our own to discover details regarding human anatomy, reproduction, and sexuality. In about the fourth or fifth grade, differences between boys and girls and the nature of relationships between them, became of interest to us. Awareness varied among individuals. I was one of the slower ones in this regard. Our discussions of or references to these things occurred mostly between peers within gender segregated groups. Boys only talked about it to boys, and girls to girls.

A Walk in the Rain
Partial awareness came to me suddenly one rainy, spring, fourth grade, morning. Mary Drake lived one block from me. She was one of the neighborhood kids that were all growing up together. We had been pals since our earliest memories, played games in each other's yards, attended each other's birthday parties, and chummed around together in school. Except for stereotypical differing interests in those days, physiological differences between boys and girls were not much on our minds. We didn't understand why our parents became hysterical if they caught us adolescents playing "doctor." As we grew older this began to

change, especially within expanded circles that school attendance provided.

To get to school in the early days, I walked one block down Chestnut Street beside our house, crossed busy Washington Street, continued one more block to Canaris Street, then turned to walk the final block north to the school building. Mary lived at the corner of Washington and Chestnut Streets. She often came out of her stately, large, white house with wraparound front porch just as I was passing by. We walked the rest of the way together. On one particular day it was raining when I left home. My mother handed me an umbrella as I headed out the door. Passing Mary's house, she came out in a bright yellow raincoat and hat but had no umbrella. As we walked, I shared my umbrella with her. Neither of us realized it was a bit later than usual. Leisurely, we walked and talked in the rain.

When we arrived, our class members were already seated at their desks and the day's lessons were about to begin. As we entered the classroom door, fellow classmates started laughing and chanting "Hubba, hubba," and "Ooh la la, ooh la la." Watching our stroll through the classroom window, they saw it as something romantic. I had no clue and was just trying to be nice, shielding Mary from the rain. Later in the day, during recess out on the playground assembled in our segregated boy-girl groups, we both faced more teasing and questions about our relationship. Slowly, for me at least, the light bulb in my mind began to glow. I began to understand what the fuss was about.

Always good friends, Mary and I never dated. In fact, her parents (especially her father) were quite strict in that regard. She was not allowed to date until she was 16 years old. It wasn't until our senior class train trip to New York city that Mary really came out of her shell. She had a _really_ good time. All through school she worked hard, studied continuously, and became Valedictorian of our class. But once we were on that train, all bets were off.

Teacher's Pets

Our grade school classrooms had large black, slate chalkboards that filled the front wall. Teachers and, when called forward, students used long white sticks of chalk to demonstrate penmanship or write math problems on the blackboards. When finished, we erased our work using thick felt erasers. This wiped markings off the board but left a film of chalk dust behind. About once per week, our teachers decided it was time to wash the blackboards. Each classroom was provided with a metal bowl and cotton cloth to use for this purpose. Those students that had grown tall enough to reach the upper blackboard areas were recruited to perform the task. We were also asked to clean the erasers. These activities were often split between genders. A couple of the boys were selected to go outside with the erasers and slap them together to knock the chalk dust out of them. We were given strict instructions not to pound the erasers against school building brick walls. That left a messy chalk dust splotch on the building. The girls took the bowl to their washroom, filled it with water, then returned and used the cleaning cloth to wash down the board.

When wetted, the blackboard became a reflective mirror. It was never really established, but to boys sitting back in their seats watching, it appeared as though the girls were looking themselves over rather thoroughly as they worked. We concluded they were checking out their body shapes, which by this time were starting to develop. Whether they were or not, we boys certainly were. During schoolyard discussions we boys concluded that the girls with the more fully developed shapes always volunteered to wash the board. It seemed to us that girls with less to look at, or display to boys in the back rows, usually didn't raise their hands when the teacher asked for board washing volunteers.

One day, testing the theory, a couple of the most forward boys stepped up and asked a group of girls that didn't often volunteer whether or not this was true. They replied, "No, of course not, the girls who always raise their hands are just trying to be teacher's pets." Nonetheless, boys were beginning to notice girls, *"Just Doin' What Comes Natur'lly."*

The Underground Library

Gatherings of us adventure seekers in the tall grass vacant lot hut next to Tony Witek's house began to wane as our physical size increased. But in later days, the storehouse of literature appearing there began to change. No one seemed to know, or admit to, where the "girlie magazines" came from. They just showed up. In addition, now and then, small pocket sized "eight-page bibles," as they were called, surfaced and circulated among the pack. One in particular portrayed "Popeye the Sailor Man" exploring his own anatomy and graphically described his exploits with "Olive Oil". They were handed off from person to person. No one wanted to keep them very long for fear of being caught with one and having to explain where it came from. One day, a member of the group handed the "Popeye" book to me. I didn't want to take it, but the bearer insisted that I had no alternative. It was simply thrust at me. I shoved it into my jeans pocket and tried to figure out how and where I would get rid of it. Since I was the last of the group to see it, there was no easy target for the hand-off. What was I to do? I left it in my pocket and took it with me the next day when my family traveled over to southeast Michigan to visit relatives. When I gathered with my boy cousins out in the cow barn, I showed the book to them and tried to get one of them to take it. No one would do so.

It turned out that I became ill the next day, a Monday, stayed home from school, and lay in bed nursing a cold. The night before, I had taken off my jeans and left them lying on the bedroom floor. I had forgotten all about the little book. When my mother came into my room, she picked them up and took them out to the wash. Checking my pockets, she came across the booklet. She burst into my room asking, "What is this? Where did it come from?" She demanded details. I didn't admit that it came from the hut or name those gathered there. I said, "It was handed to me at school." I added that I didn't want it and was trying to figure out how to get rid of it. She said, "I'll get rid of it," then clomped down the basement stairs, opened the door to the blazing coal fired furnace heating the house, and threw it in. Little more was said. I was admonished not to ever bring anything like that into the house again or show anything like that to my sister!

Down by the Riverside and Boy Scout Trips
It was a mixed age group of boys who gathered, unsupervised, to fish down on the riverbank. The older, wiser, and more experienced fellas were eager to share knowledge on topics not suitable for discussion in supervised or more formal settings. Mixed boy-girl relationships were a favored one.

Likewise, Boy Scout outings became venues for free expression of thoughts or questions coming to pubescent minds. Through some magic, the older boys seemed to have acquired knowledge about why their bodies had changed and just what that meant when they looked at girls. They also expounded on their understanding of changes that had occurred within girls' bodies, including those not visible on the outside. Support for these conversations was provided, in part, by circulation of literature between tents. While comic books were still primary volumes passed between scouts, some turned out to be "girlie magazines." The origins were never fully identified, and they could be quickly absconded by our leaders, thereby enhancing interest in them.

The younger members of the group wondered if any or all of this information was true and asked lots of questions. The "experts" were pleased to answer. "They do what, with what, where?" we asked. For some of us, these questions would not be more completely answered until we sat through brief discussions regarding human anatomy in junior high level general science classes.

Our riverbank fishing trips became a "classroom" setup for additional "ad hoc" lessons. The area directly beneath the Washington Street bridge was a convenient place for small groups to gather. Between the bridge abutment and the edge of the river, the sloping gravel floor provided on the ground theater style seating for observers. Lecturers stood at the water's edge to make presentations. These were older fellas who professed to have had personal sexual experiences. Sometimes their descriptions of exploits became quite graphic. Some included specific mention of willing female partners. Most of the time, audience members left these "presentations" wondering about their authenticity. But in a couple of cases, the evidence later became obvious in the form of teenage pregnancies.

School Dances

A major milestone in boy-girl relationships occurred when we entered seventh grade. We were eligible to attend Friday night school dances. The first of the new school year occurred shortly after school started in September. It was the annual "Get Acquainted Dance" held in the gymnasium and was a really big deal. We all had to go if we were going to place well within the school social structure. And we had to form a group we would "go with," we couldn't just show up on our own. For the younger crowd it wasn't a dating situation. Most of us hadn't yet reached that level of sophistication. Separate groups of guys and gals arranged to meet at the event and take it from there.

We also had to decide what we would wear. This was just as important for the boys as it was the girls. School colors were red and white. So, a red pull-over sweater or, for the more suave, a red sweater vest over a white shirt would work. Of course, we wouldn't wear jeans. It had to be dress pants or khakis. Girls had a wider variety of choices, but it had to be a skirt or dress, no pants, and "bobby sox" were important, especially when paired with black and white saddle shoes. From these basics, the more adventuresome, and perhaps those with cooperative parents, could venture into super-style territories. Macho guys picked up on trends that included white bucks and pink shirts or sweaters! Girls could go with frilly white blouses and "poodle skirts," often topped off with a cardigan sweater. The number of attendees showing up wearing trendy styles varied. Older students sported more of these than junior high folks. In total, it was a growth experience, one where we watched boy-girl relationships develop. The primary objective of attendance and attention to styles was to be noticed by the opposite gender.

After arrival and assembling with peers, first dances were awkward for us. What were we supposed to do? Who would we ask to dance? How would we go about that? No one knew for sure. Small groups of guys and gals stood in separate circles around the perimeter of the room, gibber jabbering and watching older members of the crowd dance out on the floor. Then, the MC (Master of Ceremonies), generally an older high school student and most likely a member of the Student Council, called for a "traffic dance."

Ah, here was our chance. The girls formed a large circle in the middle of the floor. The boys formed a second circle, outside the first. While the music played the two circles revolved, girls to the left, boys to the right. After a revolution or two, the MC blew a whistle, stopping the circles. Whomever we stood in front of in the opposite circle became our dance partner. That made it easy. We didn't have to ask anyone to dance. We just started off with whomever we had been paired with. It could even be an older student, someone more experienced who could give pointers on how to dance. It was also helpful If our partner was a person we really wanted to ask to dance but found that hard to do. That was a real bonus. Alternatively, if it turned out to be someone we would not have wanted to dance with, we learned how to be polite, go with the flow, and maybe learn something about that person we didn't know. Whatever the outcome, it didn't last long. Before the song was over, the MC again blew the whistle, couples separated, rejoined their circles, and another round began. The next whistle brought new partners together. We danced with two or three different partners during each song played.

As the evening wore on, fewer traffic dances were called. Groups of couples danced on the dimly lighted floor or gathered among sets of chairs that ringed the room, some in the darkest corners. By walking the room perimeter, we could see who had paired up with who and check up on what they were doing back in the shadows. Teachers chaperoning the event patrolled the dark areas, stopping to talk with groups or pairs that were getting too serious or involved with each other.

Getting the Styles Right

One of the first members of my circle to sport latest style trends was Jim Smith. He came to dances and sometimes to class dressed in his pink sweater vest over a white shirt, khakis, and white buck shoes. He always looked sharp and was very self-assured. I wanted to make sure I fit in with the crowd and pressured my mother into letting me get some white bucks. Once she agreed, the problem was my very wide feet. As usual, when I went shoe shopping the one pair of EEE's the store had was not likely to be a pair of white bucks. As we visited shoe stores in both Elkhart and South Bend, Indiana, it looked as though this was going to be the case. Mother was ready to quit, saying, "We tried." But I was determined. I insisted "Let's try just one more store." That one worked. We finally came up with a pair.

These suede, supposedly buckskin (hence the word "bucks") shoes looked sharp when kept clean, but it didn't take much to soil them. They came with a small cloth packet of white chalky powder packed right in the box. When dirt or some other black smudge appeared on the shoe, we took the packet of powder out of our pocket and tamped it on the smudge to cover it up. Brushing the suede with a soft brass wire brush and working over stubborn soils with gum-rubber erasers was also required to keep the shoes looking somewhat clean. We thought it worth the effort and were willing to do whatever it took to attract the attention of the girls.

Another trend was hairstyles. It wasn't just the girls who put effort into making or keeping hairstyles in tune with trends. Some boys also worked to make statements through coiffures. A few appeared to want to be known as tough guys. They grew out the sides and backs of their hair, greased it down, and combed it back into what was termed a DA, short for "duck's ass." Tight jeans, white T-shirts, and black vests completed the "look." Outside of the school building, the hardcore rolled packs of cigarettes into the sleeves of their T-shirts. We called these fellows "hoods" and tried to ignore them. But we walked a fine line with that. We needed to avoid getting on the wrong side of them for fear of becoming one of their targets. It was a balancing act and lesson in how to try to get along with everyone.

The Jocks established their own hairstyle trend, the flat-top. They said they didn't want to have to stuff lots of hair into their thick leather football helmets, making them hot during warm sunny after-school practice sessions. When off the field, sitting in classrooms, walking the halls, and certainly at the dances, it gave them an identity intended to attract girls. I wore traditional hair styles but was really particular about my choice of hair dressing. My father used Red Rose Hair Oil. I liked the smell of it, but thought it made my hair look too greasy. I chose Wild Root Cream Oil. If I was careful to not use too much, I could keep my hair in place without a greasy appearance.

Getting the Music Right

Choice of music played at school dances was of interest to both students and chaperones. The rock and roll music era had just begun. There were mixed opinions about this new style and certainly how to dance to it. Variations between slow tunes and faster, louder rock tunes produced differing reactions on the dance floor. Some moves drew attention. The kids liked them, but chaperones shut them down. Elvis, with his "swivel hips" had just come onto the scene. His moves were highly controversial. During one dance, a group of kids from Three Rivers brought a record they asked the DJ to play. They took over the dance floor and demonstrated something called "The Dirty Chicken Dance." Local kids crowded around. We hadn't seen that before and didn't get to see much this time. With its suggestive moves and lyrics, chaperones shut it down and escorted the visitors out of the building.

On another occasion, I thought the music played was leaning too heavily towards rock and roll. I loved big band music and collected recordings made by the big band greats. Harry James was one of my heroes. I strived to produce the sweet sounds that came from his trumpet. I also collected records produced by Buddy Morrow, Les Brown and His Band of Renown, Benny Goodman, Les and Larry Elgart, and king of the genre Glenn Miller. I suggested the DJ play some of these tunes. He said he didn't have any among his records. I walked home and brought back my soundtrack album from the *The Glenn Miller Story* movie (Universal-International). The DJ was annoyed but played two or three of those. The Chaperones loved it. The kids, not so much. I was not invited to bring it back and certainly not asked to serve as dance DJ.

Follow-up to a Night Out

Postmortem sessions following each dance were important for comparing results, assessing experiences, and plotting next moves. Groups, often segregated by gender, gathered briefly outside the school building to rehash evening events before walking home. Girls discussed who danced with whom and how many times. Older boys were more likely to brag about feelings of arousal that occurred while dancing with certain young ladies.

However, a more detailed review occurred the next morning in mixed boy/girl groups gathered at Armstrong's drug store. There, among the booths and tables at the back of the soda parlor, the entire evening was fully analyzed. Once I gave up my paper routes, I worked most Saturday mornings at the dime store. One of my closest confidantes on these topics was Tom Flatland. When heading up to Armstrong's to join the group, he usually stopped to check in with me. We shared personal experiences that occurred the previous evening, then moved on to Armstrong's together to capture broader assessment views.

Generally, we listened more than we talked. There were some things that didn't need to be discussed with the group at large. But as the beat wore on, the information collected was carefully filed away in our minds suggesting whose attention we might try to attract at the next dance.

Fishing Trip or Spring Dance – What a Dilemma

My dad loved taking me with him on his hunting and fishing trips. I loved spending time with him and appreciated the opportunities that these outings provided. However, of all of the things we did together, fishing was the one I liked least. Dad could spend hours sitting in his boat quietly fishing in all sorts of modes. He used long cane poles with simple long monofilament lines attached to the end, a bobber affixed to the line about six feet from the end of the pole, a hook tied to the end of the line, and a big fish-tempting juicy worm neatly threaded over the hook. While waiting for a sunfish, bluegill or perch to bite on this set up, he hooked a casting plug onto the end of a casting rod line and tossed it way out into the water, then slowly cranked it in, using his favorite Shakespeare reel. He hoped to hook a largemouth or smallmouth bass during retrieval. When the new spinning rods and reels came along, he had yet another tool to use during his favorite pastime. Occasionally, when conditions were just right, Dad also assembled his Heddon Pal split bamboo flyrod and made a few fly-fishing casts out onto quiet waters. He loved the action associated with carefully pulling in and netting a fish of any species that grabbed his dry fly.

Though I wasn't very good at it (I experienced a lot of tangled lines and casting "backlashes"), I found the action associated with casting or fly fishing more interesting. I enjoyed catching an occasional fish, but mostly, I liked the boat rides out to and back from the fishing spots best. Overall, I found the time spent sitting in the boat waiting for action boring. There was a lot of that.

Each year, Dad considered the last Saturday in April a holiday. It was opening day of the Michigan trout fishing season. On this day, he needed to be standing out next to, or in, a small stream somewhere, fishing for trout with his flyrod. There were a few local "trout streams" in undeveloped areas near our town. But the ones of most interest were up in the northern, heavily wooded areas of the state. Dad and fishing buddy, neighbor, and School Superintendent Clarence R. Lubbers (CR) arranged annual outings to the north woods, near Petosky, Michigan, searching for productive trout streams.

CR and Dad began planning these trips in February. By the time I was old enough to join the outings, CR had left Constantine to become school Superintendent in Lawrence, Michigan, about 45 miles to our northwest. Though he had moved, the two of them continued to plan and take their end of April trips. Planning was intense. It included map reading exercises to decide where to fish and where to stay, listing food provisions to take along, inventorying fishing gear needed, and work sessions to tie fly line leaders and select the varieties of wet and dry flies they would use. Some they bought, some they tied themselves.

I made two of these trips with them. The agenda included packing the station wagon with all imaginable forms of potentially needed gear, leaving town on Friday evening right after supper, and driving through the night to arrive at the first fishing site before dawn. We napped in the car until sunup then headed out to the stream to start fishing. We fished until mid-morning then took a break for brunch at the nearest diner. For Dad and CR, the break was as much about contacting locals and quizzing them about best fishing opportunities as it was eating. For me, it was about getting out of the woods into some place warm, being able to sit down, and finding some warm food.

When finished, other fishing locations were explored, and a place selected for late afternoon/evening fishing. We finally came out of the woods at dark and sought overnight accommodations. On the next day, Sunday, we were up and out fishing by dawn, fished until mid-day, then began the trip home. In all that time at the water's edge, we may have caught a few trout. Dad and CR caught many more than I did. I spent a fair amount of time untangling my fly line from overhanging tree branches.

I enjoyed the comradery and loved listening to the tales and conversations between the two sportsmen. CR, in particular, provided lots of interesting stories, talked to his fishing gear often, and kept things from getting totally boring. Dad was ever so pleased and proud to have me along and show me the ways of the outback. But I had thoughts running through my head about what was going on back home amongst my peers. There were things I was missing. <u>And,</u> this time of year was also the weekend for our school's annual Spring Ball.

It was during early March of my sophomore year that annual trout fishing trip preparations and school buzz regarding the upcoming Spring Ball collided head-on. The ball was a big deal. For the boys, it was a chance to exercise manly roles and ask girls for a date to that special event. It also gave them opportunities to demonstrate prowess to peers by wooing desirable date candidates. It was a major steppingstone towards attending the Junior-Senior Prom in coming years. For the girls, it was important to be asked. The anticipation or desirability of that invite stretched downward into older junior high girl ranks. Boys often asked younger girls to be their dates.

I was truly torn. My peers were egging me on, urging me to ask a girl to the ball. My dad had been talking up plans for the fishing trip for weeks. But there was one young lady who, though still in eighth grade, was very attractive, played clarinet in the high school band, and had an air of maturity about her that I had noticed.

Her name was Connie Brown. Mary Mann, older than I by one year, worked in the dime store after school. She was a real good friend of Connie's and told me that Connie had become interested in me. I had started to pay some attention to her on band trips and received positive vibes in return. Once I admitted these interests to my peers, they really began pressuring me to ask her to the ball. They pointed out that if I didn't do it, certainly someone else would. I would be left behind. In addition, Mary Mann was working behind the scenes, serving as matchmaker.

One Friday when band period had ended, we were putting instruments away before heading out the door for lunch. I worked up my courage, stepped forward, and asked Connie to the dance. She smiled, tried to look surprised, and quickly replied, "Oh, I'd love to, but I'll have to ask my mother first." I was elated. I had finally found the courage to ask and could report to my peers that I had done so. That would get them off my back. I walked home for lunch with a feeling of satisfaction, but also troubled by how I would break the news to my father that I would not going on the fishing trip. Then I thought, "Oh well, she has to ask her mother. Maybe her mother will say no and that will end it." I had a weekend before I was likely to find out, so I went on about my business, preferring to deal with the issue later.

On Monday, when we gathered for band at the start of fourth period, I paid close attention to the clarinet section. Connie arrived, took her seat, removed her instrument from its case, then looked over at me, flashing a smile. I smiled back but felt a knot in my stomach. "Does this mean yes?" I wondered. If so, my life had suddenly become quite complicated.

Band period seemed a lot longer that day. When I approached Connie at the end of the period, she immediately said, "My mother said I could go, but we have to walk. She said no cars were to be involved." I said, "That's not a problem, I don't have a license yet." As I walked home alone for lunch, I agonized over how I was going to break the news to my dad. As I entered the house and took my seat at the table, Dad was just finishing his lunch and getting up to head back to the store. He needed to be there during the onslaught of school kids who crowded into the store during the lunch period.

Since our school building had no lunchroom, students either took their lunch to school or walked home and back in that one-hour period. Older students, especially the out-of-town ones, often walked downtown, grabbed a Coke and bag of chips at Armstrong's, or visited the candy counter at the dime store before walking back. To accommodate all of this, Dad and Mom came home early, had a quick lunch, then headed back to tend the mob. My sister and I finished our lunch quickly and after cleaning up the kitchen table, headed back to school. Since I didn't have time to deal with "my issue" during the brief period when everyone was together, I decided to let things slide until later.

When I let my friends know of my success in securing the date, I confided in them that I had created a real conflict for myself. They were glad this dilemma was my problem not theirs and went on lining up their own dates for the ball.

Several days later, as I was sitting in the kitchen rocking chair, I said to Mother, "I have a problem." She asked what it was. I said,

"I invited Connie Brown to go to the Spring Ball and it's on the same weekend as Dad's fishing trip." She, paused, nodded and said, "You do have a problem, don't you?" Then she added, "You're going to have to tell your father, I'm not going to do it for you." I nodded and we agreed she wouldn't say anything to him about it. It was all on my shoulders.

The days ticked by. I spent after-school hours at the dime store performing my usual Vice President of the Broom tasks. Every time I had a chance to talk privately with my dad about "my issue," I chickened out at the last moment and found some other topic to talk about. When I got home at the end of the day my mother asked, "Did you tell him yet?" I just shook my head no and went on to other things. After several days she said, "Time is getting short, you need to be telling him." I nodded and vowed to do so soon. The next day while I was sweeping prior to store closing, Dad came in the front door. He had been over to Smith Hardware looking at fishing tackle. As he came in, he was smiling and waving a small box held in his hand. Proudly, he said "I thought you needed a new flyrod reel for the fishing trip. I think this will be a good one." I quickly stopped in my tracks. There it was, I couldn't avoid it any longer, I had to tell him. I stuttered and said, 'Ugh, I can't go on the fishing trip." He looked shocked and asked, "Why not?" I said, "I've asked Connie Brown to go to the Spring Ball." He didn't know what to say. He walked on to the back of the store, and I finished sweeping. It was a quiet ride home that night. When we got out of the car and went into the house, Dad said to my mother, "He's not going fishing with us." She smiled and said, "I know."

That was pretty much the end of the discussion. Mother said later that she and Dad talked about it and she explained to him that I had grown up. He agreed it was inevitable. A few days later, when Dad packed his gear and headed off to pick up CR, I had mixed feelings. I hated that I had let him down and was admittedly going to miss the comradery. And though I was quite nervous about successfully pulling off my first date, I was really looking forward to attending the big event with my friends.

As I made preparations, Mother was most helpful. She helped me pick out the shirt and tie I would wear, reminded me of all the polite things I was to do while escorting my date to the function. She gave me tips on how to, or how not to, dance. When the time came, I walked the several blocks to Connie's house on Centerville Road. I had delivered their newspapers and knew the neighborhood and her family well. Her father, Pete, drove a local fuel delivery truck and was the one who had once rescued me when I ran out of gas while riding my Cushman scooter on country roads.

Dressed in my light blue flecked wool flannel suit, I arrived with a Valjon's corsage. Connie met me in a flowing ball gown. After conversations with her parents, we started our walk to the school building and the Spring Ball. We walked the few blocks down Centerville Road to Washington Street then turned towards the school. As we walked past Washington Park, Jim Smith and his date, Judy Milhahn, drove up in the charcoal and coral, '55 Chevy hardtop, with all windows rolled down. They asked if we would like a ride. We remembered the no cars rule, but the glamor of the moment was overwhelming. We got into the back seat and off we went, arriving at the school dance in great style. We made quite the picture, the four of us dressed up in our finery stepping out of that immaculately detailed car. The only thing missing was a red carpet leading up to the school building front entrance.

The evening went well. I was proud to have escorted this attractive young lady to the dance. Given the "no cars" rule we walked home. Following this first date, Connie and I had a couple more during the early part of that summer. I walked to her house, and we walked to the Park Theater to take in a movie. When cruising around town on my Cushman scooter, I often drove up Centerville Road to see if I could catch a glimpse of her when I passed her house. If she was sitting on her front porch, I stopped to chat. She had a small record player set up out there and was into the latest pop music craze, rock and roll. She liked Elvis and listened to other emerging artists, including Bill Haley and the Comets. She was anxious to play her latest 45 rpm records for me. Her friend Mary Mann was a serious piano student. Mary and I both liked classical music and thought Connie should as well. We conspired to try and convert Connie but were unsuccessful.

It was later in that summer that Dad hired Dave Daughtery and me to paint our garage. Once we took the Cushman Scooter newspaper delivery ride over to the newly arrived Kolb family's house, I focused my attention on 125 Cherry Street, Barbara Kolb's house from then on.

Party Times OK – but Keep the Lights On

In our older teen years, we were driving, and outings or get togethers were always mixed boy-girl events. The Congregational, Methodist, and Lutheran Church youth groups held joint events. We went to movies and enjoyed skating nights or bowling parties in nearby communities. Couples often emerged from or were previously established between these groups. Birthday parties and other gatherings were held in our homes. All of this provided additional intermingling of mixed age/gender folks. A few homes emerged as frequent popular assembly points for groups to gather. We knew we could count on someone often being at these places and stopped by. One was the Dudd family home at the corner of south Washington and East fourth Street. Class member Becky was a popular outgoing but serious student, talented in many ways. She organized things in an instant. She had two sisters and a brother, all younger than she. Her sister, Jackie, two years younger, was also very outgoing and a bit more high-spirited. Both liked to socialize. Between the two of them, there was always something going on at the Dudd home. A nice finished basement room complete with fireplace was a nice gathering place. They also had a second popular place. Their father, Harmon Dudd, owned and operated the marina at nearby Klinger Lake. Gatherings on the beach complete with bonfires were popular. Across the lake, the Bush family's year-round home also provided a nice spot for outings. Swimming parties in summer and ice-skating events in winter were well attended.

For the most part, these events were chaperoned by parents who kept their distance from the masses but checked often to see that lights were left on, and boy-girl pairings didn't get too close or comfy. Nonetheless, hormones were working, and steamy relationships sometimes developed. The proof was the one or two teenage pregnancies that occurred each year among our 200-student high school population. These always resulted in community-wide debates over whether or not the students involved were to be allowed to stay in school or would be expelled. School officials did not want pregnant girls walking the halls or sitting in classes, fearing it would prompt a wide-spread student body epidemic. Nor did they want to publicly talk about the situation. Often, the girls, and sometimes the boys involved, were quietly sent to schools in neighboring communities to finish high school careers.

The presence of parental supervision didn't make our gatherings quiet affairs devoid of high-spirited action. Boys will be boys and mischievous activities, including some by girls, frequently occurred. A popular perk associated with parties at the Dudd marina were the Chris-Craft boats Harmon sold. He always kept an inventory of sleek and powerful beauties tied to his dock. Becky offered to take groups of three or four out for rides. She knew how to make those boats perform. Sharp turns and quick starts/stops were her specialty. Those rides thrilled the adventuresome and scared the daylights out of the timid. I was always relieved when we returned to the dock after her thrill rides. I thought for sure the tall wall of water she could raise up alongside the boat during one of her speedy sideslipped turns would come crashing down into the cockpit swamping us. I was only a so-so swimmer, and of course we never wore life vests.

On one such outing, I took a load of kids out to the marina in Dad's station wagon. On arrival, I parked across the road from the marina, we all exited the car and the party began. No one thought of locking parked cars in those days. As the group was breaking up and gathered to get paired with rides home, I noticed that several folks were hanging back waiting for me to get loaded and back on the road. I wasn't blocking other cars, so that didn't make sense. I dismissed it, nonetheless. I started the car and off we went. I hadn't gone far when I noticed that the car wasn't running very well. Snickers and jeers came my way as I drove on. The engine kept going even though it sputtered quite a lot. I began to wonder if we would get home, especially when we had to climb a hill. However, I got back into town and dropped my passengers at their homes. After pulling into the garage, I went into the house and reported that there was something wrong with the car. "It isn't running right," I told Dad. He got up out of his easy chair and went out to check. Confirming the rough running he opened the hood to take a look, something I had not done. There, dangling from one of the spark plugs was a car bomb that someone had installed while I was at the party. It had failed to go off and create the smoke and noise that these devices were designed to produce. Dad unhooked it and the car ran fine.

I was elated. On that occasion, perpetrators of a prank pulled, as usual at my expense, had been disappointed. Their scheme failed and I won that round. I was not able to get anyone to tell me who put it there. It just became one of the tales that circulated about what had gone on at the latest gathering of the gang.

Other Vices, Alcohol and Cigarettes
Alcohol was not a big part of our small-town adventures but did hang in the background. Most of our parents were at least moderate drinkers, held adult parties where alcohol was served, and kept a stockpile of beer, wine, and cocktail components on hand. Our teenage group sometimes held impromptu gatherings at one of our homes when parents were not present. Curiosity being what it was, the teen host provided a peek at whatever liquor was available in kitchen cupboards or tucked away in "secret," out of the way places. Some sampling or consumption occurred, but mostly only by the bolder members of the group. It was a "Hey watch this," experience that gave some folks an opportunity to boast about experimentation and exaggerated outcomes.

The nearby state of Ohio made 3.2 percent alcohol content beer available to anyone 18 years old. The Ohio boarder was just a one-hour drive away. Some schoolmates boasted of teaming up with upper-classmen and making runs to border communities. There they could either buy 3.2 beer for later consumption, or boldly sit down in a bar and "order a few," so they claimed. After-the-fact boasting may have been a bigger part of the experience than the actual drinking. For those seeking the attention, it worked. However, there were consequences for getting caught drinking underaged. Perpetrators were black-balled and banned from parent organized events, and punishments such as being barred from high school sports teams or other events, including graduation exercises, kept all but the most rambunctious on their toes, blunting some activity in this area. It wasn't until our senior trip that much of this took place.

The same was the case with smoking. Though there had been some experimentation, serious cigarette smoking was pretty much left to "the hoods." They strutted outside the school building proudly displaying their rolled-up T-shirt sleeve cigarette packs. Those engaged in athletics were ineligible if caught smoking.

In our preteen days some experimentation occurred when we tried to "roll your own" smokes from corn silks and toilet paper. Riding around town on our bicycles on a late-summer afternoon, someone in the group came up with the idea of smoking corn silks. Not wanting to get "caught in the act," we set off on an out-of-town mission for the occasion. The chosen venue was a cornfield about 3 miles out of town alongside U.S. 131 (the main highway to Three Rivers), near the base of the "Big Hill." We got there by riding out Centerville Road past the edge of town. We turned onto Constantine Street, rode to Withers Road, then peddled onward across the St. Joseph River to the cornfield at the intersection of highway 131. It was not clear why we had to go so far out of town. We passed other cornfields on the way. Nonetheless, we followed the leader. My assignment was to bring the toilet paper. Arriving at the cornfield, we laid our bicycles down in the tall grass, gathered under a big maple tree at the edge of the field, and two or three members of the group went into the field to collect silks from ripening corn ears. They distributed large handfuls to each of us. I distributed strips of toilet paper from the collapsed roll I had sneaked out of the house. Our ringleader, experienced in this area, described how to tightly compact the silks then roll them into homemade cigars. Another participant provided matches, distributing several strike-anywhere "firesticks" to each of us. We struck them against the rough bark of the big maple tree and tried lighting our newly minted cigars. After using several matches, a few members of the group claimed success. No clouds of smoke were produced in the process, and it was questionable whether any of the "cigars" actually became lighted. But we laid in the tall grass pretending to be smoking and swapped stories about other smoking experiences we had tried. I didn't have much experience to relate. I could only boast about how many packs of Camels my grandfather could go through in a day. I didn't find any reason to roll a second cornsilk cigar, as some did. As we left, they took them along for future consumption.

Smoking was pretty much a social norm for adults in those days. My father smoked both a pipe and cigars. Mother didn't like smoking but for a short time tried cigarettes in social settings. My sister and I laughed at her when she tried lighting up during Sunday afternoon restaurant outings. We said, "You don't know how to do it," as she awkwardly held the cigarette she tried to smoke. We had learned the correct techniques from cigarette ads on our newly acquired television set. The Old Gold dancing cigarette pack ads were very popular.

Besides Camels, my grandfather on Dad's side of the family chain-smoked other heavy-duty brands such as Chesterfields and Lucky Strikes. At Christmastime when shopping for gifts, I headed to the A&P to buy a carton for Grandpa. The clerk willingly sold it to me, understanding and believing the story I was buying it for Grandpa. But Dad, willing to let me buy them for him, always counseled me to "never start smoking cigarettes." "Otherwise," he said, "You'll end up hooked on them just like he is. He can't sleep through the night without getting up and having to smoke before going back to bed." I had witnessed that myself. When staying at my grandparents' house overnight, I was always awakened about two or three o'clock in the morning by Grandpa going out on the front porch to light up. I took my father's admonishment as good advice and never became a smoker. The cornsilk smoking adventure didn't encourage me to go much further in that direction. Later, as an adult, I submitted to social pressures and tried an occasional cigar. But that always left a bad taste in my mouth, making me regret or brush off the experience as one I didn't wish to repeat.

The Senior Trip

As was customary in those days, right after graduation, our senior class headed off on a class trip. During our junior year, we had chosen New York City as our destination. A travel agency in Elkhart made all the arrangements. We had earned much of the money to pay for the trip through class fund-raising events held since our freshman year. We sold school calendars, operated the concession stand at football games, and in our junior/senior years held community paper drives.

I served as organizer for paper drives. I sectioned the town into several areas on a map, then recruited groups of students to go door to door asking for donations of old magazines and newspapers. We piled collected wastepaper into car trunks and my dad's station wagon, then took it to the local paper mill to sell for a few dollars per ton. I liked organizing the events, driving around town to collect the paper, then hanging out at the paper mill when we delivered it. Our class fund raising efforts covered about half of our class trip expenses. We or our parents had to come up with the rest of the money.

Heading off on the adventure, we assembled at the White Pigeon railroad depot and awaited arrival of a New York Central passenger train. Two of our teachers and their spouses accompanied us as chaperones. It was evening when we boarded our private coach. There were no compartments or beds in our coach. We sat and slept in our seats. Our suitcases, one per passenger, were stowed in overhead racks above us. As we rode through a spirited night, not much sleep was had by anyone. Those expected to be the "live wires" of the group did not disappoint and provided many jovial moments. Chaperones broke up a poker game or two in the back of the coach. No money was to be placed on the table. Some typically calm or quiet individuals came out of their shells and acted out in surprising ways. Mary Drake was not the reserved Mary we all knew. On that train ride, she had a really good time.

On the second day, we stopped briefly at Niagara Falls, New York. Some "free time" was provided to walk to the falls and back. We counted off in groups of four or six and were to follow chaperones to the falls. Most complied, but returning to the coach, we learned that a group of adventuresome lads had planned ahead. Previous research revealed the New York State drinking age was 19. Figuring they "looked old enough," they diverted to a couple of bars instead of walking to the falls. Their fun had just begun.

We spent three days in New York City. Preassigned groups roomed together at our hotel. We toured the city on a private bus, visited attractions such as Times Square, Central Park, the Empire State Building, and the United Nations building where my father's movie camera I had taken along survived a drop on the plaza steps. I was impressed by the show we saw at Radio City Music Hall, the high-kicking Rockettes, and thrilled by the huge sound of the great theater organ.

We also had brief periods of free time. Some of us went for lunch at the Automat, a novel place where we could stick a few coins into various machines to buy sandwiches and other lunch items. (I was recently reminded of that rubbery food while having lunch at one of the New York JFK Airport automated restaurants.) Again, our "mature looking" fellas returned with stories detailing which or how many bars they had been seated in or were bounced from. Though I didn't participate and didn't want word to get back home that I had done so, I didn't want to be seen as the prude of the group either. I made sure I was present during story-telling time to laugh jovially when the exploits were described, trying to blend in as a background bad boy.

My real problem came during our long train ride home. We had been back on our private coach for several hours, again riding through the dark. Chaperones, seated in the front of the car, detected suspicious activity in the rear. Investigating, they confiscated a bottle of whisky. Thinking they hadn't retrieved the entire stash, they ordered everyone to get their suitcases down off the overhead racks and open them for inspection. Of course, my suitcase was "clean," but I wanted to be treated like everyone else. I proudly opened and displayed it on the seat next to me. The inspectors started at the back of the coach and worked their way forward. When they reached my seat, they waved me off saying "That's OK you can close it up." I was enraged. I wanted to be treated like everyone else. I insisted that the inspector check mine too. He did so but gave it a quick cursory look before heading off to check the next suspect. It was hard to shake loose from earned reputations. But some, like Mary, succeeded. Returning home and fully graduated, we dispersed into separate lives, some focused on following carefully planned paths, but some of us were just *"Doin' What Comes Natur'lly."*

Chapter 12

The School of Hard Knocks

The village of Constantine occupies just 1.8 square miles of space on the face of the earth. Today's footprint is nearly the same as it was during the 1940s - 1950s post WW II era. Village limits boundary signs still sit in nearly the same locations as they did back then. The population of the community at the time of the 1928 centennial celebration was listed as 1500, the same number as during the 1950s, and not markedly different from the 2018 census figure of 2020 residents. Some building facades and entire structures have changed. Outlying landscapes have become mega-farms rather than the individual family farms of the past. But, to those of us who grew up there, the area still "feels like home."

The community was Initially named Meeks Mills after the village founder. **Mr. Miles Smith** (who opened the first store) later convinced villagers (many reluctantly) to change it to Constantine. The date of the change is unclear. History recorded in the 1928 publication *Constantine Centennial, A Souvenir Program and History* states, "For a long time the place was known as Meeks Mills and the people nearby were loathe to give up the name for the new high-sounding name of Constantine." Also "No special reason can be given why this name was adopted….it may be that they thought Constantine would be, at some time Great…" A second account in Mary Jeanne Dowty's Western Michigan University 1967 Master's Degree Theses titled *A Geographic Interpretation of the Growth and Development of Constantine, Michigan,* suggested the town was named after an early resident who sold real estate.

I prefer the first. My generation, did consider living in Constantine as "great." During my school days, I sat in my classroom gazing at a geography book cover that pictured Roman ruins. I liked to think that our village name may have been chosen in deference to the Roman emperor **Constantine the Great.** Indeed, though the population and physical boundaries have not changed much, the references reviewed for this book show that people from or associated with the community have had influences far beyond the town's humble boarders. Many stretching all around the world.

Founders and Notables

The prairie lands that became St. Joseph County, Michigan were attractive to those traveling westward on the old Detroit to Chicago trail. When **William Meek** arrived in 1828, he was impressed by the area's waterpower potential and established a sawmill providing the impetus for community development. However, he didn't stay long. Moving further west in about 1835, he spearheaded development of a gristmill, sawmill, and woolen mill in the area that became Bonaparte, Iowa. Other entrepreneurs expanded Constantine's river-based trade, capitalizing on its suitable flat topography and port location near the end of navigable portions of the St. Joseph River. Additional mill developments followed. A notable but short termed partner in these endeavors was the famous statesman and orator **Daniel Webster**.

In 1831, **John S. Barry** moved westward from Vermont. After first dipping down into Atlanta, Georgia, he headed back north into the region and took up residence just south of Constantine in the area that became the village of White Pigeon. He moved to Constantine in 1834 and operated a general store in what was said to be the town's first frame-built building. Utilizing his law degree, he served as Justice of the Peace, was politically active, and participated in the 1835 convention that drafted Michigan's first constitution. He served as a state senator, winning elections in 1836 and 1840 and became Michigan's fourth Governor in 1841. He was re-elected in 1843. His popularity served him well and he occupied the office for the third time, as eighth Governor, in 1849. Two unsuccessful campaigns followed in 1854 and 1860, but this man from Constantine had made significant contributions to both the development of the village and the state of Michigan. His home on North Washington Street is listed on the National Register of Historical Places and now serves as a museum operated by the John S. Barry Historical Society.

Between 1832 and 1840, **John Judson Bagley** lived in Constantine. Born in New York, he had moved to the eastern side of the state of Michigan when he was 13 years old. On January 1, 1873, he became Michigan's 16th Governor.

Henry Hiram Riley became a lawyer in Constantine in 1842. He served as prosecuting attorney, and representative from the fourth district court for three terms. For many years he had been a contributor to the *Old Knickerbocker Magazine* where he presented his *"Puddleford Papers: or Humors of the West."* This volume survives today as a work "selected by scholars as being culturally important" and "part of the knowledge base of civilization as we know it."

Joseph R. Williams moved from Massachusetts to Constantine in 1839. He served as Michigan's Lieutenant Governor in 1861. He also served as the first President of the Michigan Agricultural College. That institution became Michigan State University. Williams lived in Constantine until his death from influenza in 1861.

Franklin Wells was an intensive farmer who lived near and in Constantine. In 1873, he was appointed to the Michigan State Board of Agriculture, a position he held for 30 years. Oversight and direction of Agricultural College of Michigan financial policy was one of his contributions.

Levi G. Hull was born in the state of New York, brought to eastern Michigan at age eight, became orphaned, was self-educated, and apprenticed in the printing trade. He brought the first newspaper to the village in 1851 and was a long-term editor of the *Advertiser Record*. An active founder of the Michigan Republican Party, he also served as a member of the Michigan State Constitutional Commission in 1867. Other offices held by him included township clerk, justice of the peace, county agent, collector of internal revenue and a member of the state legislature.

Edwin W. Keightly moved to Constantine in 1867, becoming a law partner with **Judge S. C.** Coffinberry. He was appointed Judge of the 15th Circuit Court of Michigan, was elected to the 45th U.S. Congress, and appointed as the third Auditor of the United States Treasury Department by President Rutherford B. Hayes.

Frank Dwight Baldwin, a resident of Constantine, served in the 19th Michigan Infantry during the Civil War, earning the rank of Captain. He received a Medal of Honor for actions in the battle of Peachtree Creek, Georgia on July 20, 1864. Serving as a First Lieutenant in the 5th U.S. Infantry, he received a second Medal of Honor during Indian wars at McClellan's Creek, TX on November 8, 1874. Following service in WW I, he retired as a Major General in 1919.

Major General Harry Hill Bandholtz was born in Constantine in 1864. He served as a United States Army career officer during the Philippine-American War, Spanish-American War, and World War I. Awarded many medals and special decorations, including a Distinguished Service Medal, he was elected Governor of Tayabas Province Philippines. His actions to save artifacts held in the Hungarian National Museum from looting by the Romanian Military were noted 100 years after the fact during a U.S. Embassy remembrance event in Hungary. A statue of Major General Bandholtz stands in front of the U.S. Embassy building in Budapest.

Dr. George Sweetland provided much of his extensive influence in the world prior to moving to Constantine. Born in New York in 1872, he was an avid and talented athlete and scholar. After earning advanced degrees in both physical education in New York and medicine at the Grand Rapids Medical College (which later became part of the University of Michigan Medical School) Sweetland served in the Spanish-American War. Following military service, he began an extensive coaching career at high schools and colleges located in Michigan, Iowa, North Dakota, Washington, Oregon, and back in New York. He always produced exceptional and winning teams. In 1916, he moved to Constantine to take over the medical practice of his brother **Dr. John J. Sweetland** who had died in an auto accident. He remained active in athletics and donated the money needed to build the Constantine High School athletic stadium, naming it in recognition of his youngest child who died of polio in 1937.

In more contemporary times, **Elliot Marantette "Pete" Estes** served as President of General Motors from 1974 to 1981. Born in nearby Mendon, Michigan, Pete and his family moved to Constantine when he was 10 years old. Upon graduation he worked at the local creamery for a brief period churning butter. Always fascinated by mechanical things, he enrolled in General Motors Institute in 1934, went on to obtain a mechanical engineering degree, and worked his way up through the GM ranks, becoming a very popular corporate president. He had significant roles in the development of the Oldsmobile Rocket V8 engine, the Chevy Camaro, and pioneered GM's electric car technology. Some of that was ultimately utilized in development of GM's first modern electric vehicle, the EV-1.

Worldly Businesses and Industry

Constantine's businesses and manufacturers have also made significant contributions to society well beyond the community's modest boundaries.

The New World Washing Machine Company

Hand-operated washing machines were manufactured in Constantine prior to 1895 by George Tweedle in a water powered industrial plant that later became the Constantine Casket Company. These machines were improved upon and later produced by father and son W. W. Harvey and W. N. Harvey, under brand names "Home Comfort" and "The New World Washing Machine Company." The latter company was still active during the 1928 Constantine centennial year, supporting customers from as far away as Pennsylvanian and Washington State.

Crater Razor Company

O.E. Crater organized the Crater Razor Company in 1917. His guarded straight razor design became known, sought after, and copied all around the world. Its combined ultra-sharp straight razor blade and spring steel guard protected the face as the beard passed through it. Becoming obsolete when lightweight T-handle razors and electric shavers came into common use, their unique design made these instruments world-wide valued and rare antiques.

Constantine and Drake Casket Companies

Relying on waterpower to support manufacturing processes, two casket factories were located in Constantine. The first, Constantine Casket Company, was organized in 1895. The Drake Casket Company was founded in 1914. Both distributed their products widely from warehouses they maintained as far away as Indiana, Ohio, Minnesota, and Pennsylvania. Drake operations continued through the 1970s. Both employed numerous local citizens and distributed their products well beyond home state boarders.

My neighbor Harold Lintz, living right next door to us, worked at the Drake factory. He was a short jovial fellow who walked with a significant limp on one artificial leg. He raised chickens and rabbits in a small garage, outdoor rabbit hutches, and a fenced-in chicken yard behind his house. He sold eggs and rabbit meat from this home-based enterprise. He also maintained a huge garden that produced all kinds of vegetables and was rarely seen without a big cigar sticking out of the side of his mouth. It was hard for me to imagine him working at casket factory sewing machines, stitching together fabrics used to line the inside of coffins. He seemed much too manly to be performing such tasks. But he was skilled at this craft and a real pleasant, down to earth hardworking man. I had great respect for his demeanor.

Classmate Mary Drake's father was one of the owners of Drake Casket Company. She arranged a tour of the factory for our elementary school class. It began in the large, complex woodworking shop where raw rough sawn lumber was converted into finely finished casket exteriors. Next, we visited the big sewing room where Harold and others produced casket interiors out of smooth satin fabrics. He looked altogether different in that setting than he did when working in his back yard. The tour ended in Mary's favorite area, the show room. Many members of the class found this area to be a bit creepy. Of course, one or two rambunctious boys wanted to jump inside and try out the products. Our teacher put a stop to that.

Constantine Board and Paper Company
Robert T. Weir started a paper mill in an old brewery building on the banks of the St. Joseph River in 1900. Just two years later he built and moved operations into an expanded new mill that included a dam on the Fawn River. It produced electric power needed to run the plant. Initially producing paper from straw obtained from local farms, the mill began to make paper for the American Can Company in 1921. The company employed 50 to 70 people. One product that folks working at the plant and community residents liked to boast about was paper used for the tops and bottoms of cylindrical Morton Salt containers sold in grocery stores nationwide.

Even the Phenicie dime store had a role in producing this product. "Water boxes" used on the mill's papermaking machinery to produce the distinctive yellow color were lined with oil cloth purchased at the store. Dad, who loved talking about important products produced in town, was proud of what he considered to be his role in producing Morton Salt boxes. When mill employees came into the store shopping for oil cloth, he always gave them a special price on patterns or colors that had not sold well. They didn't care what color or patten they used to line their water boxes.

Other products included paperboard to make shoe boxes and dry food or cleaning product folding cartons. They were used to distribute these products nationally. In that era, the mill was operated by Frederick and Robert Weir, two descendants of the founder. Both men and their families were well known in town and contemporaries of my parents. Though the two lived in different neighborhoods, both were also on my paper route. This gave me a connection to the mill. I felt comfortable organizing community paper drives to raise funds for my high school class since I could personally call on the mill owners to accept and pay us for the paper we collected. On paper drive days, I backed Dad's station wagon, loaded with classmate collected wastepaper mill loading docks, unloaded it into a mill cart, pushed the cart to the pulper and threw the paper into a giant Waring blender-like machine where it became slushed pulp used to produce new paper.

My other connection to the mill was a man named Howard Klett. Howard worked there as a steam engineer. The plant's equipment was powered by an industrial steam engine. Howard tended boilers that produced steam for the engine and operated the engine itself. After work and on Saturdays, he often stopped at the dime store to chat with Dad. Howard loved to fish and also collected unusual rocks. Both activities were favorite topics of my father. The two of them had a lot to talk about, and both liked to talk. Howard bought a small bag of candy then hung around the store eating it and carrying on conversations with Dad. When Dad had to step away to help other customers, Howard talked with me. He knew I was interested in the paper mill and steam engines. He always had tales to tell about the latest operational snafus he faced at work. Given this fond connection with the mill, I frequently rode my bicycle or motor scooter to the mill, stopped in the road in front of it, then rode up the adjoining alleyway to check things out. Using what I could observe from the outside and Howard's descriptions of his workday, I pasted together mind's-eye visions of what might be going on inside.

The dam located on the backside of the mill attracted the attention of kids in town. It could be viewed from a Centerville

Road bridge that crossed the Fawn River just downstream of the dam. We enjoyed standing on the bridge watching the water flow over the dam, tumbling 20 or 30 feet into the river below. If we felt more adventuresome, we could walk a short distance alongside the stream, climb a fence, and gain access to a walkway that took us right up to the edge of the dam. Signs on the fence read "No Trespassing" and "Keep Out," but we ignored those. We wanted to see how close we could get to that falling water. Some of my cohorts tried fishing from the walkway. I don't know if they ever caught anything.

Unfortunately, this attraction became tragic. One summer day, word quickly passed around town that a young lad we had not known well had been fishing from the walkway, fell from it, and drowned in the river below. As part of the follow-up investigation, several of us were interviewed by the town policeman and thoroughly interrogated by our parents. We had not been there that day. He was apparently all by himself. Security measures on the walkway were greatly increased and future visits to this site were curtailed.

Constantine Cooperative Creamery
The Constantine Cooperative Creamery was established in 1915 by local farmer Charles Brody as a cooperative nonprofit producer of cream and butter. It provided a needed market for farms located within Constantine Township. Under organizational rules, the original 113 cooperative members had to also be producers of agricultural products. Members could own just one $15 share of stock each. By the time of Constantine's 1928 centennial, just 13 years later, the organization had grown to include 1600 members. From there, membership increased to several thousand, services were expanded to the entire southwest Michigan and northern Indiana

area, and both liquid and dried milk products were added to its output.

During the 1940s – 1950s, Constantine Butter was considered a premium brand. For many years running, the product received first prize at Detroit's Michigan State Fair "best butter" competition. Today, the creamery continues as a cooperative business. Held by the Michigan Milk Producers Association, it has been greatly expanded. Not only is it still making butter, but it also produces the latest in ultra-filtered and lactose-free products used by food processors throughout the country. It has always been one of the village's major employers. Many were quite noticeable. Walking to and from their 8:00 a.m. and 4:00 p.m. shifts, they wore white T-shirts and white pants. Those who worked near the powdered milk spray dryer came out covered in white milk dust. To me, they appeared anxious to get home to bathe or shower and get the material out of their hair.

On one school day, our class went on a field trip to the creamery. We watched the workers knock the tops off of dozens of 10-gallon milk cans, pick them up and physically dump them into large stainless-steel vats then pump it to other parts of the plant. We saw large tanks where milk was pasteurized, the large room that made up the spray dryer, and finally the oddly shaped revolving stainless-steel churns that produced butter. We were surprised to see how butter was removed from the churns. Operators opened the hatch on the side of the churn, reached in with both arms and pulled out armloads of the yellow creamy mass. They literally wallowed in butter from the waist up during their entire workday shift.

One employee not covered with white milk dust or butter at the end of her workday was my piano teacher, Mrs. Chrisman. She worked in the offices as a secretary or clerk and was also one of my paper route customers. She always worked Saturday mornings, the time when I made weekly collection rounds. I had to go to the creamery office building and climb a long flight of stairs up to her desk to collect from her. On the way up and down, I passed the entrance to the creamery's laboratory. Each batch of raw milk received from farmers was tested for butterfat content. They were paid somewhere between 25 and 30 cents per pound of butterfat that their milk contained. The laboratory was always spotless and a busy place. A technician or two scurried around performing the tests. I could observe this activity by stopping at the door and chatting with the technicians each time I walked by. They willingly described what they were doing and peeked my interests in laboratory sciences. I was thrilled to see samples of milk placed in strangely shaped glass laboratory containers called Babcock bottles, watch as sulfuric acid was added, and the bottles spun in a centrifuge. This separated butterfat from the whole milk allowing the amount to be read from a scale etched into the bottle stems. I impressed my science teacher by being the only student who could describe this test procedure when we studied it in general science class.

Williams Manufacturing – Breneman and Hartshorn Company
The Constantine Casket Company East Water Street buildings located next to Drake Casket Company, was occupied by the Williams Manufacturing Company in the early 1940s. It produced American basswood woven blinds. Founder L. D. Williams, a talented engineer, made important modifications to weaving looms used to produce their product. In the 1950s, he sold the company to

Breneman and Hartshorn, a Cincinnati, Ohio and Muskegon, Michigan company that had developed window shade rollers. Blinds of this style are made today by Columbia Shades USA in Dallas, Pennsylvania, a company that proudly states they operate "50 years behind the times."

Mr. Williams lived in a stately white frame house directly across the street from the plant. He too was one of my paper route customers, and as it turned out, I found myself working at his plant during the summer of 1959. I had finished my first year at Ferris Institute in Big Rapids, Michigan (now Ferris State University). Dad thought I should get a job that brought money in from outside the dime store to help pay college expenses. The Breneman and Hartshorn plant was managed by our across the street neighbor, Art Whitington. The two of them conspired to line me up with a job. This "factory job" was a whole different experience for me. I had to report to work promptly at 7:00 a.m. each day, "punch-in" on a timeclock using my personal time card, report to my workstation, and quickly get to work.

The roll-up porch shades produced at the plant were made of wooden slats cut from basswood boards. The company purchased raw, green, rough-cut basswood lumber that arrived in boxcars at the Constantine railroad yard. The boards were unloaded from the boxcar, brought to the plant, stacked onto heavy duty carts and rolled into a kiln for drying. Once dry, the lumber was planed to proper thickness then cut into slats. These were fed into the special looms that tied them together edgewise forming the wooden "fabric" that was trimmed and finished to become individual shades.

My job included unloading lumber from the boxcar, stacking it on dry kiln carts, rolling carts into and out of the dry kiln, and planing them to proper thickness. It was hot sweaty work on warm summer days, and the plant had no air conditioning.

Rolling open the door on a boxcar loaded with green lumber after it had been sitting in railyard under the sun for days was a very steamy experience. My work partner, an older employee, wanted to make sure I didn't miss any of this. He and I took turns working inside the car. We handed individual boards out to our co-worker who stacked them onto the company's old International stake-bed truck for transport to the plant. It was nearly impossible to breath inside that boxcar. Back at the plant, stacking boards onto dry kiln carts was also done outdoors under the beating sun. The dry kilns were by design very hot. When pushing carts in or out between drying cycles, we didn't spend much time in there. Running dried boards through the planer as fast as the machine would go was also a hot job, but at least we were inside out from under the beating sun when doing this.

Plant manager and neighbor Art continually cruised the shop making sure all 20 or so employees were working efficiently, not wasting time, or goofing off. Since my folks often talked with Art, I had to be seen as one who was always on my toes and working hard, or I would hear about it at home. I made it a point to always be on the job, only taking breaks when the plant whistle blew, signaling break time. That occurred once in the morning and once in the afternoon. Since I could hop on my scooter and quickly run home for lunch during our one-hour break, I always waited to use the bathroom when I got home. I didn't want to create any questions about how often I used the plant floor partially screened facility. The ride home and quart bottle of milk I chugged during my quick lunch cooled me off from the morning's hot work.

When my co-worker and I got caught up on lumber processing tasks, Art assigned us to other jobs. There was always a lot of cleanup work to be done around workstations. I was often directed to clean up sawdust and wood scraps piled on the floor by plant workers. The big problem was several of them chewed tobacco while they worked. I had to be careful when handling these waste materials with bare hands. They frequently spit tobacco juice into the piles.

One morning I got what I thought was a reprieve. As I was carefully picking up waste lumber scraps and dodging tobacco juice "clams" Art came to me with a smile on his face saying, "I have another job for you." I was glad to drop those scraps back onto the floor and let my co-worker handle them. I followed Art outdoors behind the plant and into the basement boiler room. Sawdust and wood scraps were burned in the boiler to produce steam needed to heat the lumber dry kiln and the plant in winter. In summer, more sawdust was produced than needed, causing the sawdust bin, where this material was blown from plant equipment, to become full. Art pointed all this out and handed me a large scoop shovel. Then he pointed to a wheelbarrow and said I needed to empty the sawdust bin. I was to shovel the material into the wheelbarrow, push it down to the riverbank, and dump it into the river. I took load after load down to the river and dumped it as instructed. By the end of the day, I had emptied about half of the bin and Art said I could stop. By the time the bin was filled again and in need of cleaning, a cone shaped "teepee" sawdust burner had been installed behind the plant. New ductwork routed excess sawdust directly to the burner. This time I was instructed to wheel unneeded bin sawdust over to the "teepee" burner rather than dump it into the river. In my mind, this was a huge improvement. Years later, working in my forest products industry environmental improvement career, I helped sawmills find beneficial uses for waste sawdust so the use of teepee burners could be avoided. They had become an air pollution concern.

That summer was hard work, but I learned a lot about wood products operations, how to get along with co-workers and, at a pay rate of $1.25 per hour made a little money. I knew several of the full-time employees at the plant. They knew that my background had not included factory work and hassled me a bit, calling me "College Boy" rather than by name. That issue was exacerbated when my Allied Truck Lines buddy, driver Chuck, stopped to make a delivery at the plant one day while we were all sitting by the entrance time clock on a break. He spotted me and yelled, "Muscles, what are you doing here." I then had to explain why and how I knew him so well and spent the next week living down that experience.

I learned to brush all that off and not let it bother me. I also got to thinking about that weekly paycheck of about $45, after tax withholding. Knowing that my co-workers had families to support, I wondered how they did it on that amount.

E. L. Nickell Company
Elwood Nickell came to Constantine in 1944 and established the E. L. Nickell company. They produced commercial refrigeration system pressure vessels. These heavy walled tanks and the other system components were made of advanced metal alloys. This required highly skilled welding techniques. The company became widely known and highly respected for these capabilities. Located on the banks of the Fawn River mill pond on the east side of town their products were shipped nationwide. As I traveled my paper route in this "across the tracks" neighborhood, I passed the Nickell plant. As I peddled by, I often saw the large tanks being loaded onto flatbed trucks or sometimes rail cars. It was always a busy place. I often stopped

to watch the action for a few minutes. I was never inside the plant but was impressed by the welding arcs I could see through open doors and windows. When visiting the community's downtown diesel-powered electric generating plant, operators there said, "We can tell when the welders at E. L. Nickell are kicked on." The sudden increase in electric loads was substantial. I always recall that comment when watching the Chevy Chase movie National Lampoon's *Christmas Vacation* (Hughes Entertainment). When Clark is finally successful in plugging in his colossal outdoor lighting display, the power company has to scramble to start up an idle nuclear power plant to meet the added demand.

The most important impact the E. L. Nickell Company had on me personally was the hiring of Walter Kolb to serve as their purchasing agent. He had worked as a traveling salesman for the Bostwick-Braun hardware supply company based in Toledo, Ohio. While traveling the Ohio, Indiana, Michigan tristate area selling hardware items, he called on E. L. Nickell Company. When they offered him the job as their Purchasing Agent he jumped at the chance. He was tired of all the traveling. In the summer of 1956, he moved his family from the Fort Wayne, Indiana area to the new house built essentially across the street from ours on Cherry Street in the community's new "Russel Addition." Several years later, in follow-up to that first motor scooter ride into their driveway, when I "helped" Dave Daugherty deliver their newspaper, daughter Barbara became my wife of 51 years.

A Town with Five Churches

Life on the frontier was hard. As the community took shape in the 1800s and early 1900s stories report that numerous bars and watering holes lined business area streets and ways. The *Constantine Centennial Souvenir and History*, published in 1928, included Elder Little John's 1850 *Prayer*, said to be from or reprinted by the Constantine Methodist Church. It reads in part, "Oh, Lord, there is great wickedness and much drunkedness in our young and rising towns." It cites Milwaukee, Chicago, Michigan City, LaPorte, South Bend, Niles, Mishawaka, Elkhart, Bristol, and Mottville as cities and communities where "wickedness is in need of redemption." The prayer ends with, "And lastly, then, dear, good Lord, even bless Constantine, where Governor Barry sells whiskey at three cents a glass! Amen."

Starting in 1830, "religious meetings" were conducted by a Methodist missionary Rev. Erastus Felton. The community's first building used for social or governmental functions, and these services, was built in 1832. They were conducted by the Baptist Church Society. The "first class" of Methodists met in the school building until 1846 when they moved into the newly constructed Presbyterian Session House. In 1878 the Methodists completed the building that still stands on the corner of Centerville Road and White Pigeon Street. It is the only remaining original church building in the community.

The Lutherans completed their building at the corner of Canaris and Fourth streets in 1872. Reformed and Presbyterian congregations had been independently active but merged in 1888 to form the First Congregational Church. The building they constructed, with three large stained-glass "rose windows" was the largest worship space in the community. Baptist worship services were discontinued in 1860.

During the 1940s and 1950s, the Assembly of God and Missionary Church buildings were constructed. The Assembly of God building consisted of only the basement portion. Upper stories were never added.

Including the basement worship space, the community had five churches. My father was proud to tell visitors that. He thought given the small size of the community the number of churches in town was a positive statement regarding the moral character of its residents. Congregations varied in size. Methodist and Lutheran groups outnumbered the Congregationalists. The three congregations collaborated frequently and held joint functions throughout the year. During the Lenten season, an afternoon Good Friday service was held on a rotating basis in one of the buildings. School was closed for the afternoon to allow attendance. Downtown businesses closed during service times. Attendance was robust. Worship leadership included each of the ministers, combined choirs, and a mix of lay persons. Joint youth group events were popular among teenagers and provided cross-denominational dating opportunities. My faith background and its foundation were formed and nurtured by membership in the Congregational Church and participation in ecumenical events held at the others.

The Missionary and Assembly of God churches were oriented towards charismatic worship experiences. Large numbers of people attended these services. Many came in from out of town. In addition to Sunday services, both conducted mid-week sessions and held summer revival meetings. Sitting on our back patio at my home on a summer evening, we heard sounds from the Assembly of God tent meetings three blocks away. Held on several consecutive nights, they were lively worship experiences.

Fraternal Organizations and Service Clubs
In addition to the churches, an active set of fraternal organizations brought people together to "work collectively towards spiritual and common wellbeing" (*Constantine Centennial Souvenir and History*). They included Masonic Lodge, No. 35, F. A. M. (founded in 1849), Eastern Star Chapter No. 306

O.E.S. (1902), the Knights of Pythias Lodge No. 241 (1907), Olympic Temple No. 100 (1912), Constantine Odd Fellows Lodge No. 22 (18 47), Rebekah Lodge (1926), Knights of Maccabees Hive No. 734 (1878), Ladies of the Maccabees (1886) and Constantine Grange No. 236 (1875). In its early days, the downtown building known as Eureka Hall, and location of my family's dime store from 1944 through the 1970's, was home to two of these organizations, the Pythias and the Grange.

My father was a Mason. He joined as a young man. Both his father and grandfather were active in fraternal orders. His mother, via his father's Odd Fellows membership, was a very active Rebekah. My father never claimed to have taken a very active role in the Lodge. He called himself a "belly Mason – one who just shows up for meetings when food is served." However, he did acquire his Master Mason degree. My mother was quite active in Eastern Star. She served as the Chapter's Organist for many years. In support of her participation, Dad became the O.E.S. Chapter's Worthy Patron for one term in the late 1950s. He and I talked about my becoming a Mason. I regret that neither of us took the initiative to make that happen.

Dad was also a charter member of the Constantine Rotary Club established in 1945. Rotary International is a service organization founded in Chicago in 1925 by Attorney Paul Harris. He sought "opportunities for community leaders to meet together for the purpose of filling social needs locally, regionally, and throughout the world (*Rotary International website*). The organization's motto is, "Service Above Self." Spreading the Rotary network, the Constantine Club was founded by the Three Rivers, Michigan Rotary Club. In turn, several years later, the Constantine club worked to start the White Pigeon, Michigan Rotary Club. Dad was very active. He served as a long-term Club Secretary and took "his turn" as Club President twice during his 30 years in the organization. Occasionally, he took me to weekly club meetings and urged me to also get involved in civic organizations. He always declared, "What you get out of a community depends on what you put into it."

I recall two memorable visits. During my high school years, I organized a brass group that worked up a couple of classical pieces to be played at a regional solo and ensemble competition event. Dad was impressed and arranged for our group to perform at a Rotary meeting. We enjoyed playing so were pleased to make the appearance. But what really impressed my fellow student musicians was the fact that we could get out of school for a couple of hours to attend, had a nice lunch, and got to sit at the table with a large group of local community leaders. Our school Superintendent was a member of the club and proudly introduced us. On another occasion, the program of the day was presented by a man representing the petroleum industry. He brought with him a mock-up of an "oil barrel" filled with props and gimmicks. The speaker rattled on about all of the products that came from petroleum and pulled example items from his barrel. At one point he pulled out a solid plastic rod about one-half inch in diameter that had been heated, bent, and tied into a knot. He held a flashlight up to one end and demonstrated how light traveled through the rod, around all the bends, and exited the other end. He called it a "fiber optic" and predicted that one day this concept would revolutionize how we transmit telephone calls and other information. I was impressed. The presentation strengthened my interest in chemistry and energy utilization, steering me towards career choices that involved both.

Backyard Creature Care and Feeding

In 1946, The local newspaper, *Advertiser Record*, reported that 413 students were enrolled in the school sessions that opened that year. Most lived within the village limits. We did have four school buses, but a student had to live one mile or more from the school building to qualify for bus transportation. Most of us were on our own to get to school. In bad weather, parents sometimes drove us, but mostly we walked or rode bicycles. Passing houses and backyards we observed that some resident lifestyles were a bit different from the majority.

A steady stream of kids walked Canaris Street sidewalks to and from our neighborhoods. Though my house was two blocks in the opposite direction, I frequently walked this route to get downtown to the dime store. Two blocks from the school we passed a house occupied by a fellow we called Peenie Romig. He pastured two horses in a field behind his house. They were draft horses used to pull his wagons and farm implements. Peenie was a local "odd-jobs" contractor. He could be hired to haul materials to the dump and mow or plow large garden plots with his horse drawn implements. Often seen driving a horse through town, we didn't have much contact with Peenie himself. He seemed gentle but remained verbally distant. He seemed to enjoy the interest we took in his horses. Walking beside the pasture, we stopped and talked to the horses, pulled up grass and offered it to them. We enjoyed interactions with these strong muscular creatures and worried about them in bad weather. They always seemed to stand out in it when they could have headed into a small barn located near the back of Peenie's house. I still have mind's eye visions of Peenie sitting atop one of his implements and driving his horse along village streets amongst the auto traffic of the day. Riding my Cushman scooter around town I occasionally came across horse droppings in the streets. While swerving to avoid running over them, I thought to myself, "Peenie's been here." If I met him and his horse on the streets, I always throttled back to avoid frightening the horse. Peenie, seemed to appreciate that and gave me a nod and small tip of the hat as I rode by. We were "town kids" but had a taste of rural life via Peenie.

For a brief period, neighbor Virginia Langworthy kept a horse in her back yard. Her family's house faced South Washington Street at the corner of Clinton Street and had a good-sized back yard. A garden shed in the back corner of the lot became a stable. Virginia spent hours feeding, currying, and cleaning up after her horse. Quite often she saddled up and rode through the neighborhood. She offered kids short rides, putting them up on horseback while she led the horse a short distance down the street. Being bigger than most other neighborhood kids and lacking any sort of athletic skills, I wasn't a good candidate for one of those rides. But not wanting to be left out, I pestered her about letting me climb into the saddle. One day she broke down and let me give it a try. The horse knew right away I had no business trying to climb up on its back. It pranced around and whinnied nervously while I tried getting my foot up high enough to put it in the stirrup. When I finally managed it, other kids standing by pushed my backside up into the saddle. Once finally up there, I was surprised to see how high off of the ground I was. Relieved that the "mount up" process was finally over, Virginia led the horse around her back yard. I didn't expect the bumpy ride. It seemed that every time the horse took a step, I bobbed around, heading downward while the horse's hind quarters were coming upward. It was quite an uncomfortable experience. Virginia took a couple of passes up and down the length of her back yard, quickly saw that I would never make it on any sort of more aggressive ride, so ended the experience. But then it was time for me to get down off the horse. That turned out to be more difficult than getting on. My foot got stuck in the stirrup and I ended up hanging from it headfirst alongside the horse. Other kids managed to free my foot and I fell to the ground in a heap.

So much for trying to ride a horse. When I got home and told my father what had happened, he simply said, "Yeah, I always wondered why something that ate hay could be so hard." He wasn't much of a horseman either.

Neighbor Harold Lintz's chickens and rabbits, along with my father's brief attempts to keep chickens in our back yard, also helped bring an urban barnyard character to our neighborhood. A small building out behind our garage had once served as the outhouse for our home. It was a fancy one, with a large multi-paned window in the front. Since a fully functional bathroom had been added to the back of our house long before we moved in, Dad repurposed the building into a chicken coop. He built roosting and nesting spaces inside, fashioned a "chicken door" opening in the side of the building, added a ramp for their access, and fenced in an area next to the coop for their run and scratch yard. He obtained a box of baby chicks from the co-op feed store, and we began the process of raising our own flock. Initially these fluffy little creatures were fun to play with. But they quickly grew into chickens that needed daily attention. My mother and I had the job of feeding and watering the brood, collecting the eggs, and cleaning the nesting boxes. A few, especially any excess roosters, became Sunday dinner. This venture, and some intensive backyard gardening, provided Dad with a sense of self-reliance and food supply security. However, it was short lived. Once the initial flock passed their productive days, no attempt was made to continue the practice. We reverted back to buying eggs from neighbor Harold.

The chicken coop then became a storage shed. To Virginia's younger brother Jim and me, the chicken coop looked abandoned. We thought it made a good target for our Red Rider BB rifles. We plunked away at the front door trying to see who was better at hitting the glass doorknob. The six-pane front window that had provided a nice view for persons using the building in its outhouse days also became attractive targets. When Dad got home, he was not impressed. I was sentenced to going to the hardware store and using my allowance money to purchase window glass and glazing putty. I learned to wield a putty knife and repair the damage. Shortly thereafter, Dad remodeled the building once again, turning it into an attractive playhouse for my sister. That modification even included electric lights.

Another in-town yard located on East Second Street near the creamery was home to several different animals. A weathered two-story house was located some distance back from the street and the entire yard was fenced in. This bare, dirt expanse was divided into separate pens. Chickens, ducks, geese, rabbits, and a goat or two lived there. We called the man who lived there "Squeaky" Fleming. He lived alone, performed odd jobs at the nearby porch shade and casket factories, and tended his flocks. He frequently walked the downtown business area accompanied by two or three of his ducks and sometimes a goose or two. They plodded along behind him, marching in line single file. When out cruising the town on bikes or scooters, we made it a point to ride past Squeaky's place to see what the latest addition to his menagerie might be. It was the closest thing to a zoo that we had in our town. Always in disarray, the property looked a little scary. Not wanting to get too close, we made our observations from the street.

Over on Riverside Drive on the west side of town another resident focused on raising and caring for animals. George Ward operated what we referred to as a purebred dog kennel estate. This large, carefully manicured, lot was gated and totally fenced in. Always attractive, it appeared to be maintained by professional landscapers. We could only catch glimpses of the long kennel building and several fenced dog runs from the street. No house was visible and whatever went on at this immaculately kept property was always a mystery. A few local folks were said to have worked back there tending kennels. But it was said they were not allowed to talk about what they did, the business, or anything else that went on there. Word was that specially bred "show dogs" were raised and kept there, they were very valuable, were shown all across the country, and became frequent competition winners. Hence the need for all the secrecy. Though everyone seemed to know his name, few people in town knew or had met George Ward himself. Dad said that he occasionally came into the store just before closing. It was all very mysterious.

In the American Kennel Club world however, George was also a champion. More than just the operator of a kennel, George was an acclaimed dog handler. In 1972, *The New York Times* recognized his dog showing skills and long Constantine based career. He was awarded at least two "Fidos," the "Oscar" of the dog-showing world. In 1985, the Times reported that the "Scottie" George was showing in the Madison Square Garden Westminster dog show had won Best in Show 183 times. The article stated he was expecting that number to reach 200 before the dog reached retirement age. His 2004 obituary characterized him as "known the world over as one of the most knowledgeable dog people in the business." Today, a lasting legacy scholarship, established in the George Ward name, supports apprentices enrolled in the AKC Registered Handlers Program.

Small Town - Big View

Always a place of action, the Constantine/St. Joseph County region is located at the base of a geologically important peninsula, lying midway between the southern extremities of the lower Great Lakes watersheds, and was the boundary between dense forests to the north and mixed grasslands to the south. Mastodons carved a trail through the region, leading Native Americans to use and expand game trails. Known as the Sauk Trail, these passageways were named for tribes that inhabited an area that became known as Wisconsin. Settlers came to and through this area when "western lands" were being surveyed and sold for homestead and farmstead uses. Some stayed and put down deep roots supporting community lifestyles. Surnames of many settlers can still be found in the community today. Others brought knowledge and experience gained during eastern settlement and "old country" lifestyles. They participated in community and societal development then moved on to repeat the process elsewhere. Lessons learned from contact with the southwest Michigan countryside spurred development in other areas.

Carrying on the tradition on a different scale, and in much different times, such was also the case for my peers and me. Our future directions were formally launched on Constantine High School graduation night. Our teachers and local education system prepared us academically and the community with its multifaceted opportunities to interact with it provided grounding and life skills that bolstered our successes.

Our May 28, 1958 my class's graduation ceremonies were the first to be held in our "new gymnasium." Class Advisor, Miss Dorothy Harvey, worked hard to focus our attention on our grand march into the facility. During several rehearsals she drilled us on how to walk down that aisle. When we reached our seats up on the stage, we sat in great anticipation of the next walk we would take. That one would take us across the platform to receive our diplomas. But first we had to endure a long program and the keynote speaker address. For me at least, critical comments and sage advice provided by the distinguished but no longer remembered speaker have been lost – except for one key question. Closing his remarks he asked, "Graduates, where will you be 20 years from tonight?" That question brought me swiftly in from the twilight zone that my mind had been wandering around in. Just what was I going to do from that point forward? That was, indeed, a question to ponder.

Yes, I knew I wanted to go to college. Representatives from several colleges had visited the school during our senior year. I had listened to them describe campus life, the hard work that lay ahead, and the need for good study habits necessary to ensure success. All of that sounded very cosmopolitan and of interest to me. The problem was, I needed to be able to get into one of those schools. My high school grades had not been stellar. I had enjoyed my school years, extracurricular activities, and all of my "about town" experiences. But for all I had learned, I had not produced the academic record needed to document my potential. Classmates and peers were heading off to the University of Michigan, Michigan State, and private colleges such as Albion or Hillsdale. One classmate had even been admitted into the Naval Academy. I knew better than to even apply to those places.

My friend and mentor Judy Cox graduated a year ahead of me and was enrolled in the pharmacy program at Ferris Institute. She counseled me to look at Ferris since this institution had a more forgiving admittance policy. She hadn't needed it, but I surely did. I had applied and been accepted, so on that night, sitting on the graduation stage, I knew where I was headed for next year or two, but 20 years out? I had not given that much thought.

My dad had always assumed I would go into some sort of business. He had talked about that for as long as I could remember. Beginning in my early five and dime stockroom days, he explained the strategy behind each sales promotion, described special pricing decisions, and highlighted unique counter displays that he put in place. "These are things you'll have to think about when you get your own store," he said. He didn't talk EBITDA (earnings before interest, taxes, depreciation and amortization) or stock prices, but did talk "apprenticeships," "getting in on the ground floor," and "working your way up the ladder." These were key strategies cited when counseling me. It's what it took to "earn a good living," he said. These principles were behind his thinking that I should become an apprentice of Johan Johansen and go into the refrigeration system servicing business. He pointed out that reliance on refrigeration systems had become an important part of our lifestyles. He also remarked several times that, "Walgreens has a good training program." "Employees can take advantage of these and work their way up to store manager," he added. He urged me to go over to the Elkhart, Indiana Walgreens store and ask the store manager about it.

I wasn't the salesman he was. I liked being around people, entering into conversations, and could go some distance towards twisting their arm to buy something. But I wasn't the deal closer he was. That was a step beyond my comfort level. It always amazed me how he could have a reasonably expensive item lying on the display shelf for a long time collecting dust, then when someone came in looking for just that item, gleefully sell it to them at list price. I would have wanted to give them a price break. But his approach had them going out the door totally pleased, and he finally getting the price he needed to make that counterspace pay as it should to support his business.

Dad's guidance led me to think, "I could run a drug store if I was the pharmacist." In my vision, I would get to stand in the back of the store, mix and dispense chemical prescriptions, wear a white lab coat, still be in charge of the store, but not have to be on the floor selling and pushing wares as he did. When I expressed some of these thoughts, Dad said, "If you want to go to college, I'll find the way to get you there, but you have to come out being able to make a good salary." "After all," he said, "you can go to work in the factories and make $3 or $4 an hour these days and not have to spend the money or take the time to go to college." So, the challenge had been made. I could go to college, if I could get in, but had to decide what profession I wanted to focus on.

Acceptance at Ferris opened the door for me, I applied as a "general studies" student with lots of questions. Could I survive the Pharmacy curriculum? Would I rather do something else? I loved playing with electronics and recording equipment, maybe I should head that direction? I had seen pictures of recording engineers working in tall "record stack" looking buildings that housed RCA Victor headquarters in California. Would I like engineering? I liked math but struggled with it. I was intrigued by the paper technology program at Western Michigan University but knew I would not initially be accepted into that program.

Where would I be in 20 years? That was indeed a heavy question for me on graduation night. I didn't know if my classmates had similar thoughts roaming their minds, how or if they were moved by the commencement ceremony speaker, but I certainly was. The next day, I sat out on the patio chaise lounge behind our house gazing into the bright blue sky and its puffy white clouds thinking, "I've really had a good deal here. I've been provided with a roof over my head, food on the table, and lot of good times, I guess it's time for me to get out on my own and make something of myself." It was an awakening for sure.

I'm not sure we recognized at the time how well our community had prepared us to step out into the world. Close contacts with community members had put important life skills into our survival arsenal. The freedom to run the streets and be known/mentored by adults had provided lessons at least as important as our academic studies. In today's more cloistered world, person to person contacts come through indirect or electronic connections including social media. It's hard for me to regard this delivery system as equivalent or better.

Time since those days has shown that when we did spread our wings and go forth into the world, for the most part we did more than OK. We became influential teachers, leaders supporting or starting businesses that employed others. Highly successful farmers feed the world though harvests. Skilled tradesman serve our communities as do our nurses, physicians, dentists, lawyers, and distinguished military veterans. We have followed the footsteps of those stalwart pioneers who toiled to raise the community out of the flat but fruitful plains. We demonstrated the benefit of lessons learned through what my mother called "the school of hard knocks." She had not finished high school but made up for that through toils, hard work, and the determination to do well in the eyes of her peers. Some of my peers remained in the area and pursued careers locally, some ventured to other locales. In either case we have made influences around the world. Now in retirement years we are being replaced by skilled and learned members of today's society. Our experiences were unique, in a unique period, but had qualities that just maybe would be beneficial if infused into today's culture.

Where did I end up? Upon finishing the Ferris Institute Industrial Chemistry Technology program, I transferred to Western Michigan University's paper technology program, and have enjoyed every minute of my 50+ years working as a paper mill chemist and environmental control systems professional. I have helped several companies stop dumping lots of things into the river and the air.

References

The Postwar Economy: 1945-1960, Postwar America, History 1994, American History From Revolution To Reconstruction and beyond, Department of Alfa-informatica (Computing in the Humanities), University of Groingen, The Netherlands
http://www.let.rug.nl/usa/outlines/history-1994/postwar-america/the-postwar-economy-1945-1960.php

The 1947 Atoman, The Senior Class of Constantine High School, Constantine, Michigan

The 1948 Falcon Ledger, The Senior Class of Constantine High School, Constantine, Michigan

The Echo, 1949, The Senior Class of Constantine High School, Constantine, Michigan

The Falcon Ledger, 1950, The Senior Class of Constantine High School, Constantine, Michigan

1953 Falcon Ledger, The Senior Class of Constantine High School, Constantine, Michigan

1957, The Falcon Ledger, The Senior Class of Constantine High School, Constantine, Michigan

The Falcon Ledger, 1958, The Seniors of Constantine High School

C. H. S. in 1959, Annual Publication of Constantine High School, Constantine, Michigan

Constantine High School 50 Year Class Reunion, Class of 1960, memoir and book

1956 Ford paint colors
http://paintref.com/cgi-bin/colorcodedisplay.cgi?manuf=Ford&year=1956

1956 Ford Thunderbird Special V8 Special Engine
https://en.wikipedia.org/wiki/Ford_Y-block_engine

1957 Quad Headlight Systems Introductions
https://www.hemmings.com/users/182767/gallery/6098.html

1955 Chevrolet Coral and Grey color scheme
https://www.flickr.com/photos/50312897@N02/galleries/72157707488834575/

DKW, Wikipedia
https://en.wikipedia.org/wiki/DKW

1955 Plymouth Belvedere Technical Specifications
https://www.conceptcarz.com/s10882/plymouth-belvedere.aspx

Brach's, Wikipedia
https://en.wikipedia.org/wiki/Brach%27s

American Greeting Cards, Wikipedia
https://en.wikipedia.org/wiki/American_Greetings

Data USA, Census Place, Constantine, MI
https://datausa.io/profile/geo/constantine-mi#:~:text=In%202018%2C%20Constantine%2C%20MI%20had,median%20household%20income%20of%20%2436%2C719.&text=NaNk%25%20of%20the%20people%20in,the%20homeownership%20rate%20is%2059.7%25.

Constantine Centennial, A Souvenir Program and History, published by *The Advertiser Record*, Constantine Michigan

Official Website of Constantine, Michigan
https://constantinemi.com/history/

St. Joeseph County Historical Society of Michigan Facebook Post,
https://www.facebook.com/sjchsmi/posts/william-meek-of-wayne-county-ohio-purchased-land-in-constantine-in-the-summer-of/10155109178915973/

Constantine the Great, Wikipedia
https://en.wikipedia.org/wiki/Constantine_the_Great

Find a Grave Website, William Meek
https://www.findagrave.com/memorial/8485578/william-meek

Portrait and Biographical Album of Jefferson and Van Buren Counties (Iowa) – 1890
http://iagenweb.org/boards/vanburen/biographies/index.cgi?review=1000

St. Joseph County, Michigan, Wikipedia
https://en.wikipedia.org/wiki/St._Joseph_County,_Michigan

History of St. Joseph County, Cutler, H. G. ed. (Harry Gardner), b. 1856., Lewis Publishing Company
https://quod.lib.umich.edu/m/micounty/BAD1044.0001.001?rgn=main;view=fulltext

Gov. John S Barry, Wikipedia
https://en.wikipedia.org/wiki/John_S._Barry

Constantine, Michigan, Wikipedia
https://en.wikipedia.org/wiki/Constantine,_Michigan

National Governor's Association official website
https://www.nga.org/governor/john-stewart-barry/

William Meek, Portrait and Biographical Album of Jefferson and Van Buren Counties – 1890.

http://iagenweb.org/boards/vanburen/biographies/index.cgi?review=1000

John J Bagley – Wikipedia
https://en.wikipedia.org/wiki/John_J._Bagley

The Puddleford Papers: or Humors of the West, Henry Hiram Riley, Good Press, 2019 http://okpress.info, EA4064066188788

Joseph R. Williams – Wikipedia
https://en.wikipedia.org/wiki/Joseph_R._Williams

History of the Michigan State University, Wikipedia
https://en.wikipedia.org/wiki/History_of_Michigan_State_University

Village council discusses fire that destroyed historic home, Cheboygan Daily Tribune, January 19, 2017
https://www.cheboygannews.com/news/20170119/village-council-discusses-fire-that-destroyed-historic-home

Constantine History, 1932, excerpted from St. Joseph County Historical Review and Business Guide, Roy D.F. Sowers
http://migenweb.org/stjoseph/history/constantine.htm

Edwin William Keightley, Wikipedia
https://en.wikipedia.org/wiki/Edwin_W._Keightley

Frank Baldwin, Wikipedia
https://en.wikipedia.org/wiki/Frank_Baldwin#Affiliations

Arlington Cemetery Archives, Frank Dwight Baldwin, http://www.arlingtoncemetery.net/fdbaldwi.htm

U.S. Embassy in Hungary, Remembering U.S. Major General Harry Hill Bandholtz

https://hu.usembassy.gov/remembering-u-s-major-general-harry-hill-bandholtz/

Major General Harry Hill Bandholtz, Wikipedia
https://en.wikipedia.org/wiki/Harry_Hill_Bandholtz

George Sweetland, Wikipedia
https://en.wikipedia.org/wiki/George_Sweetland

Pete Estes, Wikipedia
https://en.wikipedia.org/wiki/Pete_Estes

Automotive News, Sept. 14, 2008, *Pete Estes brought his 'atta'boy' attitude to GM's Presidency*
https://www.autonews.com/article/20080914/OEM02/309149895/pete-estes-brought-his-attaboy-attitude-to-gm-s-presidency

Memorial Tributes, National Academy of Engineering, National Academy of Sciences, Washington, D.C. 1991, Elliot M. Estes, pages 75-78
https://nap.nationalacademies.org/read/1760/chapter/15

Constantine Rotary, History, Village of Constantine website, https://constantinemi.com/clubs-links/constantine-rotary-club/#:~:text=The%20Constantine%20Rotary%2C%20established%20in,the%20community%20and%20the%20schools

Rotary International website
https://www.rotary.org/en/about-rotary

Crater Razor Company, John S. Barry Society Facebook page
https://www.facebook.com/JohnSBarrySociety/posts/595298963834822/

Crater Razor Company – Worthpoint Value Store Internet posting,
https://www.worthpoint.com/worthopedia/complete-crater-guarded-straight-1823348617

Crater Razor Company – Pintrest
https://www.pinterest.com/pin/96264510767721125/

A geographic Interpretation of the Growth and Development of Constantine, Mary Jeanne Dowty, Master of Arts Degree Thesis, Michigan, Western Michigan University, April 1967
https://scholarworks.wmich.edu/cgi/viewcontent.cgi?article=4251&context=masters_theses

The Breneman-Hartshorn Story, The Muskegon Heritage Society Newsletter, October-November-December 1989, Heritage Village Boomer
https://muskegonheritage.org/wp-content/uploads/newsletter/OctNovDec_1989.pdf

Constantine Casket Co. Postcard Photo, Detroit Public Library Digital Collections
https://digitalcollections.detroitpubliclibrary.org/islandora/object/islandora%3A221942

St. Joseph County Historical Society Facebook page, Constantine – Drake Casket Company (Part Four), South Bend Tribune article, July 19, 1987
https://www.facebook.com/sjchsmi/photos/drake-employee-mary-ackerman-of-sturgis-marks-the-spot-where-the-casket-lid-will/10156497297480973/

Constantine in Retrospect, a paper produced on the occasion of the 175th anniversary of the Village of Constantine, MI, Dorothy Caseman Stears, 2004

Dairy Foods Journal, April 16, 2019, Michigan Milk Producers Association expands plant
https://www.dairyfoods.com/articles/93545-michigan-milk-producers-association-expands-plant

Babcock Bottle, Wikipedia
https://en.wikipedia.org/wiki/Babcock_bottle

Columbia Shades USA, Dallas, PA, website home page, Classic Designs https://columbiashadesusa.com/

E. L. Nickell Company website
https://elnickell.com/about/

Bostwick-Braun Company website
https://www.bostwick-braun.com/specialty-divisions/bostwick-braun-hardware

413 Enrolled in Local School, *The Advertiser Record*, Volume 102, Number 23, September 8, 1946

Close Encounter with Handler, George Ward, New York Times, February 11, 1985, Section C, Page 11
https://www.nytimes.com/1985/02/11/sports/close-encouter-with-handler-george-ward.html

Scottie and Shephard Dominate Field for Top Dog, New York Times, February 16, 1972, Page 32
https://s1.nyt.com/timesmachine/pages/1/1985/02/11/041653_360W.png?quality=75&auto=webp&disable=upscale

George Ely Ward obituary, Kalamazoo Gazette, 2004
https://obits.mlive.com/obituaries/kalamazoo/obituary.aspx?n=george-ely-ward&pid=2069691

AKC Registered Handlers Program Facebook Page
https://www.facebook.com/AKC-Registered-Handlers-Program-295367916656/?hc_ref=ARRTjV3bFF-crJYOZ7HlBsueEnJ_tbP_m5FBpGNGHQgiH40MAamh_OKVoDT0Wel0GG4&fref=nf&__tn__=kC-R

Sauk Trail, Wikipedia
https://en.wikipedia.org/wiki/Sauk_Trail

Michigan Nature Association, MNA Fall Adventure to Explore the Irish Hills, Allison Raech, August 20, 2013
https://michigannature.wordpress.com/tag/old-sauk-trail/

Sauganash Country Club (Three Rivers, Michigan) website, About Us
https://sauganashcc.com/about-us/

Photo Credits

Sources for photos used in this book are listed below. The author has cropped or otherwise edited most originals.

Page	Credit
3	Constantine High School – Post card photo, Angie Birdsall, Facebook post
6	Rob's house – Bob's Local History Club, Facebook post
8	Constantine Depot – St. Joseph County Historical Society, Facebook post
40	Gambles store – Post card photo, Angie Birdsall Facebook post
78	Phenicie's Dime Store – Walter Phenicie photo
79	Phenicie's Dime Store interior – Walter Phenicie photo
81	Vernie Loomis of The Men's Store – Walter Phenicie photo
85	Bank with clock – Post card photo, Angie Birdsall, Facebook post
95	Phenicie's Dime Store candy counter – Gertrude Phenicie photo
98	Washington Street – Walter Phenicie photo
100	Monarch Marking Machine – Ebay photo
115	Popcorn Vending Machine – Walter Phenicie photo
129	Traveling Merchant – Copy, artist unknown
133	Matching shirts – Claude Phenicie photo
154	Moto Mower Ad – Purchased on Ebay
157	First Congregational Church – Post card photo, Angie Birdsall, Facebook post
164	Washington St. Park – Post card photo, Angie Birdsall, Facebook post

166	Civil War Cannon – Angie Birdsall Facebook post
177	My Race Car – Walter Phenicie photo
223	1948 Cushman Pacemaker – Internet post, origin unknown
238	Meribeth Stephenson on Sidewalk Days – Walter Phenicie photo
247	1951 Case Tractor – Dale Phenicie photo
249	Load of 1954 Buicks – Internet photo, Antique Automobile of America
252	1956 Ford Customline – Internet photo, Flickr, Richard Spleglman
257	Smith Family '55 Chevy – Walter Phenicie photo
259	1957 DeSoto Firesweep – Internet photo, Top Classic Cars for sale
276	My 1955 Plymouth – Dale Phenicie photo
316	Breneman and Hartshorn Co. – Post card photo, Angie Birdsall Facebook post
324	Eureka Hall Cornice – Katy Spade photo

Made in the USA
Columbia, SC
24 July 2022